Glorious and Dreadful

Glorious and Dreadful

Nina Tretiak-Shields

VANTAGE PRESS
New York

Published by Vantage Press, Inc.
516 West 34th Street, New York, New York 10001

Manufactured in the United States of America
ISBN: 0-533-13791-8

Library of Congress Catalog Card No.: 00-093248

0 9 8 7 6 5 4 3 2 1

In memory of my father, mother, husband, and my
exceptional generation.

Contents

Acknowledgments   ix
Introduction   xi
Preface   xiii

  1. Crimea   1
  2. Kharkov: The Roots of My Family   5
  3. Krasnaya-Yaruga   8
  4. Grayvoron, Tekhnicum   41
  5. Adult: An Important Job   122
  6. Kharkov—My Home   142
  7. University Years   159
  8. Final Thoughts   249
  9. World War II   262
10. Family Pictures and Documents   301

Acknowledgments

I am grateful to my many friends and relatives who made a direct contribution to the production and promotion of this book:

Dr. James Lawler, author of the Introduction;

Dr. Valery Kuvakin (Moscow University), advice and an article for the press;

Dr. Frances Kinsley for editing the manuscript;

Lucy Tretiak-Caruso, my daughter, for some editing and organizing book promotion;

Betty Tzetzo, a friend and former student, for outstanding promotional work;

John Ryshko, a friend and former student, for collecting lists of Russian and Ukrainian Orthodox churches in the USA and Canada, as well as other work for promotion;

Kathleen MacNeish, my step-daughter, and Bill Shields, my step-son, for help with promotion in the Boston and Dallas areas respectively; and

A group of my colleagues and retired professors from SUNY at Buffalo: Dr. Arthur Butler, Dr. George Schanzer, Dr. Emily Tall and Professor George Richmond.

Introduction

The turn of the millennium is a time to think about beginnings, about life renewing itself, about birth and rebirth. This should be a time of renewed hope for the realization of our highest dreams. Every child begins life with such hope. Some children are fortunate to find in the society around them support and encouragement for their new and boundless energies. Such are the societies that are themselves beginning anew or in the process of being reborn.

In *Glorious and Dreadful,* by Professor Nina Tretiak-Shields, we have the opportunity and privilege of experiencing what a wonder it must have been for a budding creative life, full of joy and hope and high ideals, to find in her community, in her society, in the revolutionary ideals of her nation, a climate that fully accords with the spirit of youthfulness. Nothing could be more glorious than to experience youth in a youthful society. This is the experience that Professor Tretiak-Shields describes in the early sections of her book. Hers was once the enthusiasm of youth finding constructive expression in building a better world.

This is a story not only of the personal feelings and events of a particular life, but also of the wide vista of ideas. This youthful new Soviet life was primarily a life of ideas rather than of things or of consumer goods. In the poverty of a poor peasant society, there is always the possibility of living on ideas, of savoring ideas, of reveling in ideas. We see through young Nina's experiences how the Soviet youth of the twenties and early thirties learned to see themselves in the context of the history of their people, and of the history of humanity. If their lives were poor in external wealth, they were rich in identification with the onward and upward journey of mankind, in which they felt called to play a significant role. Hence their lives were full of inner significance and meaning—before this meaning turned to confusion and dismay.

This is not only a glorious, but also a dreadful story. Into the rich and creative life of the young woman who is so vividly revived out of the memory of the author we see enter the growing shadows of doubt and confusion and finally the brutal blackness of betrayal. The youthful enthusiastic twenties full of revolutionary ideas give way to the nightmare of the thirties. The period of liberal economic and social life known as NEP (New Economic Policy), started by Lenin, passes over into the period of collectivization of agriculture, the creation of the command economy and the regime of political terror created by Stalin.

The story of the dreadful period is the story of compromises and refusals to compromise. But there was no justice. Tragedy struck not only those who refused to abandon the principles to which they had committed themselves—principles of honesty, decency and humanity—but anyone could be struck down. The first victims, however, were the honest "old Bolsheviks."

This is a complex picture of the Soviet experience. It is black, it is white, and it is gray. It is full of all the colors and tastes of life, heightened beyond the ordinary because of the extraordinary times. These were times in which a people began to create a new world out of the chaos of the collapse of the old one, and in place of the old injustices. But the old ways returned with a vengeance as the Stalinist regime built its machine of fear. The fear was not only the justified fear of a hostile capitalist world that was so terribly realized by the Nazi invasion and the devastating war. The deeper fear no doubt was the fear on the part of the Stalinist State of what the youth would do if their freedoms were allowed to grow.

This is therefore a dreadful story of mounting fear and quiet desperation, of fighting for survival, of both bitter betrayal and unsung heroism. But what gives such poignant meaning to this tragedy is primarily its portrait of a glorious youthful spirit of freedom that was so savagely suppressed. Professor Emeritus Tretiak-Shields tells her story after a career of teaching and research as a Professor of Russian language and culture at the State University of New York at Buffalo. Well aware of the one-sided American views of the Soviet Union, she has drawn a complex four-dimensional image that does not fit readily within the terms of standard histories.

Dr. James Lawler
Department of Philosophy
State University of New York at Buffalo

Preface

In this world, sorrow is most stable,
and the regal word is the most long-lasting.
—*Anna Akhmatova*

Life, without an attempt to understand it,
is hardly worth living.
—*Socrates*

"We are the children of the dreadful years of Russia." These words of the poet Alexander Blok are about the Revolution of 1917. I am one of the children of that dreadful and glorious epoch of Russian history. Used together, glorious and dreadful, descriptively present a truthful picture of life in Russia, her Revolution, and her people.

For a long time I have been thinking of telling my story about that epoch. Although my reflections seem similar to those of millions of other eyewitnesses, they are unique, the result of my own environment and lifestyle. My past is now like a dwindling and faintly shimmering flame. Faces and surroundings are fading. The voices left behind sound as a distant echo. It is time to write that chapter of my life or it will be lost forever.

The stages of my early life coincided with the stages of the Revolution. I was born just a few years before the Revolution. The first period of my life—my childhood, adolescence and early youth—were full of excitement and a belief in a Communist good human society. Life was changing rapidly, seemingly by hours. All our activities were geared toward helping to better the life of the working man. About seventy years have passed since those days, but in my memory, that time remains like a shining star leading us to a time and place where my generation strove to be good, pure, happy human beings, taking an active part in achieving the lofty aim of building a new society.

The second period, that of mature youth, also had no shortage of enthusiasm and belief in the Communist cause. However, we craved to understand what was happening in our country and why some people lacked their former enthusiasm and spirit. My sunny ideals were turning to painful questions: Why? What's happening around us? Double-think and double-talk started to characterize the behavior of some of us.

During the third period—young adulthood—disillusion and confusion grew among us. Joseph Stalin's heavy tanks, i.e., the uniformed NKVD (The People's Commissariat of Internal Affairs), rolled over us. Millions of good citizens died. Why? We questioned later how many from that great, unique and tragic generation were still alive or died peacefully in their own beds. To have lived through that time and survived was luck. Simple, unbelievable luck. I witnessed and consequently write mostly about Stalin's period in the history of the Soviet Union.

It was the most turbulent time in Russia's whole history—a time of extreme passion and faith in a good society of the future, but also a time of extreme cruelty and bloodshed. The French said of their Revolution, "Revolution is the mother who devours her own children."

My main theme of this work is the conflict between the idealistic aim we cherished and practiced and the evil means employed by the Stalinist government.

I am trying to synthesize the memories of my childhood, youth, and adulthood, adding my parents' information and also discussions among us students about past and present events, as well as using the entire gamut of information from literature, art, music, and propaganda. My knowledge and insight as a university teacher distilled all of these experiences. My aim is to bring to light some of the events, political trends, and people's mood of that period while focusing on specific times, places, events and people as a part of the national development. There is more than one way to write about the past. I write about it from the perspective of the present day.

My understanding of the past has broadened and deepened with the passage of time. With the fall of the Soviet Union and the destruction of its socialist system, the ideological contradictions possibly have not diminished, but the emphasis is shifting. The struggle now is concentrated on the control of history. That is, in part, why I want to share my story as a small token to that past. I will try to recall that past as it was—with all the pride and all the shame, without any hatred, but still with intense pain and sorrow. The lives of the families of the "enemies of the Soviet folk" left behind are relatively unknown. They quite often became "emotionally crippled" people forever. I want to present the lives of those unfortunates because I was one of them. I was questioning myself: Why am I alive? I have to tell about my and others experience, both of our happiness and our rivers of tears.

My generation, those who were born before the October Revolution or several years later, was unique; it was not repeated even in the Soviet Union. Boris Pasternak called it "The best generation ever."

Our unshakable belief in the Communist good human society and our heroic deeds in realization of those ideals with time were colliding with the political reality. That is why throughout this work one can see contradictory political feeling. I and my generation, like the majority of the Soviet people, had two simultaneously running, parallel notions: one of them was of belief, pride, and satisfaction, and the other was of confusion, disbelief, and pain. These notions repeated themselves throughout our lives and consequently must be reflected in that fashion in this work.

My second intention is dictated by globalization of the world's culture. Close relations and development of tolerance between nations and people have necessitated learning about other cultures and national characters. Political antagonism created unhealthy relations between Americans and Russians. As a result, the historys and culture of each people were scarce or unknown to the other. American journalism and television coverage was and still is predominant, in spite of the disappearance of the "red menace": one-dimensional, lacking complexity and balance, and often speculative or simply misleading.

In this work, I am presenting facts of Russian history and people's lives and their character, not in a formal way, but as a part of my experience and in an analytical way as an outgrowth of my tekhnicum (Junior College) and university studies. Additionally, I complement this with insight into higher education and the general condition of education in the first decades of the Revolution.

I touch on the moral problem of the Russian nation: How does it happen that the territories of the Soviet Union harbor millions of mass graves of Soviet citizens killed by their own government? Who has to take moral responsibility for the past "good" and "bad"? Without that, national healing and subsequent striving to become the political and economic great Nation present a problem. Boris Yeltsin placed the responsibility for these crimes on the Soviet Communist government. That means on Yeltsin himself, as an alternate Politbureau member, the highest ruling body in the Soviet Union. Is it the guilt of the entire nation, as the Germans accepted it for themselves? But nations are the historical formation, which include past and future generations. And as an individual citizen I denied my guilt in the murder of my father and husband, or anyone of those millions who were killed. These facts illustrate the complexity of solving this moral problem, and consequently establishing a peaceful nation.

I feel I owe the writing of this memoir to my father, mother and husband, to bring their tragic deaths to light. They were among those really good human beings. No less, I owe this to my great, exceptional, and unfortunate generation.

Certainly, I did not wish to write an autobiography with myself as the focal point. I strive to present through my life pictures of the human condition in a certain time and place. Recently, I have the impression that the world—intellectually and politically—is forgetting the experience of the Soviet Union. This is not far-sighted. The world will not stop in its historical development; a new economic, social, and political formation will come. Undoubtedly, the experience of Russia could be of great global importance. Probably an old thought still has validity: History is like a homely woman who wipes and wipes the surface of a mirror into which she looks so that she may look better.

Aleksandr I. Solzhenitsyn in *Nobel Lecture on Literature* (Harper and Row) states: "From human being to human being, filling up their brief time on earth, art communicates entirely the freight of someone else's long life-experience. . . . Permitting it to be absorbed and made one's own as if it actually had been . . . Thus, literature, along with language, preserves the national soul."* Because of political circumstances, "whole speechless generations are born and die off who do not tell each other about themselves, nor speak about themselves to their descendants . . . as a result of such silence, the whole of history ceases to be understood."**

My work aims to contribute to overcome this silence.

Nobel Lecture on Literature; Aleksandr I. Solzhenitsyn; pp. 19, 20.
**Nobel Lecture on Literature*; Aleksandr I. Solzhenitsyn; pp. 21–22.

Glorious and Dreadful

Family, 1995. First row: Pauline Caruso, mother of my son-in-law; Konrad Shields, my husband; and myself. Second row: Ronald Caruso, my son-in-law, and Lucy Tretiak-Caruso, my daughter.

1

Crimea

The year is 1918. I am four-years-old. We are in the Crimea, Sevastopol. This is my first vivid memory.

My father, in his petty officer's uniform, a rifle over his shoulder and a bag on his back, dashed into our small quarters, embraced my mother, and said that his volunteer regiment was leaving for Dzhankoy to guard the bridges to the mainland. My mother immediately started yelling, "I won't let you go. What am I going to do with two small children in this dreadful time? What were you thinking? Children, hold your father. Don't let him go!"

My elder brother, Kolia, and I understood that Father was leaving us and going to the front. We fell to the floor, grabbed and held on to our father's legs, and with all of our might screamed, "Papa, *Papochka*, don't leave us. We love you. Don't leave us!" Meanwhile, Mama took Father's rifle and bag from him. Father sat down on the floor with us and hugged us all.

"No, I won't go. I'll never leave you," he said. "Forgive me for this foolishness."

The four of us sat on the floor, tightly embracing and crying happily. Papa was not going to leave us.

As a petty officer, my father, Mikhael Pavlovich Shuliak, was the head mechanic of the weapons' workshop in the Sevastopol Garrison. At the beginning of the WW I in 1914, he and the others were sent to Sevastopol from the Kharkov Garrison.

During the winter of 1917–18, the Crimea had no stable political authority. Sevastopol, the base of the Black Sea Fleet, was in turmoil. Several parties were fighting for power and control of the Black Sea fleet which, under Admiral Kolchak, still hoisted the tsarist flag. The Crimea was inundated with political opposites. The monarchist army under General Alekseev (and after his death, General Denikin)

1

and the Don Cossacks under General Krasnov were assembling in the region of the river Kuban and the North Caucasus. The new Soviet government under Lenin, following the old Russian policy of possessing the Crimea and the Black Sea fleet, sent a faithful vanguard to Sevastopol—the sailors from the Baltic fleet. Surprisingly, they were under the command of a woman Bolshevik, Katerina Brishko-Brishkovskaya.

We lived close to Ushakov's Ravine, a beautiful wooded area filled with flowering bushes, and a very large green field at its center. It was the place of roaring meetings attended by hundreds of people representing different parties and groups. This was the Hyde Park of Sevastopol, only much more dangerous. The leading parties were the Bolsheviks, Monarchists, and Social Revolutionaries. My father attended these meetings and sometimes spoke in favor of the Social Revolutionaries. Twenty years later, he paid for his words with his head.

Eventually, violence broke out at these meetings, culminating in awful, senseless terror, such as Bartholomew's nights. Various factions would massacre each other throughout the nights, pile the dead bodies on barges, and dump them at sea. Frequently, out of fear, my father didn't sleep at home. The air was full of dreadful stories we children would hear and tell each other. One of those fantastic stories, my mother later told me, was true. A young officer was killed. Several days later, his young wife bought a fish at the market. When she gutted the fish, she found her husband's wedding ring. A memorial service was held at the church and the ring was blessed. My mother went to the service and when she returned, she demanded that we leave Sevastopol immediately.

Everyone was afraid of the Bolshevik sailors. They looked different from others, wearing black leather jackets with cartridge belts crossed at their chests. Their walk was brisk, energetic, and proud. Some people said they were from hell. Every time we saw them walking to Ushakov's Ravine, we'd run away.

One day when we were engrossed in our play, some sailors suddenly appeared and picked up a few of us. Many of the children started to cry. I was one of the few not crying and the sailor who was holding me tenderly asked if I was afraid of him. "No," I said. Then he asked me my name, where I lived, and how old I was. Kolia had been standing next to the sailor and helping me. When my sailor asked me who my father was, I told him he was an officer. Kolia immediately corrected me. "Our father is a mechanic," he said. All the sailors burst out laughing, and told Kolia, "You are a smart boy. You should be with us."

My sailor asked his friends if they had any candy to give us. Again they laughed and said their bullets wouldn't make good children's presents. So another sailor gave me a very small, pocket-sized book filled with beautiful pictures of flowers he had painted. I had never seen anything like it and became very excited, telling my sailor to put me down because I had to show this to my mama. The sailor told me I looked like his daughter, also a little white head, and he would let me down if I gave him a kiss. I quickly did, then ran away. I never parted with that little book, and when it perished in a house fire during World War II, I felt a great loss. My sailor came and played with us a few more times. We liked him very much.

The Black Sea Fleet was taken over by the Bolsheviks, who later sank the ships in the Bay of Novorosiisk rather than give them back to the enemy. The Soviet playwright Korneychuk wrote a wonderful play, *The Wreck of the Escadra*, about this sad and heroic event.

There is another story from that time. I don't know whether it is truth or fantasy, but it's a good story. When the Bolshevik sailors boarded the flagship, they demanded that Admiral Kolchak surrender his command and the symbol of his authority, a cutlass given to him by Tsar Nicolas II on the occasion of his appointment. The cutlass was heavily encrusted with diamonds, pearls, rubies, and sapphires. Kolchak took the cutlass from its scabbard, kissed it, and said, "You bastards didn't give it to me and you bastards won't take it from me." With that, he threw the cutlass into the sea.

A traumatic event that left a scar on my memory was the funeral for members of my father's volunteer regiment. The regiment was decimated, when they defended the bridges to the mainland and Sevastopol held a mass funeral for the victims. Because of the huge crowd, it was impossible for my mother to keep track of us two children, so Father put me on his shoulders as he walked in the funeral procession. In front of us, I suddenly saw a long, long row of coffins carried by both military men and civilians. Some of the coffins were open. Between them were the clergy, the families, the choirs, and at the end of the procession, the general public.

The impression left on the mind of a four-year-old child was shocking. To this day I remember the funeral march, that began with the words, "You fell a victim," sung and played by orchestras. Later, it was probably the second most popular song after the "International." Dmitriy Shostakovich used it in his Eleventh Symphony, the "1905," and the Eighth String Quartet. His Eleventh Symphony is considered an immortal work of art.

Pictures of chaos and human suffering are imprinted on a child's memory. Growing up during the course of the Revolution brought other pictures as well. Some of them were magnificent, depicting a free, liberated human spirit, and the enthusiastic belief of the people in the final attainment of human justice. Historically, above all else, Russians have craved and fought for social justice.

In the spring of 1918, Germany occupied the Ukraine in accordance with the agreement between the Ukrainian government (the Central Rada) and Germany. The Central Rada had accepted Germany's oversight of the area. This brought an end to the fighting between the Ukrainian Bolsheviks (with Moscow's help) and the Ukrainian Nationalists. Since railroads were once again running, our family left Sevastopol for the City of Kharkov, where my mother's family lived. Unfortunately, our baggage was lost and looted. During this period everything, especially children's clothes, was irreplaceable.

2

Kharkov: The Roots of My Family

My grandfather, Grigory Ivanovich Bilyk-Pichka, a doctor, was a wise, kind man who spent his entire professional life in the workers' section of Kharkov. He came from a family of Ukrainian Dnieper River Cossacks, and was the first one in his family to be educated. His father was a rich farmer on the outskirts of the City of Poltava. It was at Poltava where Peter the Great destroyed the army of Carl XII of Sweden in 1709. Carl XII was counting on the Cossacks' support and ventured far south to the Ukraine. But the majority of Cossacks kept their allegiance to Peter. Pushkin, a Russian poet, wrote a long historical poem, *Poltava*.

My maternal great-grandfather had three sons. He divided his estate between the two eldest and sent the youngest to study to be a doctor. Our family could trace its known roots back to 1505 to the Cossack state *Zaporozhska Sich*. This was a democratic state organized on military principles, with each regiment having its own territory. The colonel of the regiment was the governor of the territory. The leader of the state was Hetman and his government. As unbelievable as it sounds, all of the positions from Hetman down to the lowest official were elected by direct, open votes of all the Cossacks. The purpose of this Cossack state was to defend the Christian Orthodox faith and their own free state. After Byzantium (the Roman Eastern Empire) was overrun by the Turks in 1453, the Cossacks were continuously at war with the Turks and Tartars, who were trying to push through the Balkans and the Black Sea regions to take over the Dnieper River territory. The Cossacks also fought with Poland and Lithuania because of their constant quest for Ukrainian territory and the religious conversion of the population to Roman Catholicism.

In his novel *Taras Bulba*, Nikolay Gogol depicted the life, customs, and battles of the Cossacks. They were colorful knights who had a strong belief in the Orthodox Christian faith, and their state, and would fight to the death for the preservations of their way of life. The late Yul Brynner portrayed Taras Bulba, but the film was typical Hollywood. The pinnacle of artistic representations of the Cossacks is the monumental heroic opera *Taras Bulba* by the renowned Ukrainian composer Nikolai Lisenko. Also, a realistic portrayal can be found in the painting *The Cossacks Write a Letter to the Sultan*, by the famous Russian artist, Ilia Repin. As a historical postscript, they ended their letter with the very "polite" words, "Kiss our asses."

Some wealthy Cossacks had a room in their homes called the *gridnitsa* on whose walls hung the weapons of various family members who had fallen in battles over the centuries. In my great-grandfather's *gridnitsa* hung hundreds of different weapons. The first one was an old saber belonging to Ivan Pichka, who was killed in 1505 when he and his two sons fought against the Turks. His sons buried him, put a cross on the grave, as was the custom of the time, and brought his saber home. That was the start of the family history, with the weapons being the book of chronology.

At the turn of the twentieth century, my grandfather, almost as if he had foreseen the future, went to Poltava, and invited a photographer to take pictures of all the weapons. During the civil war, after the Revolution of 1917, the estate was burned and with it went both the weapons and the history. My grandfather left these photographs in my care.

Grandfather married a Kharkov merchant's daughter with a large dowry. She was a rather chauvinistic Russian. They had three daughters and a son.

My mother, Serophima, was the daughter of Grandfather's brother. He and his wife died young, leaving a girl and a boy. The two remaining brothers adopted the children and so, at the age of seven or eight, my mother came to live in Kharkov. As I grew up, my grandfather treated me differently from his other grandchildren. For him, I was the continuity of the Ukrainian family and history. The other children and grandchildren considered themselves pure Russians and had no interest in their Ukrainian roots.

When we arrived in Kharkov in the late summer of 1918, housing wasn't a problem. Grandfather had a huge flat, but life in the city was chaotic. There was no food in the stores, a scarcity of water, no coal for cooking or heating. It was a disaster for us to lose our baggage and to be left without anything during this horrible time.

The civil war between the Bolsheviks and the Ukrainian Nationalists had started again in 1918, after the German army withdrew because of their own Revolution. The major cities, Kiev and Kharkov, as well as many others, changed hands frequently during that period. Terror and destruction always accompanied these shifts.

3

Krasnaya-Yaruga

My father went to his birthplace, the sugar plant Krasnaya-Yaruga (Beautiful Ravine), in Russia proper, south of the city of Voronezh. He was Russian, and the third generation of workers in the sugar plant. His grandfather and father were *sakharovars* (*sakhar*—sugar, *varit*—to cook). The *sakharovar* was a highly qualified worker who ran the huge centrifuges in which brown sugar was turned into white sugar. Each sugar plant in the country had its own specific tint of white. The position of *sakharovar* was usually inherited, with fathers training their sons from early youth. At that time, there were no automatic gadgets. Everything depended on the *sakharovar*'s experience. Highly skilled workers, like my grandfather, were called the *workers' aristocracy* and held in very high esteem. My grandfather, unfortunately, lost his life in a work accident, leaving my grandmother with four children, ages six to fourteen. My father was the youngest.

The owner of the sugar plant, Kharitonenko, who had nearly a dozen sugar plants, ordered a home built for my grandmother in the village since she could no longer live on plant territory. He gave her a pension and sent the boys to school if they had the aptitude. After finishing the seventh grade, my father enrolled in Kharitonenko's private technical school in the City of Summy, the company's headquarters. After four years, after completing middle school and professional education, he had an official title, "diplomed mechanic," and even a special cap to wear. At the turn of the century, this was a very substantial education.

For my father, returning to the plant meant coming home. His mother, brother, sister and her husband and their three children all lived there. Both his brother and brother-in-law worked at the plant.

The plant's director greeted my father's arrival with great pleasure. Since the head engineer had recently left, the director immediately appointed my father head mechanic and later head engineer. His task was to rehabilitate the plant, damaged during the various battles and not operational since the previous winter. The peasants' sugar beets had been left unprocessed, so the peasants and the workers had not been paid.

In the spring of 1918, the peasants were asked to plant their beets in preparation for the plant's winter work. Then the unforeseeable happened. Both the head and second engineers left. Even worse, there were no new machines and no way to get parts to replace the old or damaged ones. Father brought us from Kharkov and straight away started working with all his energy. All the workers followed him, working without any pay.

We settled into the house of the head engineer. There were two spacious houses, the director's and the head engineer's, situated in a parklike setting, and built in the classical style of architecture. For us wanderers, accustomed to living in cramped quarters, this change was overwhelming. Mama told me later I kept complaining that there were so many rooms. It just wasn't cozy. I didn't want to sleep alone in my bedroom so for awhile I slept in Kolia's room.

We had nothing. Fortunately, some furniture remained in the house and our two families, the one in Kharkov and the one here, gave us some blankets, sheets, towels, and other things. We were surprised to have enough good food. The tranquility was entirely unusual for us. There was no war, no killing, no frightening stories about killing, and no quarrels between people of different political camps. We were not used to this kind of life. We could not even imagine it could exist.

Sugar plants in Russia were unique economic and social organizations. They were situated in southern Russia and the northern Ukraine where there is still a sugar beet belt. Because sugar beets must be washed, plants were situated on rivers or lakes.

Our plant was located on a lake. It stood on a large piece of land surrounded by a tall red brick wall with two watchman's gates. Inside was not only the plant but a big park, an orchard, the administration and office buildings, workers' housing, a railroad station, a school, a store, a theater, a club, and the orchestra room and library. The streets and square were cobblestone. There was running water, indoor sanitation, and coal and wood for heating were delivered.

Each sugar plant was a self-sufficient entity. Interdependence existed between the plant and the surrounding villages and their people who planted white sugar beets. The majority of jobs at the plant, both white- and blue-collar, were inherited and represented several generations of employment. Intermarriages made the plant's population a very close-knit community, somewhat like a commune.

Even during this time of civil war, there was no shortage of food here, but there were serious shortages of clothing, footwear, and household items like soap, thread, nails, utensils, and many more. For doing laundry, centuries-old ingenuity provided a simple washing solution. On hot wood ash boiling water was poured into a wooden tub. Clothing was left in this solution overnight, then washed, boiled with some herb roots, and finally rinsed. The laundry looked beautiful! We washed our faces and bodies in a formula of water, egg yolks, various boiled roots, and homemade vinegar. Fruits and vegetables were available during both summer and winter in the *poghreb*, a room dug deep in the ground used for cold storage. Usually, only a ladder or stairs could reach this room.

Sauerkraut with carrots, cucumbers, apples, tomatoes, mushrooms, and various berries were usually pickled fresh in barrels or jars using various solutions. I liked doing these activities but my favorite was the preparation of preserves.

The standard of living for workers in the sugar plants was generally much higher than that of the working class in the cities. All employees had inexpensive housing, vegetable gardens, and big orchards owned by the plant and available to the employees. They had chickens, turkeys, pigs, and some even had cows in stalls outside the plant walls. There was a small clinic hospital staffed by a doctor, a nurse, and a midwife. Literacy was high. All of this helped develop a high level of class awareness among the workers, creating the right ground for Marxist teaching and the acceptance of the Revolution with Lenin as its leader.

As the civil war still raged, the reconstruction of the plant proceeded with great difficulty. Father was trading with the other sugar and industrial plants for needed machinery and parts. In fact, it was like a circus balancing act. For example, to get much-needed machinery and parts from the Voronezh industrial plant, grains had to be borrowed from the peasants with the promise that once the plant was working, they would be paid. The grains were then bartered with the Voronezh plant for machinery.

Finally, at the beginning of the winter of 1919, the eagerly awaited event occurred. The plant reopened! A happy, enthusiastic celebration ensued. Hundreds of people gathered, including peasants from the villages, workers, the administration, and the political bosses from the district. Speeches were made. Father and the directors were celebrities. Everybody was very tired, having worked up to eighteen hours a day. It was triumph in the midst of fear. The White Army was moving from the south toward Moscow, and the foreign armies were on Russian soil.

People looked poor in their old worn-out clothes. Nothing had been in the stores for years. The children were in the worst predicament in their outgrown and dilapidated clothes. Soon the picture changed. The director allowed sugar sacks to be made into clothes for the children. Our school and important event dresses were made from high quality sugar sacks that were almost white and very durable. Our afterschool dresses were made from second quality sacks used for brown sugar. They were light brown and very coarse. We all looked alike, like prisoners in the same outfit. But our winter clothes were a colorful parade of everything possible, the most popular being Grandma's and Grandpa's old boots and coats. Summer was heaven, since we could run around barefoot.

My Family Life

We liked to play outside the plant walls in the forest where the gardens belonging to the plant workers were located. Shortly after our arrival, some children told us, "Let's pull out some carrots and pick some pea pods." We ran over these gardens like savages, not so much picking as destroying. Kolia and I didn't realize that we were stealing and proudly brought some carrots home. Mama was perturbed and immediately called Father from the plant. Father was outraged and yelled at us as we had never been yelled at before. Since we were not used to this, we cried loudly. Our parents explained to us that we were stealing. The gardens belonged to other people, and each garden meant survival from hunger. Father said he and Mama wanted to be proud, not ashamed of us. Then Father found out whose gardens we had savaged, went to each of those families, and apologized. My father's actions made a good impression on the com-

My father, Michael Shuliak, at
twenty-one years old.

Serofima Bilyk, my mother, at
nineteen years of age just
before her marriage.

munity and set a stronger precedent for establishing the parental responsibility for any damage done by their children. For us, it was a lesson for life.

My father was a tall, well-built, handsome man. Ideologically he reflected the main traits of Russian character and tradition, a populist striving for social justice. On moral issues, he was a follower of Leo Tolstoy, even wearing a comfortable shirt called a *Tolstovka* designed and sewed by Tolstoy himself. As a true Russian, he liked singing and entertaining guests. Father's kindness was well known and sometimes people abused it, much to my mother's anger.

I heard people say my mother was beautiful, proud, and *gorodskaya*—a city lady. She was not tall, though not big. She was quite strict with us and demanded polite behavior and honesty. She disliked women's gossip and sitting in each other's homes drinking vodka. She was very practical and calm. Some of these qualities she passed on to me. For that time, Mama had a good education—six years of gymnasium.

Happiness, I still remember with nostalgia, was our family evenings, especially during the winter. Outside it was cold, down to forty degrees below zero. Inside it was warm and cozy. Mama and Marya, a fifteen-year-old orphan from the village who lived with us for ten years, prepared dinner. Kolia and I would do our school assignments, and Papa would be reading. After supper, Papa would read us either fairy tales or some selections from children's literature. Then there would be a discussion about the readings, with clear-cut distinctions made between the positive and negative heroes. Our favorites were Afanasiev's Fairy Tales, the Brothers Grimm, and Hans Christian Andersen. As I understand, fairy tales are the best-known form for developing a child's imagination and good morals. Our problem was a lack of books. The school library had a few books but the plant's library was completely empty. Various people may have owned a few which we borrowed. We were lucky. We found a source of books next door at the director's home. I think this was the first time in my life I saw a big library. The director's wife was a very private lady from the gentry. She was highly intelligent and liberal. She had fun helping us. She would make her orderly library totally disorderly until she found the books she thought were right for us. Later, as we read better, we would spend hours lying on the floor reading and looking at pictures in the oversized history books. I loved these books. That was the beginning of my love of history. It was also the first time I realized our world was so big.

End of the Civil War—Life is Normalized

During the summer of 1919, the Red Army crushed General Denikin's White Army at Orel, a city near Moscow. The White Army officers were sure that Moscow would be in their hands in just a few days so a competition started among the regiments for the honor of being the first to enter the city. As has happened more than once in history, reality can be cruel. In fact, this happened to Adolf Hitler in 1942. Hitler ordered that a victory banquet be held in the *Leningrad Hotel* as soon as the city was taken. A strictly German menu was ordered, but fortunately, was never to be prepared. At the end of

1919, the armies of General Yudenich, near St. Petersburg, and General Vrangel, in the south, supported by England and France respectively, quickly passed into history, leaving behind them destruction and tears. All together, fourteen foreign countries were involved in the war against the Soviet Republic.

The civil war in our central Russian region was finally over. The outside world regarded the Russian Revolution as a defeat of the values and morality of the civilized world. The most terrible sin of the Revolution was its total disregard for the international bankers and the industrial companies, the expropriation of banks and factories. The civilized world—England, France, Italy, Japan, the United States, and others—sent their armies, fleets, equipment, and money supporting the White Russian generals and their armies for the purpose of reestablishing that "civilization," its values, banks, and factories. It didn't matter that millions of people were killed and the country nearly demolished, its culture and the arts on the brink of annihilation. And that she, Mother Russia, lay half-dead like a huge prehistoric animal. But unexpectedly, she got up and, supported by millions of her enthusiastic citizens, shook off the invaders and stepped into a new age. Was it better? Worse? The same? It is history's task to answer that. Both sides were wrong about this world-wide upheaval. Lenin was convinced a world revolution that had started in Germany would come. The Allies were equally sure the Bolshevik regime of amateurs would disappear, like lightning in the sky.

The romanticism of the Revolution, the innocent belief in the goodness of free human beings eventually resulting in a just human society, was blooming like a fantastic flower. The first period of Revolution, of a new civilization is usually unifying, when the great majority has enthusiasm and heroic courage for the collective interest. New beliefs, customs, morals, and organizations are developing, and above all, endurance, patience, and a great trust in its leaders. Some philosophers, including Compte de Saint Simon, have called this period "organic," which in time evolves to the "critical" period. This second period is characterized by division, followed by criticism, skepticism, individualism, and personal greed, often with selfish leaders representing mainly the strongest group or class in the nation.

Russia was in the first glorious period. Some historians have assumed this new society was launched on two different premises that both had the same aim. The first goal was the realization of the ancient messianic ideal of Holy Russia, the transformation of mankind into God's just society. The second mission contained the ideal for a new kind of human—the Communist—launching a working-class revolution to establish a communist, fair society. Those historians have said that the new Bolshevik ideal was grafted onto the old Russian religious ideal. I am not going to discuss the validity of this assumption. Suffice it to say the ground was fertile for the acceptance of this illusion or reality.

Krasnaya-Yaruga, a large village, surrounded the sugar plant. People from the plant belonged to the main cathedral located just across the lake at the top of a hill. Historically, Russian churches were built on hills with high cupolas and a tall cross. Russian churches served another purpose, like a lighthouse for seamen. The cupola and cross could be seen over the horizon of the forest as good orientation points for traveling peasants, especially in winter. My mother was religious and took us to church. Usually, my grandma came along. This was my first introduction to church. In the early 1920s, the government had not yet taken any drastic measures against religion other than antireligious propaganda and the policies of disestablishment. This ordinary cathedral impressed me with its colorful icons, religious paintings and frescos, the sounds of the choir, and the solemn ritual. I kept asking how they had painted Jesus and the angels so high in the cupola.

Kolia and I did not understand all of the priest's sermons but understand that Jesus said all people are equal, the poor are no worse than the rich, and that God's just world on earth will come. Later in school, in the Young Pioneers and in the Komsomol organizations, I heard similar sermons, but without Jesus. What we didn't understand was, if the teachings of the church and the Young Pioneers and the Komsomol were similar, then why were the Communists against the church?

I listened to my *Babunia*'s (Grandma) praying. She often talked to St. Mary, Mother of God, saying that she was a sinner and asking St. Mary to help her with something. Later, I noticed what appeared to be a pattern with all older women. They would talk to their saints, asking them for something and in return, promising them something, like good behavior and not arguing with their neighbor.

In the Orthodox Church, singing plays a dominant role. Prayer

15

and the liturgy are often described as "singing to God," and singing is an element of worship. Musical instruments are not used, only the human voice, the soprano flying high to the sky and the bass pronouncing the earth-bound human qualities.

School

In the middle of a big park stood a beautiful white building, the home of the plant owner, Kharitonenko, which he used only for a few days when he visited. Prior to the Revolution, he gave it to the plant to use as a school. With his financial help, it was turned into a school with several good-sized classrooms. The big fancy hall with large mirrors and elaborate ceiling was left unchanged. The students learned to be careful and not do any damage. After all, it was our school. There were seven grades with between one hundred ten and one hundred thirty pupils. There were seven teachers, including a director.

At the beginning of the Revolution, the school system was run under the slogan, "Liberation from the old regime's shackles and prejudices." Physical punishment of pupils by teachers was forbidden. Programs changed. We were freed from the study of religion, history, foreign languages. The latter two, however, were soon reinstated. Instead of history, social studies was introduced. This was indoctrination into the new Communist ideology. Examinations and grades were also abolished. The emphasis of education was to be on the development of manual skills. But, in our school, common sense prevailed and only a few of these changes were accepted.

In 1923, the Commissar for the People's Education, Anatoly Lunacharsky, a highly educated Old Bolshevik—member of the Communist party before the Revolution of 1917—intellectual and writer who was supported by both Lenin and Nadezhda Krupskaya (Lenin's wife), realized the necessity for knowledge in education. Lunacharsky put forth a directive establishing compulsory education for all children, reinstating strong basic education programs, and strengthening teachers' authority and pupils' discipline.

In 1919, Kolia turned seven and was placed in the first grade. I did all of his homework with him. The next year, Kolia went to second grade and I, a six-year-old, was allowed to sit in his class with him. Again, I did all of his class assignments. The following year when I was seven, I wanted to be in the third grade with Kolia. The director put me back in the second grade which I had to repeat. He explained and advised my parents that at age twelve, when I graduated from seventh grade, no school would accept me for further schooling because of my youth.

Our teachers were well educated and not particularly old. Material conditions for the teachers at our plant were good, better than in cities or villages, attracting better teachers. The gymnasiums and even primary schools during tsarist times were good because most of the teachers knew their subjects and many of them were ideologically members of the radical or liberal intelligentsia.

The worst problem was the lack of supplies like notebooks, paper, pencils, and above all, new textbooks. We used notebooks over and over again—writing and erasing and writing again until there were holes in the paper. Even though we had a scarcity of pencils, we did have some newspaper on which we wrote with locally produced ink. Teachers were asked to omit the old political material in their teaching and to use material from newspapers in the upper grades. We read stories from old Russian classics usually about the lives of poor children and peasants, and frequently the teachers made some changes in these stories. I remember once when I was in the third grade, we read a story about a poor homeless boy who stood outside a window watching a children's Christmas party in a very wealthy home. He was so overwhelmed by the beautiful things he saw that he didn't even feel the cold and froze to death. I had read this story before and knew that the end was different. In the "real" version, angels came down from Heaven and took the boy to Paradise. I stood up and told the class this ending. The teacher said it was not the same story. I stubbornly persisted, insisting that it *was* the same story. After this incident, the teacher came to our home and talked with my mother, who talked with me. Mama explained to me that my behavior was wrong and I made the teacher look unreliable in front of her class.

The attitude of Russian parents toward teachers was respectful and supportive. If a teacher wrote or called a child's parents to school for a conference, the parent would agree with the teacher and discipline the child. There were strict rules of behavior. We were expected to come to school neat and clean, although, from a fashion point-of-view, we looked pretty destitute; or when wearing our "sack clothes," we looked like prisoners. I remember that for my birthday my godmother from Kharkov, Nina, the youngest sister of my mother, sent me a very simple *new* dress. I was so excited that I showed it to all of the kids in school and Kolia followed me around explaining everything about this dress. It was, indeed, a big event for all of us.

To say we were happy doesn't fully explain our feelings during that period. We were a part of the changes and excitement of that time. Indeed, we were a very happy collective. From early spring to late autumn we were busy playing, picking berries, mushrooms, and nuts, gathering sap from the maple trees and fruit from the orchards. Nobody asked us to do this, we just wanted to help. At one time, I believe, Nikita Khrushchev bragged that the great American sport of baseball had originated in Russia. I don't know whether Russians are really guilty of that sin, but I know we played a game called *Laptu* which had all the ingredients of baseball.

During the winter, sledding down the long slopes was our favorite activity. We especially liked the big sleds for five to ten kids. Our winter fashion parade would start with Grandpa's or Grandma's old felt boots and sheepskin coats called *kozhukh*.

Other parents often pointed to Kolia and me as good examples for their children. Kolia and I were always together. He never left my side and always protected me, holding my hand. I was a funny kid. In school, I was always one of the top students, but I was so gullible I believed everyone even when I knew they were lying. Kids would sometimes make fun of me, but they were afraid of Kolia because he was strong and smart. When they would start teasing me, Kolia would say to them, "Get away! My Ninok is the smartest kid in the school and you are fools." I depended on Kolia, believed in him, and was proud of him and myself.

Changes

Political, social, and economic life was rapidly changing. The first task of the plant was to organize a representative *Soviet (council)*, the government for the plant. Democratic voting was a new experience for everybody. I remember my Mama dressed in the only one good dress she had, and we in our best, and only, old leftovers

18

solemnly going to vote in the plant's theater. There were many people. Some were sitting in circles with their ballot, a list of the candidates, discussing them, while others had already voted and were starting to celebrate, drinking and singing revolutionary songs.

Pretty soon, a Sovietnik, an advisor, arrived. He was an Old Bolshevik whose name was Michael. People called him Michael Ivanovich. He was from this region and some people knew him. The Old Bolsheviks, members of the Communist Party before the 1917 Revolution, were highly respected. Later, Stalin had most of them killed. The majority of them were exceptional human beings, honest, idealistic, and believing in a just Communist society. They expected nothing good for themselves, but anticipated prison, possibly a death sentence, or exile to Siberia and deprivation of almost everything. Only a very few of the extremely egotistical among them, like Stalin and Trotsky, were counting on personal gain.

My father became good friends with Michael Ivanovich. He was a frequent visitor to our home, sometimes coming for dinner or just to spend the evening. He was in his early forties and unmarried, because, he said, it was irresponsible for a revolutionary without any means of support to have children. Who would take care of them if something happened to him? I really loved him. He spoke simply, with a melancholy smile, telling his life experiences. He had been a Siberian exile living in many small villages with other exiles. The police were constantly shifting the exiles throughout the *taiga* (forest), where villages were sometimes up to a fifty or more kilometers from each other. Some of his friends from exile were in current leadership positions in Moscow. He escaped from one of these villages and almost ended up dead. He was lost in the *taiga* for many days with no food or water. He was rescued by a group of Mongolian hunters who found him and took him to their home where he worked for a few years. Finally, he connected with a secret party network, the so-called *yavki*. Here revolutionaries could get the necessary supplies to exist, personal documents, and most importantly, the address of the next *yavka*. In this way, he got back to Moscow.

The Sovietnik's region was composed of many towns and villages. Mikhail Ivanovich was the first to institute a "school" of political ideology for both the plant workers and the villagers. By the age of six or seven, the names of Karl Marx, Friedrich Engels, and Vladimir Lenin were familiar to me. I knew who they were and understood that they were the best friends of working men. The Sovietnik's lectures in the theater brought full houses as the villagers came in droves to listen to him so as to understand better the new regime and the ideas of the Revolution. He conveyed these ideas: From ancient times, prophets and philosophers dreamed of a society where each individual would be compassionate, cooperative, and honest and the society and each individual would prosper. Now we had come to the beginning of that time, albeit the road would be very long and difficult.

The teachings of Marx and Engels, so eloquently expressed in the *Communist Manifesto of 1848*, lie at the heart of the revolutionary struggle. They foretold the coming of a new age in which the oppression of man by man would cease to exist. The wealth of the nation would belong to all the people. The Russian Revolution was the first in history where the class of exploiters was not simply exchanged for another class of exploiters, but in fact, abolished. The hardest task was going to be to try to change human character. The sovietnik's lectures were an unmatched phenomenon. Mikhail Ivanovich explained Marxist principles, fortified beliefs and strengthened the will to live and work. In addition, he sang currently popular revolutionary songs, and the so-called modern *chastushki*. These were four-line, comical songs based on folklore and often created by exiles.

New Political and Social Organizations

The civil war in European Russia was over. There was no more fear of the old regime being restored. Several respected workers joined the Communist Party, which became the engine for change. The sovietnik was its godfather. Sometime later, the Communist Youth League (the Komsomol) was organized. Again, only good and honest young men and women were admitted. This selection of only the best people for the Communist Party and Komsomol made both the people and the organizations highly respected, though, much later, this was to change and develop somewhat darker overtones.

The solemn ritual of the Komsomol installations was a big event for the plant and the village. The Secretary of the District Komsomol Committee arrived. The theater was packed with people, "like herrings in a barrel" as the Russian proverb says. The orchestra, as usual, played too loud, blaring the music to cover their lack of mastery and artisty for the new songs. In the on-going search for the new, the new was still hazy. Therefore, during this time of change and destruction of the old, the guiding beacons became intuition and ideas.

The Secretary called the new members of the League, one by one, to the stage where they were seated. Then people listened attentively to his speech explaining the ideas and the practical aspects of this new organization and society. After his speech, he called each new member to the podium and presented the Communist Youth League membership card. People were overcome with enthusiasm and clapping. It was the hypnotic effect of mass meetings, but also genuine. Many speakers congratulated the new members for being in the vanguard of the working people's revolution. I knew that in seven or eight years, I would be a member of Komsomol.

The first post-Revolution years brought both economic and social reforms and radicalism in attitude. The influence of the church was eliminated from all spheres of life. Only civil marriages were recognized as legal, abortions and divorces on demand were permitted, and above all, women were made equal with men in all matters. A women's organization was established, the so-called Women Delegates (Zhenskije delegatki) and this made many men fearful. They became known as a most colorful and active group, which always meant business equality for women. My Aunt Ekaterina was one of the leaders—a member of the Executive Committee. There were representatives of this group in the plant's Soviet and Father complained to Auntie that the women's demands frequently went too far.

One of the first tasks of this group was to stop the assaults on wives by husbands. They organized People's Trials, the first of which was a huge event held in the theater. On trial was a man who constantly beat his wife when drunk, for him it was a rather normal condition. He was arrested at the demand of the Women's Committee. The theater was full! The judges—the Executive Committee—were seated on the stage behind a table covered with red cloth. The prosecutor, one of the most educated of the Women's Committee members, was seated separately. A policeman (*militsioner*) brought in the accused. The prosecutor, then the judges, and finally men and women from the audience accused the man of antisocial behavior, of believing and adhering to old regime traditions, and so forth. The judges sen-

21

tenced him to public censure with the proviso if he did not improve, he would be rearrested and sent to the regional court for punishment. Trials like this were repeated at the plant and in the village.

The results were unbelievable, like in a fairy tale. Men said it was better to go to prison than to be put through this public trial. "You were laughed at, you became a public laughing stock, and the target of jokes," they agreed. But most importantly, the assaults on wives stopped! My auntie, a tall, handsome woman, and a widow, laughed proudly that, now, when a man met her in the street, he would bow to her, as to a queen, take off his cap, and say, "My respects to you, Ekaterina Pavlovna."

The Women's Organization, along with Komsomol, organized a drama group and presented "A Woman's Theater." The plays put on were usually short, funny, and simplistic about women's fate in the past and how it had changed in the present. *Delegatki* became actresses and the Komsomol played the role of the classic Greek chorus, now called the "Blue Blouse," whose uniforms included wearing a blue blouse. As in Greek tragedies, it became the expression of the new morals and ethics.

The new "famous" actresses often didn't remember their lines. This happened to my auntie. She would stop, laugh, and say aloud, "Oh! I forgot my lines. Prompter, please say them a bit louder." This always elicited lots of laughs and fun. People loved it. Indeed, this was "theater." Actually, in time, some of the actresses became quite good and staged a few of Leo Tolstoy's plays. One such play that was staged was *The First Distiller*, a humorous antialcohol morality play.

In 1921 Lenin introduced the New Economic Policy (NEP) allowing private enterprise. A profit-based economy, abolished in accordance with Marxist theory, was now being reestablished to encourage the small private enterprises. A certain percent of the peasants' harvest was given to the state and beyond that, the rest was theirs. This and other measures that were imposed resulted in rapid economic development and people's lives started to improve.

Cultural Revolution

At the beginning of the 1920s, the popular call was the Cultural

Revolution, transformation of Russia into a modern, socialist, cultural state. The old values and habits, including religion as "superstition" were discredited. The new world and a new man had to be created.

Between Communist intellectuals developed discussion and disagreements about the nature of culture. Some wanted to destroy the "bourgeois" culture and develop a new "proletarian" culture. But Lenin and his Commissar of Education, Anatoly Lunacharsky, thought culture had a general meaning beyond the class differences. People liked the idea of becoming more cultured and an enthusiastic movement flourished. The first task was the fight against illiteracy; over eighty-five percent of Russians were illiterate. Lenin's wife, Nadezhda Konstantinovna Krupskaia, was supervising this task. Demands for basic culture like hygiene, proper behavior, table manners, manners in public places, proper speech, appropriate dress, and many more. On the higher level were demands for knowledge of literature, theater, music, art, and Russian history. But, above all was the demand for mastering the Communist ideology.

From the beginning of the establishment of Soviet power, Lenin understood that one of the main difficulties was the absence of managers, professionals, and technicians. The educated class was composed primarily of the nobility, and had all but vanished. About two million people emigrated, many fell victim to the war, and the rest accepted this new regime with reservation. The task of the government educational policy was to attract the proletarian and peasant classes to institutions of learning. Professor Pokrovsky, the Deputy Commissar of Education, as early as 1918, had instituted *Rabfaks*—Worker's Faculties or Schools—which provided accelerated matriculation courses. The result of this rapid proletarianization of universities and institutes was the equally rapid decline of the intellectual and professional levels, at least for a while.

A young chemist, a very nice fellow who had just graduated from the Chemistry Institute, arrived at the beginning of the 1920s. It wasn't long before the chief chemist became extremely upset with this young man because of his poor preparation in his profession. But, at the same time, we children scored well, because the chemist, Alyosha, was a member of *Komsomol*, and started to organize the new children's organization, the Young Pioneers.

School Activities

The school was taking an active part in the Cultural Revolution.

Nina Petrovna, a teacher of Russian, strove to inculcate the love of books in her students. It seems all great thinkers are also great readers and their relationship with books resembles the relationship of the mythical Anteus with the earth. Anteus received his great strength from the earth. When he was lifted into the air, losing his connection with the earth, he lost his strength. A book helps us unite the two worlds, what "was," and what "will be."

Nina Petrovna's Russian was excellent, rhythmical, and devoid of popular slang, which was becoming a norm of speech. She was an outstanding artistic reader. Her unforgettable reading of the novel in verse, *The Russian Women*, by the poet Nikolai Nekrasov, stimulated deep and lasting emotions in us. *The Russian Women* is a highly moving, dramatic, historically truthful story about Princess Masha Volkonskaya, not yet twenty, and Princess Katerina Trubetskaya, in her early twenties, who followed their husbands into Siberian exile. Their husbands, young aristocratic princes, heroes of the Napoleonic War of 1812, were leaders of the first Russian revolution of 1825, the Decembrist Uprising. The demands of this revolution, to Tsar Nikolai I, were reforms, specifically, the establishment of a constitutional monarchy and the abolishment of serfdom. Freedom for all peasants. The two young princesses, both renowned beauties of the tsar's court, went through inhumane suffering as they traveled about 6,000 kilometers from St. Petersburg to Nerchinsk, to join their husbands where they and other Decembrists were working in the gold mines. These courageous women joined their husbands in exile to demonstrate to the tsar and the nobility not only their love for their husbands but their belief and support of their husbands' ideals.

Nikolai I did everything that he could to prevent the young princesses from going. But he couldn't prevent them from joining their husbands and, if he had, the Church would have been against him. This was the very first political exile to Siberia; the Decembrists were chained and walked together with criminals. Conditions were intolerable. It took thirty years, after the death of Nikolai I in 1855 before the more liberal Tsar Alexander II granted amnesty to the exiles and they were able to return. By this time Katerina Trubetskaya

24

had died. In her diary, Masha Volkonskaya wrote a very sincere and emotional tribute to the simple people of Russia—the peasants—for their understanding and support. I doubt that anyone who reads this poem can keep a dry eye. In class, we all cried and felt ashamed of displaying such emotion. Nina Petrovna told us that there was no shame in crying because tears open the heart and make it softer and prepare it to help others in need. She designed this poem as a dramatic play for two of her classes and each of us memorized an assigned role. We performed the play many times in school, in the theater, and in the village, with great success.

The Russian language is close to being phonetic, that is, as the word is written so it is pronounced, although there are some phonetic rules. In order to develop our memory and to appreciate the beauty of the language, we were required to memorize many poems of the great Russian classical poets like Alexander Pushkin, Michael Lermontov, Nikolai Nekrasov, Alexander Blok, and the contemporary Sergei Yesenin, Vladimir Mayakovsky, and many more. Another characteristic of the Russian language is its ability to "create perfect poetry even when it is minor; and when it is major, it is great without qualifications" (D. S. Mirsky, *History of Russian Literature*, Vintage Books, 1958, p. 74).

Russian poetry in translation loses much of its beauty and form. One of our greatest poets was Alexander Pushkin whose ancestry was Black Ethiopian. The Russian ambassador to Persia, Count Apraksin, bought a boy of about seven at the slave market in Teheran at the end of the 17th century. This young child, kidnapped by slave traders, was the son of a tribal chief. The ambassador was very impressed by the boy's intelligence and good conduct, so he sent him to Peter the Great as a gift. Peter liked the boy so much that he had him christened into the Russian Orthodox faith (Ethiopians are Orthodox Christians) and adopted as his son. Peter sent him abroad for his higher education and as the son of the Russian tsar, he was received in all of the European courts. After he returned home, Peter married him into a *boyar* (aristocratic) family. The marriage produced three sons, each of whom held a high government position. The daughter of one of these sons (a famous admiral) married into the aristocratic Pushkin family and became the mother of Russia's pride, Alexander. Pushkin wrote a short story about his ancestry, *The Arap of Peter the Great*. The best portrait of Pushkin by artist Kiprensky shows the Negroid features: his hair is softly curly, lips a little larger, eyes almond-shaped, and skin a bit darker.

Pushkin was one of the creators of the modern Russian language. We recited his poetry in our classrooms and at gatherings and celebrations. The beauty and strength of his language makes his poetry especially unforgettable. In the late 1960s, the students of the Russian Club at the New York State University at Buffalo presented me with a unique edition of *Pushkin's Ruslan and Ludmilla* as a token of their appreciation for my work as their club advisor. This was a hand-painted edition written in German and limited to about one hundred copies. As I looked through it, I started to recite, in Russian, of course, several long passages. I asked my students, "When do you think I learned this?" There were no guesses, so I told them. "When I was in the third through seventh grades."

Their response was, "Unbelievable!" That is what it means to have that beauty of language in combination with the love of poetry—it does become immortal in one's memory. It felt good to be able to recite this beautiful poetry and I have my cousin, Nina, from Kharkov, and Nina Petrovna to thank for my training. I enjoyed performing.

Our Tragedy

I grew up in a peaceful and loving family. My parents were devoted to each other and to us. In family matters, my mother's word prevailed. My parents seldom screamed at us, rather they would explain why it was wrong and tell us not to do it again. We had quite strict rules even about small things such as taking our shoes off in the house and never sitting on the bed in street clothes.

Generally, protracted discussions about behavior rarely occurred in Russian families. The word of the parents was heard and obeyed and, if it wasn't, parents would yell at their children. To do a comparison between my family and the contemporary American family would be senseless because of the cultural and time differences. Many years later, when my daughter, Lucy, was a teenager, she was strong-willed and independent. I frequently felt ill-equipped to deal with her because of these same cultural and time differences. Besides, it seems

Portrait of Alexander Pushkin by D. Kiprensky, 1827.

that growing up in a peaceful family leaves one less prepared to deal with life's hardships and ways to approach and resolve differences.

A tragedy devastated our family. Kolia fell ill with encephalitis and died. He was eleven years old. Mama, Papa, and I never overcame this loss. This probably had a profound influence on my development and character. Kolia, a good-looking, tall, intelligent boy, was always by my side. He was my protector, especially from the nasty boys. Now, I stayed away from them. I wasn't afraid of them or anyone, but it hurt if they laughed at me for being so naive to believe them. I've never been able to overcome this character trait completely. I didn't want to complain to Mama and Papa and make them suffer more, so I learned to keep this to myself.

Mama and I went to Kharkov where her family was very helpful. I remember *Dedia* (grandpa) taking me to the opera. At that time, Kharkov was the capitol of the Ukraine and had first-class theaters. We saw Rimsky-Korsakov's *Snow Maiden*. At nine years old I was so impressed that the beautiful images of that "realistic" fairy tale are still in my mind. *Dedia* explained the opera to me. A beautiful snow maiden lives a life of eternal cold that she gladly trades for a moment of human love and warmth, and then melts. Just before the overture started, *Dedia* told me, "In the beginning, the music is grim and morose, characterizing Father Frost. It then develops into a tender, delicate motif representing the coming of spring and love." This was my first lesson on how to understand classical music and see an opera.

After Kolia's death, walking alone gave me the most painful feeling and while I didn't cry, tears streamed down my face almost all the time. Every morning, one or more kids would knock on my door to take me to school and bring me back. They would also come by and ask me to come and play with them. It helped.

The Young Pioneers

One of the popular expressions of that time was about children being the future. The duty of adults was to prepare children for the hard work of building the Socialist society. Because of this attitude, children were a privileged group.

We children needed a place to play sports and games, so several *subbotniks* were organized to build a sport and playground behind the school, close to the lake. *Subbotniks* (*subbota* equals *Saturday*) were a new craze around the country. In the newspaper many pictures of Lenin were shown carrying logs at *subbotniks*. Millions of people were cleaning, building, and planting as volunteers to make the country clean and look pleasant. My papa, as always, was one of the organizers.

An inviting and beautiful sport and playground was built, but there was no sports instructor! The Komsomol sent one of them, a young man, to Voronezh, the capitol of our *oblast* (region), to take a course in sports instruction. This place drew both children and adults. It was always fun. There were always lots of competitions, and sometimes, even clashes.

Then it was our turn! One day, all we kids were gathered in the school hall and the director of the school, with Alyosha, who had become the Young Pioneers organizer, told us about this new organization which had been founded in Moscow and was spreading through the whole country. The aim of the Young Pioneers was to involve us in helping our parents build a Socialist society. We had to be good and disciplined students and prepare ourselves to be good doctors, teachers, engineers, and other professionals in the future.

Several weeks later, on May 1, I think, in 1923, the greatest celebration to date took place at the plant. It was the day the Young Pioneers took their Oath of Allegience. That day was full of excitement! After the May Day demonstration in the village square, thousands of people gathered at our sports grounds. The leaders of the new regime had learned quickly how to impress people. The ancient Roman slogan—bread and entertainment—worked magically.

I remember this day vividly. Afterward, in school we were asked to write essays about this day. My essay was published in the local paper. I was extremely proud of my first publication and kept a copy until it perished in the flames of WWII.

On a high pole, the Soviet red flag with its hammer and sickle was flying proudly. We were gathered in two lines on either side of the pole facing each other, and dressed in our new uniforms: white shirt, dark pants or skirts, and the red Pioneer necktie. The plant provided the money for our uniforms. Dignitaries from the plant and village, the District's Komsomol secretary, and the Pioneer organizer gathered in front of the pole. The orchestra played the "International" and we saluted—the right hand, with fingers straight up, was over the middle of our foreheads as a symbol that on each of the five continents of the Earth there were exploited and unhappy children. The dignitaries then gave speeches. After that, the district Pioneer organizer read the oath that we repeated while, again, saluting.

I think I still remember the oath:

I, a young pioneer of the Soviet Union, in the presence of my comrades, solemnly swear to uphold the interests of the working class in its struggle for the liberation of the whole world. I will steadfastly fulfill the rules and customs of the Young Pioneers.

The organizer finished with our motto, "Be ready," and we answered, "Always ready." Then he read the rules and customs of the Young Pioneers. They were general and humanistic: Be honest, a good student, and a kind friend to your comrades; respect your parents and teachers; don't smoke or drink; and more. Then everyone congratulated us. My *babunia* (grandma), who had a great sense of humor, asked if she could be an Old Pioneer because the rules and customs sounded much like the Ten Commandments of God. People laughed.

The director's wife said, "My dear children, remember this day and your oath throughout your lives and try to live according to it."

Like an avalanche, parents started screaming to their children, "Vanya, Vasia, Ania . . . remember your oath, remember your oath!"

Emotions ran high. Mothers were crying. I, like all the others, felt the seriousness of the moment. I had an aim in life, a task to fulfill. I grew up and matured in those few hours.

Yes, we were changed. At our first meeting we elected a council and a leader of our detachment. Discipline in the classroom, good behavior at home and elsewhere became strictly our responsibility. At our meetings we discussed, sometimes criticizing harshly, those who didn't adhere to our accepted rules. This collective ethic that made each of us feel responsible to our classmates for personal behavior also made each of us feel responsible for the behavior of the whole. Better students helped weaker students. I tutored some of my classmates. The results of helping each other were always amazing.

In the school choir we learned many revolutionary and folk songs. People loved to hear and sing along with us, so we performed them often. In school we sat at double-seated desks, a boy and a girl at each desk. We didn't feel that there was any difference between us. It's funny, but to this day, in my old age, I don't understand why girls or women have to apply a different strategy to their relationships with boys or men. Perhaps it would be better to be honest and treat them as friends first.

Of the various social assignments we received, a fight against illiteracy was the greatest responsibility. Good students from the fifth through the seventh grade received this assignment. I was eleven, and for three years I taught two middle-aged women.

The assignment of teaching was taken very seriously. We had received instruction in how to teach. Every week, for three winters, I met with my students. In the end, they read, slowly, books and newspapers, and could express themselves in writing. The relationships between these older students and their child-teachers were usually very close and, frequently, even the families became involved. My women and I were good buddies. If it was too cold outside, they would come to my house. They would often bring something to eat like Siberian *pilmeni*, which I loved. After our lessons, we'd have tea or whatever else Mama prepared. My mother had her own class of eight women in school.

In 1918, Russia had an illiteracy rate of about 85 percent. About twenty-five years later, the literacy rate was over 90 percent. The Woman's Organization, the Komsomol, and the Young Pioneers helped achieve this in great part, a result of the Cultural Revolution.

For the New Year, we entertained our parents and the families from the village by singing, dancing, reciting, and presenting short plays around the *yolka* (Christmas tree). Nina Petrovna coached us. Usually parents, mainly mothers, assisted her.

The Russians have a great sense of humor. People liked our acting in little funny sketches, lampoons or just one-liners on conditions of *nekulturnost*, lack of culture, and backwardness. Our teachers wrote them, or took them from the numerous journals like *Krokodil*:

Two boys were talking.
"My family is advancing in culture. My mother bought tooth-brushes for each of us."
"Do you brush your teeth now?"
"Of course. Once a week regularly."

On bureaucracy:
A woman asked a bureaucrat for permission to buy a railroad ticket to Voronezh to see a doctor.
Bureaucrat: "Come tomorrow. I have to think about it."

A meeting of the Village Council.
On the agenda:
The Earth circuits around the Sun.
Decided:
To mobilize the masses for support of this genius Soviet theory.

The Young Pioneers were involved at all the different celebrations whether they were at the plants, theater, in the village square, or in the school hall. Usually, we were the last to appear. Imagine! We were a detachment of Young Pioneers, neatly outfitted in uniforms and stepping smartly. At the front of the detachment was a standard bearer, two drummers, and a bugle player, walking alongside Alyosa, who was also in uniform. People greeted us with warm applause. The plant community, especially the parents, loved us. We were exemplary in our behavior. Sometime after, we would be excused and would leave in an orderly fashion. During the summer, we liked to practice military-style marching in the park, making campfires, and picnicing.

Young Pioneer organizations spread to larger villages where there were at least seven-year schools and Komsomol organizations. Reflecting on those times, I wonder how we were able to carry out all these activities. We were a happy bunch, responsible and proud. I was happy, although Kolia was always on my mind. I often ran to the cemetery, which was quite far from us in the village. I sat down on Kolia's grave and talked to him, telling him what I was doing and asking him for advice. Kids usually walked after me, waited till I finished my talk with Kolia, and brought me home. They did not laugh at me because the teachers had explained to them it was my expression of my deep grief.

The ideological indoctrination later in my life was often flat and dull. During these school days it was absorbing and exciting, perhaps because it was new. This was the program for the formation of a new character, the creation of a new person, a collectivist who was not greedy but sincere and courageous, and above all, honest.

Often, "wise men" came to our school to talk to us. The director of the plant and the sovietnik were two of our favorites. The sovietnik talked to us about courage and responsibility. Sometimes it is an act of courage to live. His own life and the lives of his revolutionary friends, among them Michael Kalinin and his wife, were examples. Michael Kalinin, son of a peasant, was the chairman of the Supreme Soviet of the USSR, equivalent to the president. The sovietnik was not afraid to use sayings from Confucius, Mohammed, and Jesus. Confucius said, "A wise, courageous man expects everything of himself. A weak, mediocre man expects everything from others." We often repeated this.

The director, during his student years in St. Petersburg, belonged to the Russian radical intelligentsia, who, in reality, spearheaded the Revolution. We listened to many interesting stories about their activities. He told us the story of Tamerlane, the Mongol conqueror, comparing him to Trotsky. Tamerlane realized that challenging the Slavic army was a mighty task, so he ordered the steppes in back of his own army to be set on fire. This was cruel, but it resulted in a huge victory, and what's important, he, himself, was in front, leading his army. Yet, courage without kindness and truthfulness usually results in brutality. Trotsky sometimes put machine guns behind the Red Army and those soldiers who did not want to fight and tried to flee were killed. These soldiers were peasants who wanted to go home to their villages and work the land, previously owned by large landowners, and just divided among the peasants according to the Bolshevik reforms. Trotsky's acts were cruel and brutal and contrary to the Revolution. Those who didn't fight in the war, but accepted and believed in the Revolution and helped in any way, were not enemies.

My father knew a lot about Leo Tolstoy and enjoyed telling "Tolstoy tales." One of the stories he told was this:

On a paved road leading to Moscow from Tula (*Yasnaya Poliana*, Tolstoy's estate, was near the City of Tula) walked an old man with a full gray beard wearing his peasant coat sashed with a colorful peasant belt and his peasant cap, a *kartuz*. In his hand was a simple wooden stick. All of a sudden, the new technical wonder, the auto machine, passed by him and the occupants greeted him with great superiority and haughtiness. Fools! They didn't know that tomorrow their wonder machine would be in the past, but Leo Tolstoy would forever be in the present. The chief chemist and Father talked to us about Tolstoy and his teachings of living a respectful life and accepting our individual moral responsibilities.

Tolstoy was every inch the aristocrat in spite of his peasant dress. After his epics *War and Peace* and *Anna Karenina* he turned to religious and philosophical ideas, presenting his moral and ethical code of nonresistance to evil. It's known that Tolstoy's teaching had many followers, one of them was the Indian Mohatma Ghandi who visited Tolstoy a few times in his estate *Yasnaya Poliana*. Tolstoy also taught the Russian Orthodox Church should abolish the religious ceremonies, and instead the Christians have to live their life simply, according to Christ's teaching.

During this time of change, uncertainty, and shortages, the quality of education was surprisingly good. We were taught to think. Teachers and the public were not yet dependent on outside "authorities" to dictate and proscribe. Our thinking was not divorced from reality, feeling, and action. Our heroes were humans with many faces.

Did the Communist Party succeed in creating a "New Human,"

a "New Man"? Yes. But with the corruption of the Revolution, the "New Men" were often also corrupted or physically destroyed. But during that initial period, distinctive, positive characteristics of the "new" personality emerged. What exactly were they?

We learned to be profoundly social-communal in attitude, both toward each other and toward society at large. Helping and being compassionate to each other was the norm. In our sugar plant, we had been nurtured, not only by our parents, but by the whole community. An accepted idea of that time was that in order to make a child a good citizen, the whole of society must be involved. Each of us felt reponsible not only for him or herself, but for the whole collective as well. We had pride in our school achievements and felt obligated to work toward that goal. The word *egoist* was the most frightful word for us. A child who was called an egoist had to explain his/her behavior at a Pioneer meeting and would be firmly criticized for that sort of behavior. As far as I can remember, this happened only once. We all dreaded being called upon for these or any other explanations before our peers. We were molded to value society and avoid conflict among ourselves. The opposing view of this prevailing group consensus is that the individual can be dehumanized in the sense of losing his/her individuality. It's possible, though this wasn't the case during this initial period of the Revolution because of our sincerity, and the prevalence of equality and freedom.

The principle of equality was already in our blood. We had an indifference to the accumulation of material goods, athough we enjoyed being well dressed and having all the necessities of normal life. We learned wealth didn't make a human being happy and good; to the contrary, it could make a person greedy and unkind. It took me many years, in the United States, to develop a respect for money and to count it carefully. The essence of our behavior reflected our respect for our community, and our community took care of us with great love.

An important influence on the development of my character was our fight against lying. "A Young Pioneer doesn't lie," we were taught. Many of us grew up gullible. We believed anything told to us. Later in our lives, the reality of Stalin's time cured us of this beautiful dream.

The Death of Vladimir Ilyich Lenin

January 22, 1924 is a day that remains vividly in my memory. We were in our classrooms when a bell suddenly started to ring even though it wasn't time for our break. The director's voice told all students to go immediately to the hall. In a few minutes, Alyosha and the director came in. Alyosha was crying. We were frightened. Alyosha and the director told us the awful news—Yesterday, Vladimir Ilyich Lenin had died. The director told us to go home and return with our parents to the meeting in the theater.

The overflowing theater sounded like a hive of disturbed bees. The muffled noise of crying didn't hide the undercurrent of the *prichet*, the crying and uttering of words, expressing feelings such as, "What are we going to do?" and "Who will help us now?" "Vladimir Illyich, why have you left us?" and "What's going to happen to us now?" There were many speakers. Sometimes the crying became unbearably loud. It was an expression of deep, deep grief and of the fear of the unknown. From the time of Lenin's death, the mood of the people changed to a more subdued one.

My father was extremely perplexed. Years later he expressed the thought that the death of Lenin changed the mood of the country. The country had gone from the idea that "We're going straight to Paradise on Earth and no one can stop us," to a more thoughtful understanding of the paramount difficulties. Specifically, it was known that the people did not trust Trotsky or Stalin as they had Lenin. Doubt, as an ominous cloud, was appearing in the sky of the Revolution.

The Russian poet Yevgeniy Yevtushenko realistically depicted that time of childish, ignorant rage in his famous poem *Winter Station*:

He boldly claimed, voice shaking with emotion,
Wielding a long quotation with his fist,
That if you'd throw the bourgeois in the ocean,
None but the little problems would exist.
Then life would build itself, all would be fine,
The International rings, trumpets tune,
Flowers would bloom, flags wave, the sun would shine.
The path leads forward, straight to Communism.

It is correct to say that Lenin was loved and trusted by the majority of Russians like no one else in Russian history.

The next day in school, we were all feeling very sad. Gathered in the hall, the teachers and Alyosha told us Lenin's biography, about his accomplishments as the leader of the Russian Revolution and the proletariat of the whole world. Lenin was still a human being then, not the demi-god as he was later presented.

Just like others of my generation, I have had a sincere admiration for Lenin. The man was a genius with one aim in his puritanical life of a professional revolutionary, namely, to help the average man to live the life of a human. According to his Marxist teachings, he believed that economic, social, and cultural inequalities and the lack of freedom would stand in the way of the realization of this aim. Only through the Revolution and the working masses taking political power would inequality be eliminated and human dignity be vindicated and become a natural part of human rights. Singular as it was, it was on the basis of this theory that he created the State. No other state in human history was created so spontaneously and directly on solely a new theory and the efforts of the people. The following lines from Kahlil Gibran's *The Prophet* could have been written about Lenin: "You are good when you strive to give of yourself. You are good when you walk to your goal firmly and with bold steps" (Alfred Knopf, Inc.).

It's not surprising that, when the idea of socialism is nullified, only the image of Lenin remains to be retracted. Yet, is it realistic to assume that the leader of a new Revolutionary state would instruct the young Soviet Army and population to send kisses of love to the enemy, military and civilian, who fought to the death to destroy this new state? There were fourteen foreign countries that were involved in helping the counter-revolutionary forces inside or took part, directly, in fighting against the Republic. Around Moscow were organized military peasant uprisings by Savinkov's social-revolutionary party. From the Ural Mountains, throughout Siberia, the Czech Military Brigade was in revolt, supporting the government of Admiral Kolchak in the City of Omsk, Siberia. The United States Military Brigade was marching in Siberia toward Omsk, but they were too late, Kolchak's forces had been crushed by the Red Army. England sent her forces to Arkhangelsk at the North Sea. The French Military Fleet was in the Black Sea, occupying Crimea and Odessa. All of these were advancing on Moscow, as well as the well-equipped White Armies in the West and South of the country.

Lenin's motto, "Who is not with us is against us," was known and used by everyone. Under those circumstances, there was no other way for the supporters of the Revolution to act. Historian Dmitri Volkoganov, a three-star general, former head of the army's political administration, and then director of the Institute of Military History, has had since, *perestroika*, access to all, including the most secret archives of the Soviet Union. He has written biographies of Lenin, Stalin, and Trotsky. The Free Press in New York published his last book, *Autopsy for an Empire*, in 1998. This extraordinary book is comprised of the political autobiographies of all six General Secretaries of the Communist Party, starting with Lenin and ending with Gorbachev. In his books, he challenges Soviet principles and taboos.

But I can't agree with his interpretation of Lenin's role. Volkoganov considered Stalin's policy as no distortion of Leninism, but its logical continuation. We knew Stalin used terror as the main instrument of his political control. This was just one fact of Lenin's policy toward people that was entirely different than Stalin's. In 1921 the civil war was still being waged in the Far East. In central Russia, the peasants, some workers, and the Baltic Fleet sailors were discontented with economic conditions. So in 1921, Lenin introduced the New Economic Policy (NEP) in spite of the fact that many Communist leaders were against it. As a result, the economic conditions changed for the better until 1928, when Stalin abolished the NEP. It is correct that the ideology, views, and aims of the Revolution and the structure of the State system with the political monopoly of the single Communist Party that were created by Lenin as a necessity for the time of the civil war, and continued with no change until the end of the Soviet Union. But the practical application of the ideology was changed by Stalin. Coercion and terror became the modes of governing.

With the end of the civil war, people exercised freedom and broad initiative in building a new society and relations. My father said more than once that, "With the death of Lenin, freedom also died." In 1918, when Lenin was shot, almost fatally by Fanny Caplan, as he lay bleeding on the ground he pleaded with the plant's workers (he had just given a speech there) not to lynch his assailant.

They stopped. Witnesses who worked with Lenin said that he detested servile flattery and adulation and that he would not tolerate cruelty toward people.

While visiting the Soviet Union in the 1980s, I still heard people saying, "If Lenin would have been alive another fifteen or twenty years, the Soviet Union would have developed differently, without the terror and extreme sufferings of the majority of the population, and people certainly would have become more prosperous." People's trust and love for Lenin was preserved, while the memory of Stalin was and will be cursed forever by practically everyone.

After Lenin's death, when the Politburo was considering a mausoleum, many members were concerned this would start a cult and be seen as a relic of church ritual. Nadezhda Konstantinovna became so upset that she burst into tears at the Politburo meeting. "This would dishonor Ilyich's memory. He never would have permitted such a thing. He wanted to be buried, simply, next to his mother."

This was the beginning of the "cult of the personality." Stalin and his Politburo already saw themselves as above the masses. Sly Stalin needed to cover this by establishing a cult of Lenin and screaming about the "Dictatorship of the proletariat in unity with the poor peasants." So Stalin happily accepted his new "cult" of the new "saint," this beloved "Father of the People."

I expressed the absolute majority of people's sincere opinion and outlook on Lenin during the Soviet period. Now, the world policy and political consideration are changed. Hence, the new, different image of Lenin has to be created.

Graduating from School

In 1928 at fourteen years of age, I graduated from school. Just before graduation, that group of us who were considered to be the best Young Pioneers was transferred to the Komsomol. It was a big honor to become a member. I was happy and proud. As usual, it was done in a solemn ceremony with speakers greeting us and entertainment in a theater full of people.

In my Certificate of graduation from the seven-year school, the following subjects were listed:

Russian language and literature
Mathematics
Geometry/Trigonometry
Physics
Chemistry
Geography
Biology
Social Studies
Music (singing)
German

Physical Education was a Young Pioneers activity.

This was the end of my childhood and adolescence. In summarizing this period, I want to emphasize the fact that essential to our behavior was a spirit of great self-esteem, based on the belief that we were the best, the avant garde in a new era of struggle for the good of the human race. For this enormous task we had to prepare ourselves to be morally pure and knowledgeable in our professions. Yes, we grew up to be good human beings! The future for us was not something unforeseeable, but clearly predictable, sunny with red stars all over Earth's horizon. Destructive cynicism or disillusionment had not yet touched us. Our healthy idealism was the opposite of disbelief and isolation. Healthy idealism is a vision, a vital principle for the existence of a nation or a person. In our youth, a trust in the world developed—specifically the world with red stars—a feeling of human bonds, to feel the other human elbow. Without these simple human interrelations, it is hard to exist. Can these facts from the far past and a faraway country help to explain the contemporary problems among American youth? Having an abundance of bread is not enough for human contentment. No less needed is spiritual food, sincere belief in an ideal that will make a human better. A human without belief loses his or her humanity. No other quality magnifies humanity so much as to be of service to others, not to be egotistic.

Do I exaggerate or embellish the period of the first twelve years of the Revolution, specifically before collectivization? I don't think so. My specific experience of the positive, although radical, developments was not the exception. The majority of the country's young generation lived through similar experiences. Certainly any revolution and civil war have a high capacity to devour human lives and their environment. Boris Pasternak, in *Doctor Zhivago*, gave a broad picture of the human sufferings and the country's destruction during such a time. Let us imagine another possibility. If foreign intervention had not taken place, then unquestionably the destruction of the country and its people wouldn't have been so devastating. This foreign intervention, as a historical continuity of many preceding invasions and destructions of country and population, had strengthened the will and psychology of the people for resistance, and strong Communist rule, above all, was accepted as a means of resistance.

4

Grayvoron, Tekhnicum

Where would I go to continue my education? My parents were concerned because I was very impractical and overly trustful. Mama insisted I go to Kharkov and stay with the family. I didn't want to do that. I loved Grandpa and *Krestnaia* (godmother). I could stand my two other aunts, although they were very old-fashioned. But *Babunia* (grandmother) was a terror for the whole family. She was constantly teaching me good manners and scolding my mother for not teaching me the old-fashioned manners she thought necessary.

Once, at Grandpa's birthday party, she sent me away from the dinner table. We arrived and the other guests—family members and close friends— came. By custom, family members and close friends are never invited for a birthday celebration. They have to remember and come. Otherwise the celebrant will feel hurt. Somehow, my cousins Nina, Valentin, and Boris, were not present. I was alone among the old-fashioned company and not happy, so I started to play with my knife and fork. *Babunia* looked at me and at Mama, who told me to stop. I did not. Then *Babunia* said, "Nina, take your plate and go eat in the kitchen. You don't belong here."

I was not ashamed, just proudly walked out, not taking my plate. Mama was greatly embarrassed. Grandpa was upset because he loved me and later had a good talk with me. I wanted to be with kids, to live in the dorms. If I stayed with the family, I knew I couldn't invite friends to my home. Icons, even a portrait of Nicolas II, were hanging on the walls.

While in Voronezh on a business trip, my father happened to meet his old acquaintance from military service in Kharkov. He was director of a new Tekhnicum—a three-year school (Junior College) providing high school education and a profession, teachers for elementary schools. It was in the small regional City of Grayvoron,

41

about seventy miles from us. My parents persuaded me to go to Grayvoron tekhnicum and later to Kharkov University, although I was not happy with that decision.

At the end of August 1928, my parents brought me to Grayvoron. It was a pleasant provincial town, on a hill over the Vorskla river. It was probably in better condition and order than other regional towns because before the Revolution it was the site of a small regiment and small military school. The tekhnicum was now in the former military school building that stood near the end of a hill. It had a breathtaking view of the river, which in the spring flooded into a wide sea, and in the summer changed into a beautiful meadow. Before the Revolution, those towns were commercial trading centers for the outlying villages, and Grayvoron had a square in the center where there was a big bazaar every Sunday. Now it was a faint shadow of the past. There was one restaurant and one small hall used as a movie theater.

A part of the first floor in the Tekhnicum building, previously officers' quarters, was now a dormitory reserved for female students. Next to the dorm rooms were a kitchen and a huge hall, our dining room. Every student was scheduled to work in the kitchen. At least three students every day helped the cooks and cleaned the dining hall.

I shared a room with a freshman, Galia, a benevolent girl from the village. She was not too loud nor too talkative. That made me happy. But I developed deep friendships with Lena and Nina, who had attended the high school where their fathers were teachers. They were not members of the Komsomol. Rather, they were conservative, very intelligent and good-looking.

I was disappointed there was a completely different atmosphere from which I was familiar. We freshmen looked like fearful rabbits; no one made us feel comfortable. Shcherbina, director of the school, spent half of his time in the village on Communist Party assignment. The teachers were just efficient and the upper classmates plain smart-alecks.

As the shortage of well-qualified specialists was still acute, several key teaching positions, namely Literature, Geography, and Chemistry, were vacant. Besides, Director Shcherbina, who had to teach Russian History, was only available about two days a week. The office secretary gave us a list of a few books, reading for the course, but we did not find even one copy of those books.

I felt especially uneasy with Zamora, the secretary of the Komsomol at the tekhnicum. A senior, he was that new type of loud, selfish opportunist who every five minutes proclaimed himself one hundred percent supportive of communism. Once, in a Komsomol meeting, he attacked me, accusing me of not looking like a *komsomolka* (female member). He said I had several skirts, probably half a dozen blouses and, worst of all, I had close friendship with two philistine (narrow-minded) girls, meaning Lena and Nina, who were not members of Komsomol.

I was speechless. I didn't know what to say against such a bizarre accusation. But Galia simply said, "Look, I now wear Nina's skirt. Nina is not greedy; she lets girls use her things."

And Victor (Vitia), who became my friend, supported Galia. "The truth is the opposite of Zamora's view," he said. "Nina shows the right behavior for a *komsomolka*. She shares with those who have less than she has. Zamora's outlook is outdated, the working class does not have to be poor anymore."

Actually, the girls were poor, usually having one or two skirts, one or two crude blouses, and one dilapidated sweater. In comparison, my clothes were high fashion, but in reality were quite simple.

Recess

The first semester was not eventful. It was recess and I was at home. One of our rooms was full of furniture. I recognized that it was from the director's house, and in my room there was a section of bookshelf with my favorite books from the director's library. Father was silent. I noticed changes in his face; his eyes had a different expression, not happy and kind. Mama told the story. Our smart and kind director, after twenty-five years of being a good, responsible administrator, was removed and a new director was appointed. The new director was a Communist, a former worker who finished three-year Rabfak. He had never even seen a sugar beet.

The intense Stalin policy to replace the "bourgeois intelligentsia" by new intelligentsia from workers and peasants had lasting impact. Those new kadres (bureaucrats) generally displayed low culture and inadequate professional preparation. The majority were Communists, who became managers of industry, or administrative bureaucrats, and soon many climbed the ladder into the Party elite. It was the so-called Brezhnev generation. Ineptness and low culture was the sign of the state administration in all its branches. Our plant was a victim of that policy.

After the new director's arrival, he gave the former director and his family ten days to vacate the house. Hastily they sent some of their furniture and library to their daughter and stored the rest in our home. They gave some books to the plant's library, and some to me. Later, Mama sent the belongings they had left to their new residence.

Papa was angry. The new director didn't know anything about the plant's work or how to run it and was not in a hurry to learn. Instead, he said to Father and the head chemist that he was making them responsible for the success of the plant and they would have to answer to him.

As the new crop of Soviet business administrators, he was poorly-educated, with the leftover civil war habits of high-handedness and impudence. Stalin's upper bureaucracy demanded merciless treatment of people because, as they said, it was necessary for the development of the economy and the change to a Socialist society.

In removing our longtime director, the Sugar Industry Trust in Veronezh had thrown out a distinguished man, an excellent administrator, a man who worked for the Revolution but was now treated as a nonentity. The director's wife was from nobility; her parents were landowners, but she entered St. Petersburg University in the so-called Women's Courses, studying medicine to become a doctor. Then she joined the radical intelligentsia movement, the Social Democrats. In this organization she met her future husband and they carried education and propaganda among the workers. They had not expected such treatment from the government and were deeply hurt. He and his wife stayed with us during their last days before moving out because their house had no heat.

I was happy to meet my friends and feel friendship and warmth again. I recall that out of twenty-eight students graduated in June 1928, twenty-one continued their education. Mama and I went to Kharkov, where there were already some shortages of food. As always, we brought a lot of food products, some for the family and some to exchange for clothes and household items we needed. Almost every night Mama and I went with Grandpa and *Krestnaia* to the opera, theaters, or to the movies.

44

Until 1934, Kharkov was the capitol of the Ukraine, with a very intensive and modernistic cultural life. In the branch of the famous Ukrainian Drama Theater known as *Berezil,* Nina, my cousin, was a leading actress and her husband, Svetlanov, was also an actor and an administrator. The whole family, except *Babunia,* went to the premier of the Ukrainian operetta *Natalka Poltavka* by the Ukrainian composer Nikolai Lisenko. Nina played Natalka. Her acting was good, but I didn't care for her overall presentation.

After the theater, Nina, her husband, and the other actors came to Grandpa's home for good food and talk. Everybody but me sang dithyrambs to Nina. I didn't know how to say anything different from what I thought, so I said that Natalka, a Ukrainian girl, was not Nina's character, although Nina was excellent in the *Three Sisters* by Chekhov. She presented Natalka as more of a sophisticated city girl. Nina's voice and acting was not natural for a Ukrainian girl. Everyone was silent. Then Svetlanov seemed to agree with me and laughingly said that he would like to have me as an artistic critic in their theater.

Second Semester, Changes

Exciting news—two new teachers were hired. The first day of classes in the morning we gathered in the school hall (dining hall) so Director Shcherbina could introduce them. There they were, husband and wife just graduated from Leningrad University. The wife was short, almost round but not fat, with light reddish, sparse short hair, a big nose, little blue eyes with no eyebrows, and a reddish complexion. The husband, on the other hand, was tall and handsome, built like Apollo from Belvedere, with dark hair and expressive brown eyes. We all looked at each other, amazed that such a combination was possible.

Shcherbina introduced them: Liia Lvovna and Pavel Petrovich, both graduated with the highest honors. With their qualifications, they could have had positions in Institutes wherever they wished, including Moscow and Leningrad, but they selected a little Tekhnicum in a provincial hole. Pavel Petrovich was a Ukrainian from the northern Ukraine not far from our city. Grayvoron was in southern Russia on the Ukrainian border. They wanted to work in a remote place. After introductions, Liia Lvovna greeted us with a nice smile and a few warm words that left a very pleasant feeling.

A few days later we had Liia Lvovna's class in Humanities and Literature, for which we waited impatiently. The upper classmates already lauded her highly. It was wonderful and for an hour we and Liia Lvovna, with her carefully leading, exchanged our thoughts. The next day Pavel Petrovich entered our class like a god but smiling, joyful, speaking with a soft, pleasant voice. He unrolled a huge geography map of the world. We never saw anything like it. We knew a great deal about the geography of the world. Now we were mainly learning about people, their lives and ways, and systems. Soon we noticed that the other teachers became more animated and interesting; the academic situation at the school improved considerably. Who would now notice that Liia Lvovna was not handsome—we thought she was beautiful!

In the next class L. L. was reading and explaining Socrates' short dialogues—a confrontation of opinions or conventions, confrontation with authoritative views on statesmen, people, heroes, poets (Homer), what is pious and honest, what is falsehood and prejudice. Out of these confrontations philosophy emerged. When L. L. read a dialogue about profiteers, we were surprised. It sounded like our thinking. The profiteer, in his unbridled pursuit of profit at the expense of another human, we learned, should not be treated with the respect due a human being. Then we became acquainted with Plato's *Republic*. After several weeks, we came to Jean-Jacques Rousseau's *Emile*. It was exciting. L. L. read and explained the passages and we discussed them. We found out that Voltaire and the French Encyclopedists down to Marx received and developed their ideas from Rousseau. Now Rousseau's thinking on human history is well-known; that the savage man was born free, equal, self-sufficient, and now he is unequal, dependent, full of false opinions and superstitions and not always honest to his duties. In *Emile*, Rousseau describes the healthy education of Emile from his birthday to his adulthood. It was an education that reconciled man's selfish nature with his duties in civil society. He said nature made man a brute, but happy and good. History made him civilized, but unhappy and immoral. Answer: the right education is a way to change society.

It is still very contemporary and may help in understanding the roots of the ills of our society, namely, inequality, resulting in loss of freedom, selfishness over compassion. Rousseau worked out a whole system of education that would change a savage human into an egalitarian honest man.

Emile had a very deep and lasting influence on me and all of us. Until now we had been exposed to Marx-Engels-Lenin's teaching about the inevitability of the working people's revolution and a subsequent society of working people. Now we learned that not the Communists, but mainly Rousseau, inaugurated these ideas, although they involved the whole of human society, with no exclusions, omitting the violent Revolution. A human (Emile) has to be basically changed. We learned that a number of philosophers had followed Rousseau's ideas, each of them in his own way. As a result, our belief in Marxist teaching was reinforced and immensely broadened.

At this time, an academic novelty, the so-called method of the circles, was introduced. We were organized in small groups—circles of five or six students—mixing the high achievers with the slower students. The purpose was to involve *all* students in discussions on subjects like history, philosophy, literature, and geography or to help each other in subjects like math and physics. It was an additional organized form of studies, and each teacher applied it with our agreement as he or she found useful. I was used to this form of studies and help. We had many assignments, which were graded by teachers, and our mistakes were explained in class. Seldom did we have tests. At the end of the semester we had exams. Textbooks continued to be a problem. More often we used the teachers' selections from different sources; sometimes they were typed with carbon paper, or we wrote down the lectures after the teacher spoke and we had had discussion.

I felt satisfied and self-confident again. In classes of philosophy, literature, and history, just a few of us—Vitia, Lena, Nina, Vania, and myself—were well-informed and well-read. I often took part in discussions, though sometimes I felt my wish fell short because the general cultural level was not high enough. No one but me went to the opera or ballet, listened to the symphonic orchestra, or even spent time in the good art gallery, although a majority of the kids read a lot of Russian and some World Literature. The students said I was L. L.'s pet. It offended me. I was shy and modest; I didn't care to be praised and could not stomach unfair blame.

As a joke, they called me "cat eyes" because I had big, greenish, very shiny, gleaming eyes. I was quite tall and slim, better dressed than anyone. I liked to be different. I worshipped books and read quite a bit. I imagined a scholar or a writer to be a highly moral and spiritual person. Later, this image, like many others, was shattered.

The upper-class students in the literature class read, among others, a book called *What is to Be Done* by Nikolai Chernyshevsky, a leader of the radical intelligentsia. This book, which he wrote in 1863 in jail, was accepted by young radicals and even liberals as not only their political guide but also as a handbook on relations between the sexes. He said, and the radical intelligentsia accepted, there was a need to give women superior privileges to compensate them for centuries of male domination. Love must be sincere. Otherwise, it is a mistake and can be corrected by humane divorce.

Many students read another book on relations between the sexes, *The Pit* by Alexander Kuprin, which was about "white slaves," the panorama of urban prostitution, a social injustice toward women. In this book, the public was subjected to vivid, naturalistic portrayals of sexuality. Ascetic Russia was not used to such graphic writing and was shocked. The early years of the twentieth century brought about a preoccupation with sex that had no parallel in Russian culture. This sensuality continued into the years of the Revolution and on to the middle of the 1920s with the famous Aleksandra Kollontay's views on sex. The students asked for and arranged a trial over those two books: Kuprin's *The Pit* and Chernyshevsky's *What is to Be Done*.

A court was organized, as in reality a people's court, with judge, people's assessors and witnesses. All of them were upper classmates. Witnesses presented the various points of the book's subject matter. Then the people's assessors analyzed the witnesses' presentations and expressed their view as a judgment. One "witness," a beautiful senior, was very vulgar and declared that she was a follower of Kollontay's views on sex and the family. We were shocked. Students asked L. L. to explain Kollontay's views, and she proposed to organize an evening event with her lecture on the subject along with entertainment. The music teacher, loved by us because he was a sincere enthusiastic man, decided with L. L. to prepare folklore songs by our choir, representing traditional forms and outlooks on love and relations between the sexes.

Meanwhile, we had a Komsomol meeting for the election of a new Secretary and Bureau (Council). I met the "famous" Misha for

48

the first time. He had graduated the year before and had been the organizer of our Komsomol organization and its first Secretary. Now he was the Second Secretary of the District Komsomol Committee. He was tall, slim, good-looking, and very pleasant. All the girls were crazy about him. Zamora made a report about activities of the Komsomol organization. His language already was different from ours. He spoke like *Pravda*'s headlines, generalizations about the difficulties of building socialism in one country when we, he said, still don't understand it and don't see the class enemies who are wrecking our country. He criticized all of us, calling us narrow-minded Philistines.

We called Zamora and a few like him *boltun*—chatterbox—and joked: "What language do they speak? Russian? No! They speak a new language, a variant of Russian, called *Boltovnia*—jabber."

After the meeting, everyone was around Misha and he called Vitia and me over, too. He said that I looked like a saint—around me was an aureole—and he had never seen such an interesting sweater. The kids laughed because they had already made similar comments to me. I was wearing a white angora wool sweater with a long fleece that sometimes, depending on the light, appeared to create a short halo around me. Later Misha liked to say that I was his second love; his first love was the white angora sweater, which for a few weeks, occupied his mind.

This meeting was important for my feelings and thinking. In my family, in school, and in the Pioneer organization, I felt, like all young people do, love, encouragement, and thanks for our behavior and help to society for a good cause. I was used to logical and humane language, but what we had heard recently was different and frightfully hateful. Unfortunately, this was the beginning of the new style, the style of Stalin's era. Certainly we did not foresee the coming changes. The communist ideals were still without blemish for us. Those "chatterboxes" we considered unpleasant servile flatterers or blamers, a manner that goes against the Russian character. A human being has to live in peace with himself and the people around him. Then why this high talk about class vigilance and enemies around us?

The year 1928–29 was the beginning of the system of the Five-Year Plans and Collectivization. It was a time of cardinal changes. The "class" terminology was omnipresent: *class enemies*; *class war*; *kulak*; *bourgeois specialist*; *class vigilance*; and more.

"Proletariat" denotes not only the social position, but political loyalty and trust as well.

"Bourgeois" and "Petty Bourgeoise," like rich peasants, priests, small shop keepers and others implies political unreliability, called "class enemies" or "alien element."

People from "bad" social background, the "alien elements," were restricted in everything: employment, education, the right to vote, and more.

Those people were fighting for their lives, and naturally they had to hide their class background, and present themselves as of the workers, poor peasants, office clerks, or teachers' social background. The long, ugly "war" of unmasking those enemies started. The millions, mainly young people of "bad" social background, left their homes for the cities where they concealed their social background and home place and tried to pass as proletarians or poor peasants.

The "witch-hunt" for hidden "enemies" and "aliens" became an obsession of all political organizations. My cousin, Valentin, who finished high school a number one student and gifted mathematician, was not accepted by any college in Kharkov, because he was the son of a priest who was killed in his church in 1920. Then he forged his personal papers, changing them to read that he was the son of a teacher. He was accepted in a college, but soon his forgery was discovered. He was "unmasked" and expelled from college as an "alien" element.

The next year, he submitted his forged papers and was accepted at the Nikolayev Shipbuilding Institute—It was his dream. Nikolayev is near Odessa, on the river Buh, and was one of the centers for the shipbuilding industry. Valentin graduated and became a leading engineer in the shipbuilding plant there. His family did not see him for five years. He was afraid to come home. His mother wrote a ficticious return address on her letters to him.

Evening Event: Misha, my Brother

Our choir was like storm troops preparing a lovely program of folklore love songs in the short time given to us. It was a lot of fun. Our school hall was quite big, but now it seemed too small for the event. Some juniors and seniors from the city's high school came, and our boys covered the floor with what was available and sat them down. Officials from the District Government, Party, and Komsomol came with their wives, as well as the teachers and other employees from the city. They wanted to hear our new school star, L. L., talk about what? Sexuality! I was quite nervous because, as a principal of the choir, I was to give a short talk about folklore and then to read the lyrics of each song before it was sung. L. L.'s presentation was outstanding. Here are a few of the main points:

The Revolution happened in the midst of a profound cultural upheaval which had started before the Revolution, and Lenin's government did not curtail it. It was the so-called Silver Age of Russian culture.

Many schools and currents developed in Russian culture since the late 1890s and now they became more rooted in Russian tradition. The main ones were Prometheanism and Sensualism.

Prometheanism was the belief that free man is capable of transforming the world in which he lives. The figure of Prometheus the Greek Titan chained to a Caucasian mountain by Zeus for giving fire and the arts to mankind fascinated the radical romantics, Marx, Goethe, and Byron among them. The Soviet Russians of this period thought like Prometheus to bring knowledge and arts to their fellow countrymen and to create a higher social type, something like a superman. Cosmic Prometheanism was accompanied by a counter-current of personal sensualism, a preoccupation with sex. Sensualism was a reaction against traditional Russian asceticism, guarded by the official Orthodox Church culture and a dominant moralism expressed by Leo Tolstoy and others, and the ascetic puritanism of radicals like Chernyshevsky and Belinsky. Although different in argumentation, it was supportive of puritanical personal behavior.

The rapid advent of a mass urban culture and the anarchy of the Revolution also caused the exaltation of sex. The leading authors and poets like Vechislav Ivanov had a different aim, to revitalize the image of Christ with the flesh that had been taken away by the Church. Fedor Sologul, in his *The Petty Demon* and other stories, displayed all kinds of sexual perversions, the world of petty venality, vulgarity—*poshlost*. Vasily Rosanov, the high priest of the new cult of sex, looked to Dionysus, not to Christ. Dionysus, the God of arts and sensualism, provided a new religion of uninhibited creativity and sensuality. Tolstoy and Dostoevsky and many others also made their imprint, although in a different way. The imperial family and court were under the sway of the notorious Rasputin.

All these literary ideas were carried on to the new regime. Among official patrons, the first place belonged to Alexandra Kollontay, the gifted daughter of a Russian general and a Finnish noble woman. She was the first Commissar of Public Welfare in Lenin's government. As a gifted writer, she published *New Morality and the Working Class* in 1919 and later in 1925 her collection, *Free Love*. Kollontay campaigned for free love in the new society. However, free love has to be socially creative love, some kind of spiritual unity, and a unity with the proletarian society. In one of her stories, *The Love of Worker Bees*, a woman character declares that sexual intercourse in itself is as simple as drinking a glass of water. Kollontay's outlook became known as the "theory of a glass of water."

L. L. expressed her views on sexuality. Her point was that every creature in the world has sexuality, but only human beings have sexuality as a part of love, so sex by itself is not love. Love is a higher psychological level of human relations and is the foundation of any civilized society.

Kollontay's views were quite popular in the big cities, although provinces and villages were not impressed, except for the ideas of women's liberation and equality, and freedom in divorce and abortion. As we know now, government tolerance of the various literary views, schools and movements came to an end with the beginning of Stalin's "building socialism in one country."

Our choir, as a contrast to the ideas of free love, presented songs as *narod*, people were singing about themselves, the traditions and customs created by the people over many centuries. In lyrical songs, *narod* revealed deep feelings, love, morality, and dreams of happiness and their grief. Characterization, especially a girl and a young man, was hyperbolized. Repetitions of words and expressions, and traditional allegories, served to produce emotional intensity.

Folklore has always been popular among all classes in Russia, from the tsars and noblemen to the peasants and workers. Russian folklore, collected in several hundred volumes, is very rich. This was the scheme of my introduction about folklore. I recited and explained every song before the choir's singing. I was told my reciting was artistically expressive. The choir's performance got very high marks from the public. The public didn't let me go, and I had to recite some beautiful love lyrics of Blok, Pushkin, and Yesenin. Here (by my free translation) are a few sample stanzas of the folklore lyrics:

About a Girl
She is a beautiful ivory gull
Ripe, sweet apple
She walks like a pea-chick
Her speech as a swan sings

About a Young Man
There is no one better than Petia-falcon
In the whole world.
He gives warmth like a sun
He holds me in respect
Takes me home from evening party

Her young husband leaving the village to go to the city for work
You, my love, brave eagle
Where are you going
Leaving me, your fine wife
Who will give me happiness?

A Young Man in Love
Girl, my girl, this is for you.
I sing with love from my heart.
Girl, my girl, don't be shy
And listen to my song
   Sun is to give warmth and light
   Songs are to be sung
   Heart is to love a dear
   Lips are to kiss, my dear.
Girl, my girl, the autumn came
Happiness to catch at spring
Girl, my girl, heart will wither
If it has no love.
   Girl, my girl, an evening will come
   After a joyful day

Girl, my girl, the sun will return
If you fall in love with me.

For the first time in my life I had some kind of unusual feeling. Misha was sitting in the first row. I felt him, his fixed look on me, specifically when I recited, *Song of a Young Man in Love*. I was in a funny, unusual emotional state and yet continued a phenomenal recitation of the love poetry because the public wouldn't let me go.

There was a lot of excitement after the performance, especially around L. L. and the choir master with us, the choir. Pavel Petrovich, Shcerbina, and many others praised us highly. P. P. embraced me and said, "Nina has a future as a great dramatic actress. Clearly she has much talent." Some also praised my costume as a tasteful addition. I wore a nicely embroidered Ukrainian shirt and so-called *plakhta*, a colorful homemade tweed which as a kind of short skirt twisted around a figure with a small embroidered apron, and my beautiful black boots. Galia had brought the costume from her village.

Misha came up and said, "Ninok, you are *molodets* (a good fellow)." In this moment everyone around me disappeared. Only Kolia's image was with me and tears like a river gushed over my face. "What happened?" All around me were asking and I was quietly repeating, "Only Kolia could call me Ninok." With all the excitement of the evening, my nerves were strained and had burst.

Misha, Nina, and Galia took me to my room and Lena stayed behind and explained about Kolia and my reaction to being called "Ninok." Misha was so kind and soft. Nina gave me valerian drops, which were widely used for calming nerves.

Then Misha asked, "May I be your older brother? Take me!"

It hit me like a thunderbolt that I again had a brother. Change happened immediately. I stopped crying and told Misha, "Yes, you can call me Ninok."

Lena and Shcherbina came. He knew the story because my father had told him.

The next day, I was the center of attention. In the evening, Misha came to find out how his "sister" was. He kissed me tenderly on the cheek as a brother and I sincerely accepted it as a brotherly kiss. I was, after all, fifteen and very naive. Misha came visiting several times. It was so nice to be with him. We laughed a lot. Kids always filled the room where he was at once. Misha was a natural, pleasant leader; he drew people to himself.

Once, when I was leaving the classroom, that beautiful vulgar senior took my hand and asked, "Do you think that your tears or my love of Misha will hold him?"

I didn't know what to say. This trait in my character when I am shaken by someone's offense, I become temporarily speechless, has given me trouble throughout my life. I went straight to Lena and Nina's room. I told them what happened. Lena was laughing at my naiveté. "Do you think Misha has just a brotherly feeling for you?"

I was very unhappy. I wanted Misha to be just my older brother, like Kolia. Nina was almost like me in her outlooks and morals, but with one difference. She was a very refined beauty and had a soft, kind character, but something about her was like a beautiful marble statue just to look at. A number of the upper-class students were interested in her, but she avoided them. Lena and a senior were in love and making serious plans for the future.

Policy Changes, Life and Activities

In 1928 the first Five-Year Plan was launched, combined with the crash program of collectivization. This was equal to the second Revolution this time launched by Stalin, and was almost as sweeping and radical as the first one in 1917.

In our school we felt it first of all in our dining room. In the autumn of 1928 when I entered school, our food was not very good but it was sufficient and consisted of a lot of vegetables, potatoes, grains, and quite often, meat. Day by day the food became worse and finally we had only bread, potatoes, cabbage, and *kasha*, a grain porridge. For breakfast we had tea (*lindentree*) and bread. We had no sugar. For lunch, we had *kasha*, tea, and bread. For dinner, we had cabbage, potato or bean soup, with tea and bread. Mama sent me sugar a few times which I shared with the girls. Many of us received some kind of food from home. As a rule, we shared that food amongst all of us. Director Shcherbina came more often from the village just to fight for food for the school.

The situation in the country worsened. Stalin curtailed Lenin's New Economic Policy (NEP) and the economy faltered. The cities again had poor food rationing. The poor peasants had little grain and consumed all their products. The more prosperous ones stored their surpluses, waiting for higher prices. Government prices were extremely low. The State started forced requisitions of grain and other food products, just as it was during the Civil War. Then the peasants didn't care to produce, to sow more. A vicious cycle was set in motion because of wrong government policy. Thousands of Communists, the same as our director, were sent to villages as the strict enforcers of the Party policy to take grain by force. Peasants hid their grains. It was some sort of witch hunt; the army units and police found it and took everything, sometimes even the last bag of potatoes, beans, or grain, leaving nothing to feed the children.

In spite of the food shortages, we were content. Difficult situations were normal for us; we were used to it. We did not yet comprehend a new political course. Our freshman class became as one body, close and friendly with each other. Boys and girls were friends; in the sense of sex relationships, we were verty conservative. Vitia more than once told me that he didn't respect girls who were "hung up" on him. He liked me because I acted sincerely as a friend.

After dinner we liked to sit at our class tables and discuss politics, newspaper articles or a new book that someone read, sing popular songs, or tell stories and jokes.

We were quite good in creating our own jokes or *chastushki*, folklore poetry. We liked singing together the most. The revolutionary songs were the psychological organizers of masses and a powerful means of revolutionary propaganda. What was characteristic of all of them was a clear rhythm, often close to the rhythm of a march, a clear and plain melody, a broad drawl which is characteristic of Russian melodic singing, conveying a feeling of spaciousness. The tradition of the old revolutionary songs and the folklore of the cities and villages had influenced the style of the contemporary composers of mass songs, like Aleksandrov, the brothers Pokrass, Dunaevsky, and many more. Also, many poets were writing songs like Demian Bedniy and Bezimensky. I still remember many of those songs. I don't think it would be an exaggeration to say that nothing united us more, made us a close collective, than singing together. It created some kind of euphoric feeling. Our favorite song starts with the words: "A song helps us to work and to live." Some of our "artists" drew the pictures—illustrations—to the songs and displayed them on the walls. For *A Song of the Convicts* who were walking on the long, long road

56

called *Vladimirka* to Siberia, one of our "artists" made a copy of the picture *Vladimirka* painted by the well-known artist Levitan. We made an arrangement of this song:

Dzin (girls' voices), Bom (boys' voices)
Dzin-Bom
The clinking of shackles is heard
Dzin-Bom
Dzin-Bom
On the way to far Siberia
Dzin-Bom
Dzin-Bom
Their walking is heard
Our comrade is led to drudgery.

A song called *Broadly Spread was the Sea* had special meaning for us. As the story goes, a group of communist Baltic fleet sailors were brought for execution on a ship deck and when the rifles of the White Army soldiers were pointed at them ready to fire, they spontaneously started to sing this song with all their might.

L. L. and P. P. quite often came for dinner. Each time they sat with a different class. Each class—senior, junior—had its own long table. We freshmen, the largest size class, had two tables. P. P. was so attentive and tender to his wife. His eyes showed his love for her. Their relationship was a wonderful example for us. Upper classmates once asked them to tell their love story. L. L. said, "No," but P. P. said, "Yes." His story ran more or less like this:

"At Leningrad University, I was dating my classmate, a really beautiful and smart girl. Everybody thought that we were already a *para* (couple). At the beginning of the last (fifth) year, students tried to get married and to receive an assignment for both to the same city or town. I felt that it was better for us not to marry in spite of her wish and her beauty. Her character frightened me: not understanding, cold and selfish, as some beautiful women are. I was very unhappy. I couldn't concentrate on preparation for the State exams. Once, I stopped in at the University club, where a movie was in progress, and sat down on the last bench next to . . . I looked. It was Liia. At the University she was known and respected, being always a member of some kind of the ruling body, such as the student council or the Komsomol Bureau. After the movie we went for a cup of tea and we talked and laughed. I didn't notice how I opened my heart, it was so natural. We met for a short time each evening. I felt regenerated, full of high energy, and plunged into studying with success. Then one day I asked myself, *What is going on with me? Ah! I am in love and I want to marry Liia*. I went to her room. She was alone, so I was straightforward."

"Liia, marry me!"

"She gave me a long look. 'No.'"

"I did not expect it, was hurt by this answer and ran away. In my room, I realized that I had not asked Liia 'why.' So, right away I ran back. Liia opened the door and I asked: 'Why?' She replied, 'Because you are handsome and good. Any girl would be glad to marry you. I am ugly; no one wants to marry me.'"

"Her words struck me again, but this time I understood it was not my fault—it was Liia's funny thinking. I started laughing so hard and mumbling words of love; then she joined me in laughter. We embraced, kissed, and in a few weeks were married. Since then we have been really happy. Remember in human relationships, specifically between a man and a woman, the main thing is the inner quality: honesty, kindness, understanding, and unselfish help. We are delighted to be here and work with you. You are an exceptional group of young people—morally good, and ideologically and politically healthy."

For many of us, this sincere story became a guideline.

On the first of May, our school, in good formation, went to the center of town for an enthusiastic parade. Many people, organizations, schools and workers from a factory were marching as well as a few orchestras. District dignitaries, among them Misha, were there on a platform. I was excited because my parents would arrive some time in the afternoon and they, of course, would bring lots of good food. I had written to them that I had a brother and, as I understood later, it troubled them.

I was so happy to see my parents. Mama asked if she would see my brother. Of course, I answered, he will come soon. She started unpacking, serving food on our small table. Papa ran to see Shcherbina with a present; he had brought some sugar for them. He came back very moved. Mrs. Shcherbina cried from happiness when Father gave her the sugar. She said her two children were undernourished and they hadn't had sugar for months. Misha came in. My parents got up, looking at him, not answering his greetings.

"What is the name of your father?" my father said.

"Peter," Misha answered.

"And your mother?"

"Rosa."

Then my father embraced Misha and kissed him and mother did the same. "Do you know I was at your christening and your parents and you were at our wedding? You were sleeping in a basket."

Now all of us were very happy, sitting around the table full of fabulous food, vodka, and wine. Misha told his parents' story.

Misha's father, Peter Nikolayevich Ostapchuk, and mine were in military service at the Kharkov Military Brigade. He was a bookkeeper. Misha's mother was a Jew and his father a Ukrainian. Her family would not allow her to marry a Ukrainian and when she married him anyway they disowned her. Fortunately, their marriage had been very happy. Now Misha's father was a stationmaster of the important railroad crossing, Belgorod, not far from our town, and Krasnaia-Yaruga.

Misha told us that he was appointed the first secretary of the Grayvoron district Komsomol organization; that's why he was standing on the platform with the district's dignitaries.

The Soviet democracy of Stalin's vintage was already in action. The district Komsomol members had nothing to do with the appointment of their secretary. The higher-up Voronezh *Oblast* (Region) Bureau of Komsomol appointed Misha and the Grayvoron's district Communist Party Bureau confirmed him.

Misha was nineteen, the district's youngest Komsomol secretary in Oblast. My parents' eyes and talk showed their affectionate feelings toward him. He was tall and handsome, with brown eyes that expressed caring and kindness, and a compelling smile. Misha believed that human beings basically are good. Just open your heart sincerely to someone, help him and you will be surprised at the transformation of even a "bad" one into a good human. He was like a magnet for young people, a crowd was always around him, lots of laughing and talking. His whole-hearted belief in socialism and working for its fulfillment were the purposes of his life. His own character and behavior should be a good example, and it was. In a year or at the most two, he planned to enter Moscow State University.

"I want to explain why Ninok is a *sistrenka* (small sister) to me," Misha said. "I love her but she still is a child—a gifted, honest child. Now I am just a brother to her. She needs one; she is too gullible. But in five years or so I want to marry her. Ninok, will you marry me?"

It was so unexpected to me that I blushed with shame and bent my head. I felt I did want to marry Misha in five or more years and I made a sound: "Uhu," which means "yes."

Then Misha asked my parents if they would accept him as a son. My parents accepted Misha's sincere words. They were very moved and kissed and caressed Misha. Late into the night we laughed and talked about life and our future. It was decided the right school for my further education would be the Theatre Institute. Finally, Misha left. In the morning my parents left, content and sure about my future.

The month of May was a very busy time for us, preparing for our exams, some of them in oral, others in written form. We considered the Russian language exam, which consisted of two parts—dictation and composition—to be the most difficult. Russian sentence order is not like German or English; it is quite free. Instead, the punctuation system is more complicated and very important. Often, we were told a story that was said to be historical fact, about a Governor of the Province, an aristocrat who knew French better than Russian. On the petition for pardon that he wanted to satisfy a petitioner, he wrote down: *Kaznit, nel'zia pomilovat,* which means, "Execute him, it is impossible to pardon." The problem was the comma. What he wanted to say was: *Kaznit nel'zia, pomilovat,* "Don't execute, I pardon him." In Russian this sentence has only three words and the position of the comma affected the meaning of the sentence. In this case, grammar traded life for death. Exams finished, I made good grades.

Once when I saw Misha, I wanted to kiss him on the lips. He put his finger on my lips and said, "Child, don't call a wolf from the forest." (A Russian proverb.) I didn't understand it and noticed Misha's irritation. "Ask your mother what it means."

I grabbed his hands and kissed them. It made him smiling and tender. At home, I asked my Mama. She was a little uneasy but explained what Misha meant. I should finish my education before having a family and children.

Misha and all his staff were in villages organizing Komsomol cells on Party orders that each village had to have one to help organize peasants into collective farms. Everyday life was getting harder; there were more shortages in food, clothes, and home necessities. Some people called this time a "dog's life." But we called it a "heroic time."

Before leaving for home, I received Misha's letter from a village. He wrote that his parents would visit us in Krasnaia-Yaruga. He would try to come just for an evening but was not sure he could make it.

Home. The Ostapchuks Visit Us

It was nice to be home. As usual in the summer, Grandpa and *Krestnaia* arrived from Kharkov. I loved to be with *Dedia* (Grandpa). He was a very wise man, told life stories, some funny, some dramatic, usually with moral emphasis.

Preparations for the Ostapchuk's visit were in full swing. I was nervous. I hated to be like Tatiana in Pushkin's *Eugene Onegin*—in the "market" of brides. But *Krestnaia* calmed me down. Grandma and Aunt Ekaterina came. Finally, the Ostapchuks arrived, an exciting meeting between friends after about twenty years since parting. After the whole company had finished greeting and kissing exercises, Mama introduced me and they opened their arms for an embrace and kiss. I was astonished when I looked into Mama Rosa's eyes. They were like Misha's, kind and caring. All that made me feel comfortable and natural and made us sincere friends.

Soon all of us were seated at the big wooden table in the back yard, which was Maria's wonder—several fruit trees, a big oak, and lots of flowers. Although Maria was married to a nice man at the plant, she had taken good care of her creation. The yard had complete privacy; on one side was the plant's brick wall, on the other a fence. The table was covered with everything possible—the pride of Mama and Maria. It did not look like the country had food shortages. The centerpiece was Papa's pride—vodka, cognac, and wines.

The wicket gate opened and a smiling Misha entered. Everyone made sounds like, "Ohh, ahh. Welcome!" He kissed his mother, kissed me on the cheek, kissed my mother, and then greeted each one present with nice words. But we saw his deplorable state, tired, noticeable loss of weight, unshaved, smelly clothes that hadn't been

61

changed for many days. Mama took him inside and later he appeared clean, shaved, and in my father's clean clothes. He sat down between his mother and me.

By custom everyone proposed a toast, many wise and funny words showing warm, sincere relationships. My mother praised Misha in her toast. And Misha's mother's toast was praising of me, and Misha and I laughed secretly at both of them flattering us. Those were the happy days of my life. The next afternoon, Misha left. There was no doubt in our minds that we belonged to each other for life. The whole world was smiling on me.

The Junior Year

At the end of August I was back in tekhnicum. What a difference compared with a year ago! Now I was among friends all wishing to tell each other what they had done during the summer, expressing some joy and lots of frustration. Misha came and said that the next day the juniors and seniors would be sent to the government farms, *sovkhoz*, to help harvest sugar beets. He told me what to wear. The next morning, the first day of classes, we were assembled in the hall. Director Shcherbina and a staffer from Misha's Bureau of Komsomol explained that the government farms didn't have enough workers to harvest beets before the rainy season. So it was our civic duty to help, that the Soviet people would have sugar. We were given instructions and responsibilities. We were organized in groups (brigades) of ten. Each elected a "brigadier": ours was Vitia. The next morning the trucks arrived and took us, juniors and seniors, to the different farms.

Our living quarters were barns, one for girls and the other for boys. We slept in rows on a thick bed of straw. We had brought our pillows and blankets. In the morning we had a simple healthy breakfast in the farm dining hall. Then they drove us to the field. Dinner was brought over to the field, usually a thick soup and bread, and supper was back in the dining hall.

Tractors plowed out beets. We gathered them around in one place, and with sharp knives we cut off the green leaves, cleaned off dirt, and hurled beets on a pile that formed a cone about six feet high. We worked responsibly and enthusiastically, besides having a lot of fun. Probably about ninety to one hundred of us worked ten days or so and harvested just about all the beets. Our appearance was beyond description, dirty, in funny, shabby, dilapidated clothes. We were not paid, although the farms had an agreement with tekhnicum to provide food, so that throughout the whole winter we had noticeably better nourishment.

A few days before the work ended, we decided to organize an amateur performance to be held on the very last evening. I was made a taskmaster. I asked the farm Komsomol organizer to take part with their amateurs. The last day we only worked half a day. The small bathhouse was steaming; a few hours were given to girls to get clean, then the same for boys. After, we were making fun of recognizing each other.

The farm had a place for meetings, a big round space, bordered with acacia trees and lilac bushes. In the center was a large platform for dancing, performances, and meetings. Around it were benches, green grass, and some flowers. That was the norm for the old economies, now *sovkhozes*.

It was an evening of competition. All the farm people were there. The director of the farm extended hearty thanks, and the people liked us and applauded enthusiastically. After my few words, competition began between our amateurs and theirs. In comparison to ours, their chorus sounded highly professional. It was customary in the Russian and the Ukrainian villages for young people to gather in certain places for singing and dancing. There was always a garmonist (who played the garmon, a simple kind of accordian). Often it was polyphonic singing—sopranos, mezzos, tenors and bass—with soloists and a conductor from their kind. I remember in Krasnaia-Yaruga that we liked to sit on a summer evening at the lake's edge just opposite the church on the other hillside bank, where the young and old gathered for singing, dancing, and fun. Once, Grandpa said, "We are listening to a fine folklore concert." It was a wonder to listen in the stillness of the night to that powerful, well-trained chorus and its echo all around. No one in particular trained them. It was a centuries-old custom that, besides possessing a natural feeling for beauty, each learned from the childhood by imitating adults. These incomparable customs disappeared now in the river of oblivion, *Lethe*. It is a painful loss.

Their chorus beat us and we beat them with our dances and recitals. It was an enormous success of friendliness and joy. Thanks from the farms were published not only in our district but in the Veronezh Oblast press as well. So our tekhnicum was put on the map and we felt deeply satisfied.

Classes Start

The most fascinating was L. L.'s class on world literature. No less interesting for me was P. P.'s class on economic and political geography. We learned about natural resources of countries and how they shaped world relations and politics.

The meeting of our Komsomol organization this time was different, not about our studies and activities, but about the right-wing Party opposition. The speaker was a staff member from Misha's District Bureau of Komsomol. Politically smart, the new kind of *apparatchic*, he did not explain the essence of the opposition. Instead, he employed a "psychological attack," using headlines from the leading Party newspapers saying that the opposition wanted to make the *kulak* (prosperous peasant) dominant in the villages, which would mean the poor peasants would have to work for them as before Revolution. This was a new form of capitalism against the Party's socialist policy. They, the opposition, were "mad dogs," the speaker said. After him, in his soft voice P. P. explained the essence of the opposition. He was the Communist Party advisor to our Komsomol cell. What was the root of party oppositions: Trotskyism, the Left wing, and the Right wing. Each of these oppositions was followed by a *chistka*, purge, and then by mass arrests, deportations to Siberia's labor camps, and executions.

P. P. explained that the introduction of NEP in 1921 brought considerable economic activities, both industrial and agricultural. It was understood that a strong country could be achieved only through industrialization. The fear of another possible attack on the Soviet Union by the capitalist countries intensified this necessity. In the absence of foreign aid, industrialization could be developed only on the basis of internal accumulation. But which class or classes could and would provide this accumulation? How would they employ it and how fast would they proceed? This was the basis of the Party discussions, disagreements, and oppositions.

Trotsky and the Left opposition demanded that the *kulaks* be destroyed and collectivization be carried out quickly so the accumulation received from collectivized peasants could speed up industrialization. The Right wing opposition—with Nikolai Bukharin as leader—was pro-peasant and stressed development of private "middle" (or middle wealth) peasants which would provide the means for industrialization and encourage the gradual transformation into socialist collective farming when industry would be able to provide a technical base, agricultural machinery. The other crucial problem was how the Revolution should further develop. Should it be according to Trotsky's theory of "Permanent Revolution," in which revolution had to spread from country to country with the help of the Soviet Union, including its military? He believed the Russian Revolution could not stop at national borders and had to pass into its international phase. Or should it be according to Stalin's notion of the "Building of socialism in one country"?

Later we learned that in those circumstances, the most crucial struggle was for power. Stalin was a man of such unparalleled brutality and unscrupulousness for the attainment of his aim—power—that he did not stop even at the price of economic and physical annihilation of millions of human beings.

With the help of the Right wing, Stalin destroyed Trotskyism and the Left wing. Then he put the Left wing program to work using extreme brutality. The fate of the opposing Right and its leader, the political theoretician Nikolai Bukharin, as well, was tragic.

After P. P.'s explanation and speeches by students, mainly the "chatterbox," we accepted a resolution in which we pronounced our full support for the Party and personally for our beloved comrade Stalin. This kind of resolution had become a standard for the whole country. The process of "The King is wearing beautiful new clothes" was fast developing.

The meeting was coming to a close when Misha hurried into the room. He asked for a few minutes of our attention and presented his project to organize the "Agit brigade of the District Committee of Komsomol," a group of about twenty or so kids to entertain and provide propaganda. His idea was that our peasants were going through the most critical time in their history. Peasants by their psychology were private owners and now in a short time they would have to change to collective ownership of land, cattle, and so on. It would be nice if we could present in artistic form something good about them and about the necessity for these changes. It would unwind them a little, make them laugh. He asked one senior, then Vitia, and me to be the organizers, to select kids who could sing, dance, and talk. He asked P. P. to oversee preparation of artistic material by teachers for the brigade and especially L. L. to make final decisions in selecting materials. His staff would do all the logistics. Finally, he asked us to be ready in two weeks.

Agit Brigade

We started working right away. Two weeks later, we had dress rehearsal in our hall. It was a big success. My recital of the *Russian Woman* by Nekrasov, which L. L. had shortened, edited, and then coached me in delivering, was as everybody thought, including Misha and the District Party Secretary, just what was needed. L. L. noted that it was not a recital but a professional one-person play. And our unprecedented experience started.

A few days later in the evening, we were taken by a small bus that was falling apart (it had become a point of jokes and laughs) to a village not far away. P. P., the music teacher, and a couple of Misha's staffers were with us. The village hall was filling up fast with men, women and children. P. P. gave the introduction, told them about our aim to raise up their mood in a time of important decisions to help our country become strong. We started with a very smart staging on the words of the *International* anthem, a really exquisite work of L. L.'s. Each of our numbers had a certain theme and complex artistic presentation—singing, dancing, recitals, music, lots of funny lines, and jokes. People liked it and became more and more animated.

My presentation of the *Russian Woman* was in the second part. I gave a short introduction about the Decembrist revolution and its aim and how two young princesses followed their husbands into Siberian exile. Nekrasov, as no other poet in Russian poetry, expressed a deep love and praise for the Russian peasant and Russian people in general. The fact that Princess Volkonskaia said those words in her diary strongly reinforced their dramatic impression. At the start of my presentation there was deep silence, then emotions, getting louder, then crying, and exclamations, "*Pravda*! (truth); *Pravdochka*! (diminutive of *pravda*)." Because of my own emotions, I stopped many times. Drama at the highest point! The last number was full of life and cheerfulness, so-called *chastushki,* humor about anybody and anything that was happening. Soloists, chorus, a harmonist, and dancers added to the excitement. The village youth joined us with their local *chastushki.* There were lots of laughs and gaiety.

When we were finished, the chairman of the village council and other village officials ran onto the stage, thanked and hugged us. No one left. We came down off the stage. A big crowd assembled around me and said, "Nowadays we don't hear anything good about us. From you we heard the truth that we are good people." I got many kisses and tearful thanks from the women. Why? Their deep pain and feelings of insult were answered, although just in the good words of a poet and princesses. What a tragic truth! The same response was repeated each time we performed in the various villages. It was usually two times a week over a two-month period. News about us got around fast, mainly through the newspapers. Misha said that every village invited us to perform and some asked that Ninochka surely be present to tell the truth about Russian women and peasants.

After our performances, as a token of their thanks the women often brought us food—bread, bacon, salted meat, pickled vegetables. We seldom took it, telling them that they needed it. Then we were informed that the "middle" and the rich peasants met forced collectivization with bitter resistance. They hid food (grain) in large quantities and slaughtered cattle, pigs, and even fowl in nihilistic despair instead of bringing them to the collective barns. Thus, in the winter of 1929–30, many peasants had enough food. Still, we seldom took it. I remember a woman with three lightly-dressed small girls once brought me a dozen eggs. I asked her how many chickens she had. "I had fourteen, but now only four are left," she said. I took the eggs and gave them to the older girl. They needed them more than we did. Then I took my black woolen scarf and put it around the youngest little girl who wore just a dress and was shivering from the cold. The mother and the women around us cried bitterly.

What was going on in our country? Simple people like us or educated people like you are kind and good, but why were we oppressed? Our good country would not survive without us.

The question "Why" also occupied my mind. Later, I often witnessed women crying if some nice words or attention were addressed to them, or even if we gave them something, a "nothing," like braid ribbon. It's understandable why, as they were saying that their hearts were aching from the injustice done to them.

Collectivization Start

It was the middle of December and we were preparing for exams. Suddenly, in the morning we were called to the hall. Director Shcherbina and a representative from the District Party Committee told us first about the difficulties and necessities of collectivization. They then stated that the Party needed our help. Therefore, we were all going to villages to help the Party and the government in this decisive campaign for our country.

"Oh, no," all of us thought, "not tomorrow." We had already prepared for the next day's Winter Carnival on the iced-over river. This was our favorite winter entertainment! But the Party's campaign had priority over everything. We were paired in twos and threes, given the name of our village, and strict instructions as to what to do and how to behave. "Don't be soft-hearted, be like steel, like Comrade Stalin," they said. We were told what to expect. Our task was mainly to keep the pressure on the peasants. How long would this assignment be? It would last through the end of our vacation, January 15, 1930. Shcherbina told us that this is certainly not the time for a vacation. Our exams would be given at the start of the next semester.

Moshchenoye

In a few days, Grisha and I were in the village of Moshchenoye. Grisha was a seventeen-year-old senior, dressed lightly, although he had on everything he owned. I was dressed just for the occasion. Misha brought me a pair of wool socks and a warm hat and I had warm boots and an overcoat. We lived in peasants' homes assigned to us by the Chairman of the village council. They were very nice people. My *khoziayka*, the houselady, took very good care of me, especially when I gave her a blouse and some other small things for her granddaughter. Grisha's *khoziayka* let him use a pair of woolen socks and a vest she had knited. The unquestionable, supreme authority in the village was the Representative of the District Party Committee, known as "R." His word was law. As I look into my memory, I try to find another man who was as bad as he. Perhaps he wasn't so bad, but circumstances made him that way. The Party's directive was to collectivize all the peasants. Those who weren't willing, especially the *kulaks*, were to be deported with their families to the various regions of Siberia. In a speech in December 1929, Stalin gave orders to expropriate the *kulaks*. This meant that about two million *kulaks* with their families were caught in a gigantic agricultural revolution that mercilessly sent both them and some middle class peasants to their doom.

Lenin envisioned free will collectivization. His concept would have taken decades, if not a generation, to implement. It meant that the *kolkhozes* would receive ever-increasing amounts of technical expertise, tools, credit, and machinery. It would provide for a higher standard of living, thus making it attractive to even middle class peasants to participate. This healthy mixture of both private and collective farms might have assured a satisfactory food supply for the entire country and funds for industrialization. Lenin's view of socialization was practical and humane. In order to solidify his power, Stalin, on the other hand, was in a hurry to prove his theory of "socialism in one country": radical collectivization and the creation of powerful industry.

In some villages, increased peasant resistance took the form of open rebellion, but they were forced to surrender at the point of machine guns by the GPU (the political unit of the NKVD) and the Red Army units. Russian history has seen many mass peasant rebellions that were the result of the peasants' utter despair.

Every morning, we would come to the village Council House where a "Representative" would have a "talk" with about ten peasants who had been called in. The peasants' faces were the color of burlap and they were obviously confused and in pain. The "talk" went something like this:

"Why are you still not in the *kolkhoz*?" Each peasant tried to respond in some way. "You are the obstructors of the Party's great plans for you."

Here he would start to paint a beautiful picture of life in the *kolkhoz*. Then he would place a list with their names before them and say, "Sign it and become a good member of the *kolkhoz*." The peasants would mumble something and some would try to leave. Then the Representative's demeanor changed, his face taking on a frightening expression, and he would scream, "You are the enemies of the Soviet State. You are the snakes who are poisoning the good people in this village. I give you three days, and if I don't see your names on the list of *kolkhoz* members, you will be arrested and together with your families, you will be sent to . . . you know where!"

Once, in the school hall, there was a meeting of all the peasants who had not yet joined the *kolkhoz*. "R" drew his gun and shot, first into the ceiling and then just inches above the peasants' heads. They fell to the floor, one on top of the other. Fear, despair, and confusion was in their eyes, but not a word was said. They just got up and ran away. It was a heartbreaking scene. Why was it necessary to offend and humiliate these strong, wise, and for the most part, good people? They were the providers of life supplies for the whole country.

We had two assignments from "R." The first was to work with the Komsomol youth and educate them about general party policy, specifically, as it applied to the peasants. The second assignment was to visit the homes of the peasants to educate them and reinforce the pressure that was being put on them. "R" gave us the names of the streets he wanted us to go to first because he said these were the streets where the "middle farmers and a few *kulaks* still lived." Some *kulaks* had already been sent to Siberia and their homes given to poor peasants.

The south of Russia is often called the black soil or the rich soil region. Some regions in this area had a mixed population, i.e., Russians and Ukrainians. While the language was Russian, it was Russian with some Ukrainian characteristic, such as accent, or Ukrainian words pronounced in a Russian way. Nikita Khruschev was a product of this region and his language made him the brunt of many jokes. In this part of Russia, the architecture of the houses was somewhat different from the *izba*, log home. This region was basically a steppe, so wood was more scarce and, consequently, not many homes were built from logs.

There was a difference between the style of the Russian and the Ukrainian houses. Russian houses in this region were mainly long structures made of peat and turf, whitewashed, and divided throughout by a long corridor. The Ukrainian *khata* was neater looking, more like the Russian *izba*, but the outside was white stucco with a light brown house base.

The first street we were sent to was a Ukrainian-looking street. Each house had a fence around it. We opened the first gate and a big, wild dog rushed at us. We ran out and waited beyond the gate, but no one came out. The next house was the same and by the end of the street, none had let us in, but they were looking out at us from behind the windows.

The next day, we went to a street of Russian-looking houses. At the first house, the gate was open and there was a dog on a chain a safe distance from the house. We knocked on the door and waited. Finally, the *khoziayka* opened the door and invited us in. We saw a big, quite clean room with white walls and wooden floorboards. There was a large table with benches along the walls, a few coarsely made stools, and a large wooden trunk for clothes. The icons in the left corner were draped with linen, embroidered towels. Not far from these icons was a portrait of Lenin. The most important feature was a huge brick stove, topped by bedding for the most privileged members of the family, usually, the grandparents and babies. Between the stove and the front wall was an enormous, stationary, wooden bed which could accommodate the entire family. Lush houseplants, mainly geraniums, were at the windows. Each home looked practically the same on the inside with very few, insignificant differences, but this one represented the better homes.

The *khoziayka* woke her husband who was sleeping on the stove. This man had an inquisitive mind and we had a good conversation. At one point, he put small heaps of different grains on the table and asked us to name them. We felt that he had us in a corner even though we could name some: millet, corn, and buckwheat. We couldn't tell the difference between rye and wheat, or between oats and barley. He was surprised that we were so smart, even though we looked like city people. "Look, they sent you to teach us peasants how to live and tell us what's best for us, and you can't even identify the grains your bread and porridge are made from," he said. He kept asking us questions about peasant life. Naturally, we didn't know the answers. We started laughing together and developed a very good rapport.

The word must have gone around that we weren't "chatterboxes," and that we respected the peasants and didn't try to teach them. We visited many homes. Sometimes we were invited, and often, were treated to food. However, our discussions were often very intense and painful. We usually began with the known political formula: socialism is the predictable outcome of our socialist Revolution. Our government started to lay the economic foundation for this new society, its industrialization and the elimination of small capitalist enterprises, the private farming and instead organizing the socialist agriculture. It would bring sacrifice and hardship, but the big rewards would come later.

We had an exchange of opinions about what the Soviet State accomplished and what the peasants and workers gained. They expressed both satisfaction and painful bitterness. We had been told during our instructions that the peasants now are smart people, are literate, read newspapers, listen to the radio, and many were acquainted with Russian history, especially since the Revolution. They praised Lenin's policy, since he provided them with land and raised the prices of agricultural products.

The women were especially against Stalin's collectivization. "They ordered us to take the cows that feed us to the collective barn. They also made us bring our pigs, sheep, geese, ducks, and even our chickens. But they put lazy women in charge of the animals. The fowl started to die so we brought our chickens, geese, and ducks back home. 'R' threatened to punish us. They are selling milk and eggs, some we are getting every day, and some is going to waste."

Sometimes we meet in someone's home, a small group having a drinking party. Their *samogon* was the Russian equivalent of moonshine. They always invited us to join them. We would thank them for the *samogon* but we wouldn't refuse the *zakuski,* cold food. This would invariably make somebody comment that we must have good parents who brought us up properly.

When they got somewhat drunk, they'd begin to talk openly: "Stalin is destroying us. We will die of famine or be sent to Siberia. Our grains were taken from us by force. But why have we killed and keep killing our livestock, our calves, pigs, sheep, goats, even our geese and chickens? We've already sold some of our horses and cows. We have enough food now, but what will we eat next year? We may be members of the *kolkhoz*, but how will we plow our fields in the spring? The only way left may be to harness us and our wives to the plow. That's not a joke. The *kolkhoz* doesn't have a single tractor or any machinery. Stalin won't save us next winter and we'll have to blame ourselves as well."

"Some *muzhiks* think we have to take up our weapons and start an uprising. It's stupid talk. Instead of villages, there would be flat, empty places and instead of us, the wind would blow away our ashes. Our children won't be spared. We still remember, ten to twelve years ago, there was complete chaos. Not only was the landed gentry killed, but peasants killed each other. Not only were the stately homes of the landed gentry burned, our *isbi*, houses, also went up in flames. On the other hand, do we want to have a strong Russia? Yes! Then our country has to be industrialized. Who is going to give us money for that? Only we, the peasants, are the workhorses. The whole of history is like that and it won't change."

Perhaps the majority of the peasants subscribed to this practical conclusion. Their understanding of the situation in the villages across the country was certainly correct. All of them displayed a mystical love for Russia and a painful, almost angry patriotism. They were afraid Stalin and company were not real Russians (Stalin was a Georgian; the others were Armenians, Jews, and Poles) and they would bring about the destruction of Russia. They believed that their communal spirit, now, as well as in the past, was the foundation of their relationships and would help them overcome these almost impossible circumstances.

They were right in some ways. From their early history, Slavs were organized in communities and worked in teams. Great Russia-Siberia was colonized by peasants and monks mainly, military force came after them. When the Mongols occupied Russia from the Volga River to Kiev in 1240, large groups of peasants, sometimes entire villages, moved to the northeast into no man's land beyond the Volga River and still farther, beyond the Ural Mountains. In order to survive the harsh climate, build the houses, and prepare the forest terrain for agricultural use, a communal effort was necessary. After Alexander II abolished serfdom in 1861, it was decreed that peasants owned the farmlands jointly, in communal villages called *mir* or *obshchina*. Even though the old communal villages and the new *kolkhoz* may have appeared similar, the peasants were smart people and clearly understood the difference. In the old commune, each houshold owned a parcel of land, livestock, and the fruits of its own labor. But members of the Soviet *kolkhoz* were required to give everything to the *kolkhoz* as well as their work and to be paid for a day's work only at the end of the season.

Once I read a poem to a company of people in someone's home. It was *Who Lives Well in Rus'* by Nikolai Nekrassov. It's a long poem, about one hundred and eighty pages, and is an artistically excellent, socio-culturally truthful presentation of the peasants' life. The poem is about six peasants from neighboring poor villages who were quarreling about who lives well in Russia. A Russian peasant had called on a "philosopher." They were inclined to discuss the problems of truth and fairness. Those six first discussed, then quarreled, then fought, and then made peace and decided to walk throughout Russia to find out who lives well and happy in Rus'. I received many invitations to come and read the poem, and usually the house was filled. There were a lot of laughs and some tears and discussion. More than once I heard such laughable comments as:

"Listen *kum* (*kum* is a godfather of one's child), do you remember when we were quarreling and fighting?"

"Yes *kum*, then we looked into each other's eyes and I asked you, 'Why are we fighting?'"

"'I don't know,' you said. Then we shook hands, came to my home, and drank for a peaceful solution and since then we have tried not to quarrel badly."

The Russian peasant more often expressed his thought not directly but in traditional people's sayings, proverbs, tales, and songs. Here is one of those, a historical story told by one peasant:

"The Fieldmarshall, Prince Kutuzov, who won a victory over Napoleon in 1812, called to his headquarters the partisans-peasants who were fighting Napoleon's army. He wanted to see these real heroes.

The French are good soldiers, but their spirit is weaker than ours, partisans said to Kutuzov. Napoleon's mistake was that he thought he could take Russia by fear. Now he is turning back in fear. Even our *baby*-women became partisans and are chasing Napoleon.

Then the peasants asked Kutuzov about the main pain of their hearts. "Maybe after this victory land and freedom will be given to the peasants?"

Kutuzov couldn't conceal his confusion. What could he tell them? If it were up to him, he would do it. The partisans saw his embarrassment. "Your Serene Highness, these are two different things, to take land from *bare* (landowners) can wait. But Russia, its independence and well-being is an overarching concern and can't wait."

"That is exactly as it is now," my peasants said.

Being in the company of the women was truly pleasant. They congregated together, just like the men, bringing their children with them. Dutch treat is an old Russian custom. The women also liked to sing. Frequently, I would sing old folk songs with them or teach them some new ones. We would recite *byliny* (old Russian epics) and at their insistence, I would recite parts of *The Russian Woman* and other poems. Being among them I felt great human warmth and sincerity, and that famous Russian togetherness, especially on a spiritual and emotional level.

Once, I was invited to the home of a well-to-do activist peasant, a member of the village council. The *khoziayka* was the picture of a peasant beauty. She was tall, strong, well built with arched brows over brown eyes, and pink cheeks. Their conversation was full of pain and grief.

"We don't even talk about our cows and chickens anymore. Our children's fate worries us deeply. We don't know if we'll be able to feed them next winter."

"We're very afraid. We don't know what's going to happen to us. We had such good order and such a good life in our village. We observed our traditions and customs, as well as the new law."

"What are we now? I cry every time I go into my yard. It's empty. Just a few weeks ago, my yard was full. My geese, ducks, chickens would run to me, and they'd talk to me in their own way and understood when I talked to them. When my cow would hear my steps, she's greet me with a moo-moo. I was a proud *khoziayka*: a full house, my children looked healthy, my barn was full and so was my yard. Now we have nothing and we are nothing! We have a lot of free time so we sit in each other's homes and eat our hearts out. Our husbands look like they've lost their minds. They drink, talk politics, and sleep. At the *kolkhoz*, they work two or three days a week in the winter."

There was apprehension about the unknown. Their personal world was becoming hard to manage because of the uncertainty.

One morning, I noticed that my *khoziaeva* were in a very gloomy mood. Grisha came very late and looked upset. Since the school day was already over, we went to school so we could have a private talk. Then Grisha told me what happened the previous night.

"Yesterday, 'R' ordered me to be with a group which was to expropriate *kulak* 'X.' The group consisted of two policemen from the district, a local communist who was the leader, two members of the committee of poor peasants, and me. At about nine p.m., we went to the home of 'X' and woke the family. The communist read the order from the village council to expropriate the family as enemies of the Soviet people. He gave them an hour to take their warm clothes and some food. Everything else was to be left since it wasn't their's anymore. This was a family of seven, the *kulak* and his wife, their son and his wife and two small children, and an unmarried daughter of about twenty. The old woman and the two children were screaming. The old man got out of bed, sat on a bench like a statue, no sound and no tears. The other three adults started to gather their things and food and put them in bundles. The son's wife opened the large family trunk that contained all their clothes. At this point, the communist stopped her."

"'These aren't your's anymore,' he said.'"

"'They're mine as long as I'm here.'"

"And with this, she took some clothes. Members of the Poor Peasants Committee tried to wrest them from her. They pushed her to the floor, but she got up, and together with her sister-in-law, started fighting for the clothes. The communist drew his gun and shot at her but missed. The policemen stopped the scramble. After all, order had to be maintained."

Grisha said he was so upset and mad that he screamed, "Let them take the clothes for their children and warm clothes for the adults."

"Finally, they took what they needed and dressed the children. Dressing the old man was almost impossible. He had lost his mind and his speech. Sometime after midnight everybody was dressed, their bundles ready. The old woman took only a fire iron and a large kettle so she could cook the family *borshch*."

"They got into a large, waiting sled into which their bundles were thrown. They were all screaming. It was a horrible nightmare. Our group followed in another sled. We brought them to an open field alongside the railroad tracks where other families were already gathered waiting for a freight train. It was snowing and the temperature was about minus twenty degrees Celsius. There were children and old people in this group. The railroad station was quite nearby. Why not take them there to wait where they could at least be warm? This had to be kept secret!"

Grisha and I were very upset and we couldn't comprehend the Party policy. These were good, hardworking people. Some had become members of the *kolkhoz*, so why this cruelty toward them? Was this Stalin's policy or just a local perversion of the Party's directions? The painful questions in our minds were not answered.

The village policeman told his wife in secret (certainly, the whole village knew this) that an old man and two babies had died, probably from the cold, while waiting for the train in this open field. Their relatives buried them in the snow.

By this time, I was already subconsciously upset about people's attitudes toward the dreadful things that were happening to all of them. They took it as a matter of fact. The Russian peasant is helpful toward each other, but now their behavior was different. Why? It was much later that I understood people's minds and their psychology. They had lost their sensitivity because of the unusual circumstances of life in the previous fifteen years: WWI, Revolution, Civil War—all of these not only devoured human life like "hot dogs," but created new views and conditions for life.

The Christian faith, which had been the supporting point in the peasants' life, the basis of their brotherhood, was now declared a power hostile to people. Instead, an idea of class struggle pitted people, one against the other. And the richer peasants, often good people, were thrown off their land, taken from their ancestoral homes, left without any rights and nobody really understood why.

Not having a reasonable explanation for all this, only one cause was left, specifically, "God's punishment." The logic was that in Holy Russia the ancestors lived according to God's teachings and had a good life. Then people started to forget God's law. But, God is kind. He will forgive the sins of His people. The people thought they had to pray and live a righteous life. That was one of the reasons they became passive and left themselves in God's hands. The other, more powerful cause was the hopelessness of their situation; the force of the State would crush them to death if they showed any rebellion.

The New Year Celebration

The New Year was approaching. "R," Grisha, and myself decided to organize the celebration, so we helped the small Komsomol cell to organize it. The secretary of the cell was a wonderful guy, Serioha (Sergey), known in the village as an accordian player, dancer, and joker. The teachers, with the help of the children, set up the *yolka*.

Serioha organized the orchestra—an accordian, guitars, balalaikas, tambourines, and peasant "instruments," like spoons, bells, and grates. The women brought a lot of *zakuski* such as fresh bread and *pirozhki* filled with meat, cabbage, and cheese. They also brought bacon, ham, pickled vegetables, and fruit. The men brought *samogon*. All of this was arranged on tables in large classrooms.

The school hall and the classrooms were filled with village youth, parents, and grandparents. "R's" talk was pleasant—quite different from his usual. Perhaps this was because the village was quite advanced in its efforts toward collectivization. Although I was busy and happy organizing this event, I felt lonely without my parents and Misha. In my mind, I kept calling Misha, "Come, please. I want to see you."

The party was in full swing: dancing, singing, and jesting. Many came already *na veseliye*, slightly drunk. The women danced, mostly in groups, doing difficult and loud footwork. When a woman danced with a man she had to display smoothness, plasticity, and femininity. Men most frequently liked to dance alone. They would stand in a half circle and each dancer, in turn, would display his special tricks and abilities. Many of these were nothing to laugh at. It was a part of their competition and the men would judge each other, making straightforward remarks with strong expressions.

One has to observe a Russian party in order to understand better the Russian character. As many historians have noted, Russians are endowed with a "broad nature," expansive, generous and passionate, and hard to restrict within a legal formula. Russians display dynamism and excess in their behavior, and unpredictability is not excluded. The spirit of simplicity and togetherness is unique. Instead of becoming violent or crying because of the hardships and injustices in their lives, they prefer to congregate, drink and sing. But, when even their limitless endurance has ended, their dynamism and excess goes into full swing, in rebellion.

The women and I were dancing. Suddenly, the music stopped and Serioha screamed, "Misha came!" He and everybody else ran to greet Misha, as well as "R," the Chairman of the Village Council, and the Chairman of the *kolkhoz*. Misha, as the District Secretary of the Komsomol, was a member of the Bureau of the District Party Committee. A Bureau consists of seven or nine people who are the highest ruling authority in the district and each member of this group is a very important person. They decided everything about the whole life in a district.

This was all too much for me and I sat down trying to restrain my excitement. Misha, with a crowd around him, saw me, came straight to me, kissed me on the cheek, sat down next to me, took my hands and our eyes told us all. I heard "aahs" and the "oohs" all around us, as well as praise.

The *Komsomolki*, female *Komsomol* members, invited everyone for *zakuski*. First, they invited Misha and me because an old Russian custom required that the *Vitiaz i Princessa*, the knight and the princess, be the first honored guests at the table. We sat at the back of the one room with Serioha and the young people. We ate, drank, and talked mostly about collectivization and why there was such a rush that went against all conventional wisdom and against the interest of the people and the country. Everybody trusted Misha, so they spoke openly.

The dancing and singing of *chastushki* continued until quite late. Serioha composed *chastushki* about Misha, and in no time, everybody was singing it. Using Russian sentence structure, it went like this:

Night. The moon is shining.
The wolves are howling.
Who is hurrying alone through the frosty night?
Misha. What is the cause?
Nina!

In Russian, "what is the cause," *kakaya prichina* and *Nina* are a perfect rhyme.

Finally, those who could still stand helped those who had lost that ability and dragged them home. Misha and Serioha walked me home and Misha stayed at Serioha's house. Misha's behavior made a very good impression on both the young people and the parents. The parents said that the youth leader, Misha, showed everybody how a young man who was in love should treat his girlfriend.

A week later was the Russian Orthodox Christmas. The church in Moshchenoye had been closed for about a year, so the believers attended a church in a neighboring village, about eight kilometers away. This made the elderly men and women extremely unhappy.

The complete separation of Church and State was marked by the thorough exclusion of the Church from political life. The Patriarch Tikhon, who had been elected by the Church Council in 1917, energetically opposed the atheism of the Bolsheviks. This resistance from the clergy made the religious battle increasingly bitter. The persecution of the Church, which included killing priests and confiscating church treasures, was brutal. Patriarch Tikhon was arrested and, I believe, died in a labor camp.

There were some among the clergy who demanded a compromise with Bolshevism. The groups they formed were called "The Living Church." The State welcomed this trend: In July 1927, the Patriarchal Vicar Sergius, in his encyclical letter, ordered the faithful to pray for the Soviet State and government. Religious services were permitted to some extent, but by 1929 Stalin's policy of industrialization and collectivization and the increasing battle against all the bourgeois elements in the country dealt the Church a crushing blow. Churches were closed and rare artistic treasures such as icons, frescos, mosaics, embroidered towels from around the icons, and priests' robes were destroyed or given to museums. Buildings were destroyed or given over to utilitarian functions such as storage or for the Association of Militant Athieists, which was led by the Communist intellectual, Yaroslavsky. Resistance? Just the old women, bitterly crying.

The villagers celebrated Christmas in the old way, which meant for at least a week. But in previous times, people were in Church from early morning until mid-day, standing and praying. After Church, they would celebrate the birth of Christ. Now they were confused, asking, "Where is the truth? Marx and Lenin taught us that the truth can be found only if social equality and justice provided for all working people. But this involved class struggle. On the other hand, our Christian Orthodox belief taught us how to live in friendship and love with each other."

Another ambiguity: During this holiday season, children would join together in groups and walk from house to house singing *Koliadi*. This was an ancient Slav, pre-Christian agricultural rite which had found its way into the Christmas and New Year folklore. These are "glorifying songs, sung during the Christmas holiday season by groups of singers in villages. Their function was originally magical, to promote good crops, happy marriages, childbearing, and wealth" (*The Study of Russian Folklore*, edited by Felix J. Oinis and Stephen Sudakoff, p. 320). Now these were children singing:

Mister Peter bright Ivanovich
Is the shining moon
Anna Kirilovna is the gleaming sun.
Their children are the close set stars!
To the master and the mistress and the children, we wish good health
For ages and ages, for many years.

As at American Halloween, Russian children begged for donations at Christmas:

Tausen, bausen
The sausage is done
It sat in the stove
It looked at us
If you give us no pie
We grab your cow by the horns.

Grisha and I walked with a few of these groups and asked the children why they were doing this, especially since they were young pioneers. "We want to collect lots of food for our party in school."

The next day we went to that party—it happened to be the normal young pioneers meeting. There was lots of food, singing, and dancing. The old and the new had met.

I was invited to join numerous families for Christmas. I went to the home of an older couple where I met a small group of their friends in the same age group. They were very wise people who knew a great deal about Russian history. The Orthodox religion was their hearts' passion. They were pessimistic about the future of the *kolkhoz* and felt it would not work. Later in my life, more than once I would recall

81

this conversation and be amazed by the correctness of their predictions. These people's hearts were still broken over the destruction of their church, which had been built in the eighteenth century and was of the wooden style of architecture. It had housed many priceless treasures: icons, stained glass windows, and chronicles, the history of this region.

"It was the embodiment of our village spirit and history," they said. "All our ancestors, as well as ourselves, were baptized, married, and buried there. The graves of our fathers, mothers, and everyone who was dear to us were in the church graveyard. Nothing is left. This is a disaster for Russia. We have lost our history. We don't know who we are or where we came from."

The close relations with people, learning their thoughts and beliefs, later raised doubts in my and my friends minds. Are Russian peasants religious or more superstitious as adhered to by the anti-religious propaganda? We learned that people still believed in the Orthodox Church's teaching, which was, they think, the last sanctuary of the original Apostolic Christianity. Holy Russia of the fourteenth to eighteenth centuries was the expression of that teaching. Hence, the idea of the Messianic role of Russian Orthodoxy to rejuvenate the world's Christianity to its Apostolic form.

Another idea among some Russian and foreign scholars was *dvoeverie*, dual faith, the pagan and Christian elements in Orthodoxy. It's natural because Christianity was imposed on dying paganism. The last still has roots in the people's customs. But the Church has a strict adherance to Christian dogma, the sacraments, and liturgy.

The old customs were still prolific. I especially liked the way they sent season's greetings. The women made cookies called *prianiki* in many different sizes and forms, but before they were baked, using a wooden plank with a message carved in high relief, they would press it into the dough. I received several large, heart-shaped cookies with the different messages: *Kogo Liubliu, Tomu Dariu*—I am giving this to the one I love. I brought some home and Mama saved them until WWII. It so happens that now I have one on my dining room table in a big crystal bowl. In 1996, my friends Valery Kuvakin and his wife Julia, both professors at Moscow State University, sent me the same heart-shaped *prianik* with the message *Kogo Liubliu, Tomu Dariu*. It gave me a wonderful feeling.

From the beginning of their history, Russians liked storytellers, many of whom were women. These people were naturally intelligent, highly gifted, artistic, and remembered immense quantities of folklore: byliny; historical songs; lyrical songs; fairy tales; lullabies; proverbs; jokes and much more. This mythology teaches about life's wisdom and morality. The jokes were very popular, especially among men, and frequently these jokes were anti-Soviet. Fortunately, in the 1920s no one was arrested for telling them. However, later, many people would unexpectedly find themselves in Siberia for that hearty laugh. To my surprise, I found many of these anecdotes published, certainly not in the Soviet Union. Let me share a few:

—*Do you know the difference between Capitalism and Socialism? Certainly, capitalism means exploitation of man by his fellow man. In Socialism, it's precisely the other way around.*

—*Stalin's own words: What is the difference between Capitalism and Socialism? The basic principle of Capitalism is the maximum exploitation of the toiling masses. The basic aim of Socialism is to catch up with, and surpass, the most advanced capitalistic state.*

—*On Balance: Stalin was smuggled into Hell. Alexander II, a liberal Tsar who abolished serfdom in 1861, came to see him.*
"Welcome, Yosif Vissarionovich," Alexander II says. "And how is Mother Russia?"
"Doing well, your Majesty," Stalin answers.
"Do the peasants own the land now?"
"Yes, it looks as though they do."
"It was the same in my day. And how about the press? Is it free?"
"Absolutely free. They mustn't write against the government, of course."
"Yes, that is how it was in my day, too. And how about our vodka? Is it still forty proof?"
"No," Stalin says proudly. "It's forty-five proof."
Silence while the Tsar muses. After awhile he speaks up. "Tell me, was a silly five percent in vodka worth the whole bloody upheaval?"

—*A group of peasants come to Michael Ivanovich Kalinin, the chairman of the Supreme Soviet.*
"Comrade Kalinin, our lives are getting very hard. We have no clothes and we are walking barefoot."

"Have patience, comrades. There are countries where people are completely naked."

"Oh, my God! In those countries, the Soviet government must have been in power for at least fifty years."

A Traditional Wedding

Once, Serioha took Grisha and me to the home of his friend Kostia, who had just arrived from a big plant construction site. Each village had to send several young men to help build industrial projects. Kostia had been recruited for the project, and now he had come home to marry his fiancee and take her with him. He seemed a very nice fellow, strong, good-looking, friendly, and trustworthy. A number of people had gathered at his home, including his fiancee, Anastasia-Nata. The table was covered with *zakuski* and vodka. Kostia told us about some of his experiences.

"The railroad train filled up with only us young men. There were no women. After several days of traveling, we passed behind the Volga River and stopped in an open field. The command was, 'Disembark, and take your belongings with you.' There was nothing around: no houses, just snow-covered fields, although it was the end of March. We came to a mountain of building material, primarily boards and planks. The building technician gave us the plans of where and how to build our barracks. At once, we started working constructing several barracks. The first night, we slept on planks under the open sky and had to watch each other to make sure no one froze to death. The next night, we already had the walls and roof of the barracks constructed. A few days later, our homes were done and we started building the plant located a few kilometers from our barracks. This was great work and our enthusiasm was high and kept us moving. We understood the urgent necessity of this work for our country. Yes, the Komsomol under the most difficult conditions built huge plants, hydroelectric stations, railroads, and even cities, without any complaints. It was for the Motherland!"

Several days later, we were watching a modified traditional Russian wedding. A traditional wedding was a very complex affair that historically developed based on the religious, magical, and aesthetic outlook of the people in patriarchal villages. The expression *svad'bu igrat* meant to have a wedding game. It was a very colorful game with all of the personages having to act in very specific and traditionally prescribed ways. Each character has a name: the prince and princess are the bride and groom. The *druzhka* and *svakha* are the best man and the maid of honor. There are also some very specific word formulas which must be used. It is an extremely ornate and highly prescribed wedding activity that expresses respect for each member of the wedding. The "official" wedding game continues for three days.

After both families have agreed on the wedding, then the bride and her girlfriends start preparing the dowry and the gifts she has to give to the groom, his family, all the girlfriends, and her family. For weeks, they weave, sew and embroider, working at the bride's home. They would work and sing, usually beautiful folk lyrics, and on certain evenings the boys could come to visit them.

Kostia and Nata's wedding was on Sunday. The guests gathered at the bride's parents' home where the bridesmaids dressed Nata in a colorful, national costume with a crown of white flowers. After she was dressed, the *svakha* sent a message to the bridegroom's home: "We are ready for the bridegroom's procession." The procession was on horseback. First came the *druzhka* with an embroidered towel over his shoulder and across his chest, then the groom with several groomsmen on either side of him. Sleighs carrying the groom's parents and then the relatives followed them. The procession was very ornate with many ribbons and small bells.

The gate to the bride's home was closed. The *svakha* announced the arrival of the groom and his procession and the *druzhka* demanded that the gate be opened for the prince. The brother of the bride asked for an entrance payment to which the groom agreed. Inside, at the main table, are seated the bride's mother and father, the *svakha*, the bride, and next to her was her brother and all her bridesmaids. The *druzhka* asked the prince to sit next to the princess. Usually, at this point, there develops a comic interchange between the bride's brother and the bridegroom. The guests laugh and take sides. Finally, the groom pays a ransom, in order to be able to sit next to the bride.

The members of his *poizd,* procession, are seated according to very specific rules that relate to their position in the family and in the wedding party. The father, the mother, and the *druhzka* are at the main table. Now the *velichanie* (songs) begin, with very dignified, elevated lyrics that are sung to each principle member of the wedding, including the bridesmaids and the groomsmen. The person to whom the lyrics are addressed stands up, takes a low bow, and thanks the singers in very nice and flowery words.

After this the bride and groom stepped up to the Chairman of the Village Council, who had been sitting alone at a small table, and he performed the civil registration of the marriage. He then congratulated the bride and groom and made a speech about the great future of the country and the newlyweds.

In an instant, as if by magic, the tables were filled with food and vodka and the feast had started. There were many toasts made, started by both fathers. As people began to feel "better and better," they shouted, "gorko," bitter—an indication that the bride and groom should kiss and make the vodka sweet by doing so. There was a great deal of singing as the bride gave her gifts to the groom, both families, bridesmaids, and "officials" in the wedding. There was the singing of moving wedding-rite lyrics, when the bridesmaids unbraided the bride's single braid, which, by custom, girls wear, and braided her hair into two braids, arranging them in a crown around her head to symbolize she was a married woman. The bride's mother cried. The bride bowed deeply to her parents and thanked them for their love and care. This is a very beautiful and highly emotional custom.

Late in the afternoon, the groom took the bride to his house. His father invited all the guests to their home. There was an old and very elaborate custom, at this point, of taking and carrying the gifts and dowry. But not at this wedding. The feast continued at the groom's home with many different customs. Finally, the married couple left. A wedding is considered splendid if the guests could not use only "two" to get home, but "four" and crawl.

After they all left, the young people danced until morning. I was dancing a ritual dance with the other girls. During this dance, if a boy extends his hand to a girl, she takes it, stops dancing, and he embraces her, meaning they are in love and there will be a future wedding. One of the boys whom I knew well, just as I knew all the Komsomol members, extended his hand to me. I didn't know what to do and looked at the girls who became very angry at the boy.

"Don't you know that Nina has a fiancee, Misha? How dare you act like this. It's dishonest and immoral."

He left. This affirmed that the villagers still had a strong moral culture.

The wedding left a profound impression on me. It displayed the cultural tradition of the harmony and respect toward each other in the community. It also showed the fine aesthetic feelings and the immense love of gaiety of these people.

Over forty years later, I was in the USSR on a cultural exchange program studying the Russian wedding tradition and how it had changed and why. Unfortunately, this rich moral and cultural tradition had practically disappeared, as it happened in all civilized societies of the world. With this, as well, went the naturally upheld spiritual norms and understanding of human behavior. Naturally, not everything from the past was acceptable in our time. But the peril for humanity is that the human being is losing his spirituality and getting to be more just a material vehicle of life.

Back to School

We were back to school on January 15, 1930. We were glad to see each other, but our mood was very subdued. The experience of the last month, witnessing the suffering and confusion of these simple, good people and the disintegration of the peasants' old ways had made us more realistic and mature. Not many of us spoke with pride about taking part in the *kulaks'* expropriation.

Still, it would be over thirty years before Solhzhenitsyn's *One Day in the Life of Ivan Denisowich* would be published, a book which aroused in honest people a feeling of historical guilt for the fate of the Russian and Ukrainian peasantry. But some of us, including myself, already had that feeling of guilt. We were subjected to a new political thinking in categories, ranging from the important people to the "not people at all," like *kulaks*. And the number of categories for "not people" was increasing, till they became collectively defined under just one all-embracing term as "the enemies of the Soviet people."

In our after-dinner conversations, only a few of us were talking with self-pride about Stalin's ingenious policy of collectivization and his destruction of the "blood-suckers." Vania was one of them, though I wondered if he was sincere. Vania had just become a secretary of our Komsomol organization. He was unnoticeable, plain, with reddish hair, eyebrows and eyelashes, small blue, close-set eyes, superficial and primitive. But his voice was loud and authoritative and he used phrases like "we will take measures" and "embrace the teachings of the genius Stalin." He learned perfectly the style of Stalin's *apparatchik,* which he later became. But in his "out of stage behavior" he was an infernal bore. He paid more than normal attention to me, which made me sick.

The moral and political problems troubled us, raising questions like "Who is telling the truth?" However, our belief in socialism and in the Party's policy was unshakeable and we were on Stalin's side. We had agreed that Trotsky's theory of "permanent revolution" would provoke the Party and the masses to skepticism, as the prospect of world revolution moved to the far future, and it meant that the fate of Russia would depend on the situation abroad. Stalin's path of Nationale Communism, with his theory of "socialism in one country," which quickly became dogma, required that country to be developed, industrialized, and collectivized. However, the means which were employed for achieving this aim were not in harmony with official theory. This was especially true of collectivization, which was carried out by force. This fact bothered us and our idealistic beliefs. It is interesting that years after Stalin's death, Soviet historians permitted themselves to be open, admitting that Stalin's agricultural collectivization program had been premature and coercive, but agreeing with the goals of the program.

We knew that P. P. had been a Party Representative in a village. But he was back in the tekhnikum. Soon we found out that the Grayvoron's District Party Committee called him from the village because he did not follow the Party's directive. Specifically, a small number of peasants were collectivized, *kulaks* were not expropriated. It was said that he was a "soft intelligent" who did not fit the Communist Party, which meant that he might be expelled from the Party and then from his position at the tekhnikum. We were very agitated to hear about this possibility and asked L. L. what we could do to prevent it from happening. She sent us to ask Shcherbina about it. He told us, "It's not your business. It's better if you don't talk about it."

We noticed that L. L. and P. P. were very sad. About a month later we heard good news. On the agenda of the Bureau of the District Party Committee was the P. P. question. A group of communists, among them Shcherbina and L. L., were allowed to come to the Bureau meeting and they stood fast for P. P. But the decisive vote was Misha's. As a member of the Bureau, he was against expulsion from the Party and for a reprimand only. Misha again was our hero.

I compared two representatives of the Party: P. P., who was branded a "rotten intelligent" and almost expelled from the Party because he had moral integrity, and the representative in Moshchenoye, a real rotten, heartless, careerist who was highly praised for his inhuman treatment of the peasants. Discipline, unity, and obedience were the first requirements for the members of the Communist Party which believed "The Party is always right."

The exams were cancelled and regular classes started. Misha came and was very upset, for the Oblast Bureau of Komsomol rejected his request to relieve him of duties as the District Secretary, allowing him to go to school at Moscow State University. Instead, they ordered him to be in Voronehz in a month's time for work in the Oblast Committee. I was crushed. We had planned that in July, Misha would take the entrance exams to Moscow University, a five year school. Then, in two years, I would take the entrance exams to the Moscow Drama Institute, a four year school. Misha calmed me down, saying that the Oblast Committee promised to let him go to school in one year. That's how it was: the society's interest had priority over personal interest.

Misha left at the end of February. I felt very lonely and realized how deep and strong my love was for him.

On March 2, 1930, Stalin played one of his famous tricks. He proclaimed that the Party officials who were carrying out collectivization had become "dizzy with success" and had overdone it. He pretended his orders had been misunderstood and that it was the officials who had used an excess of zeal and set up *kolkhozes* by force. Those who did so, he proclaimed, were reactionary fools and had to be punished. A stop had to be put to all excesses. Peasants were made to understand that membership in a *kolkhoz* would now be strictly free will. So it would be all right for those who didn't want to be in a *kolkhoz* to take back their livestock.

On the tekhnikum side on the outskirts of town was a *kolkhoz*. A group of us ran over there to see what was happening. It was an absorbing picture of mass disorder and tragic comedy. The big barn was divided into spaces for each group of fowl: chickens, turkeys,

89

geese, and ducks. But now all of them were mixed together, running and flying. The poor women and men were running after them, trying to catch their scared creatures. Other peasants came and took their cows and pigs home. So Stalin suddenly and shrewdly slowed down the process he had originally speeded up. And he became a good friend of the peasants. But was he?

In any case, this "agrarian revolution from above" had catastrophic consequences. Peasants slaughtered or sold their horses and cattle. As a result, in the spring many tracts of land were left untilled. A famine in 1931–33 engulfed the richest agricultural areas of the Ukraine, the North Caucasus, the Lower Volga, and some of southern Russia.

The Second Semester of Junior Year

As before, the most popular class was L. L.'s—Russian literature and culture, a three semester course. We had already had as prerequisites an Introduction to Philosophy and a course in European Literature and Culture, to better understand Russian culture and its connections. The course started by viewing the culture and literature of Russia as results of its early Christianization. The next two semesters, we examined the modern period from Peter the Great through Soviet time.

Finally, the history teacher arrived, a graduate of Voronezh University, quite smart. At the beginning, he was uneasy and a little shy. His three semesters of Russian history followed the same sequence as L. L.'s course. These two courses considerably influenced our outlooks and strengthened our pride and love for Russia and Russian people. Specifically, our views were changed on the role of Russian Orthodoxy in shaping the character of the Russian people and the Russian State. These courses were pleasant eye-openers in a sense. We used to hear that the Russian Empire oppressed and annihilated working people. The Tsars and their officials were despotic or not smart enough to rule, or they were of foreign origin and hence did not care about the Russian people. Nicholas II had a permanent epithet, *durachok*—a fool. Now we saw a different picture of the past. Not everything was black; a lot was white and bright colored, which made us proud rather than ashamed of our past.

What forces formed our own culture, as well as any culture? There were three in particular: the natural surroundings and climate; the history; and the beliefs, from pagans to the Christian heritage. Russia had contact with and influences from both the Eastern and the Western worlds. In the last seven hundred years, Russia had emerged as a powerful, distinctive, creative civilization. In the tenth century, Kieven Rus' was sufficiently powerful to accept (without sacrificing her independence) Christianity from Byzantium—a powerful and exquisitely cultured country called the Eastern Roman Empire. In the year 988, Vladimir, the Grand Prince of Rus' was baptized, married a Royal Princess of Byzantine, and issued an edict to the population to be baptized. What were the results of these actions?

a) Most importantly, this religious fusion developed the ethnic and political unity of Rus' and forged a consciousness in each individual of belonging to the same Christian community and civilization. It helped people to survive the Mongols' domination and further social-political oppression.

b) Abstract theological ideas did not play a dominant part in Russian Orthodoxy. Christ was accepted as a God-man which meant that every human was able and obliged to fulfill his teachings. To be Christian meant to live according to Christ's and the saints' teaching, not to discuss them. The thinking was that Christ's teaching didn't need any justification, only fulfillment. Naturally, Russians did not support the Roman Church's practice of theological disputation and controversy.

c) Written language, architecture and religious art were brought from Byzantium and other Slavic Christian countries. The Cyrill-Methodious (Cyrillic) alphabet was introduced, and the Greek liturgy and scriptures were translated into the Old Church Slavonic language, which all Slavs understood. This fact had far-reaching historical consequences.

First, listening to the Holy Scriptures and Liturgy in one's own language, which was not the case in Western Europe, stimulated the people to accept the holy teaching not only rationally, but deeply emotionally. Soon, people called themselves simply *Khrestiane*—Christians. So a peasant in Russia is still called *Krestianin*. Hence, later the country was called Holy Russia.

Second, there was no need even for the clergy to learn Greek or Latin and with time it helped to cause Russia's alienation from Greek culture and the Latin church and culture, a separation from the classical tradition of rational theology.

The initial stimuli for the native culture and literature were the translations of many Greek religious and secular writings—books on the Byzantine civilization, specifically the Chronicles, writings on history. In general, this was the process of diffusion of the Byzantine civilization in the Slave world. Slowly, native literature accumulated local historical facts. The most famous of these chronicles is the *Russian Primary Chronicle*. Among the other forms were sermons and hagiographies. There were also princely biographies like *The Life of Alexander Nevsky*. In heroic poetry, the earliest were "*byliny*," which glorified the exploits of the *bogatyri*—knights, in defense of their beliefs in the Orthodox faith and the Motherland.

Our boys somehow obtained the old *gusli*, a type of harp played while it rested on the knees. L. L. read excerpts from a *bylina* about the most popular and strongest *bogatyr*—Illya of Murom. And some of us, including myself, chanted a monotonous recitative to the accompaniment of the *gusli*. Who would have imagined it, but it made us very emotional to think that about 800 or 700 years ago the Russian patriots had composed and recited them. An unforgettable education experience for us was the heroic poem *Lay of Igor's Campaign* about a historic campaign in 1115 led by Igor, Prince of Novgorod-Seversky in southern Russia against the Polovtsy invaders who were nomads of the steppe. In that campaign, Igor's army was defeated and he was taken prisoner. The poem is highly artistic and musical, its author unknown. The composer Borodin wrote the beautiful opera *Prince Igor* in the 1880s. L. L. and our music teacher combined their efforts, so that L. L. read excerpts from the *Lay* and the music teacher played them on the piano with his comments about music. We sang along for some of the parts, like the famous chorus of slave girls, the Polovetsian dances, and especially Igor's aria—*O! Give me! Give me freedom!* For us who had never seen or listened to an opera, this was a real educational and spiritual treat.

In 1240, the Mongol-Tartars (pagan nomads) took Kiev, finishing the occupation of Russia. The whole country was reduced to ashes and young people were taken into slavery and harems—perhaps this is one reason why so many Turks had blue eyes. The country was cut off from the west and the flourishing Byzantine Christian civilization was stopped in its development. The country was turned around to face the east instead of the west as it traditionally had done before. Instead of Kiev as the center of Rus, Moscow slowly secured the first place among the equal Principalities. The only force that united Russians and saved Russia was a common Christian faith. An enemy gave them a common purpose and they accumulated spiritual energy for a victory over them.

We were fascinated with the *Tale of the Grand Prince Dmitri Donskoy*, written in the middle of the fifteenth century. Dmitri, a Grand Prince of the Moscow Principality, united almost all Principalities and defeated the Mongols in 1380 at the River Don. The exceptional role in organizing the victory belonged to Father Sergius, the founder and Superior of St. Sergius Monastery at Zagorsk, near Moscow, now the holiest Orthodox place.

We were no less impressed with *The Life of Alexander Nevsky*. He was the Prince who crushed the invading Teutonic knights and before them the Swedes on the river Neva. The famous Eisenstein made a movie called *Alexander Nevsky* about a battle between Russians and the German invaders, with music by S. Prokofiev. This was the crown of Prokofiev's epic music.

The development of the country shifted into the northeast, with Moscow as a center. Profound changes occurred in the culture. Although, "the ritualized forms of art and worship and the peculiar sensitivity to beauty and history all remained constant features of Russian culture" (Billington, "The icon and the axe," p. 16).

The second church, built in the 1100s in Kiev, was the St. Sophia, a copy in stone of Constantinople's St. Sophia with spherical domes. "The uniqueness of the new Great Russian culture that gradually emerged after the eclipse of Kiev is exemplified by the tent roof and the onion dome: two striking new shapes which by the early sixteenth century dominated the skyline of the Russian North" (Billington, p. 47). These vertical buildings were needed for snow-shedding roofs, but also for spiritual intensification, because those gilded cupolas rising over the forest lines were the spiritual and practical beacons for travelers and believers all around.

Another indigenous form in architecture was developing—a simple heavy structure in white stone. Limestone and mortar were replacing brick and cement. This made it possible to ornament the outside walls with sculptured reliefs depicting scenes from the Bible and with animals and flowers. The Kremlin's churches represent this style with some deviations. The supreme Muscovite style exemplified in the wooden Church of the Transfiguration of Kizhi is likened to a giant fir tree because of the superimposed twenty-two onion domes and *kokoshnics* (women's head dress). The famous St. Basil on the Red Square represents this style in stone.

Not only in church, but in each home and wherever people gathered, there was an icon (Greek word for "picture") as an omnipresent reminder of the faith. The omnipresent holy picture provided an image of higher authority before which anyone swore oaths, resolved disputes, and received blessings before battle. The icon became not only the object of worship and authority, but also the artistic expression of theology—of Christ and the saints' lives. It was the so-called "Bible of the Poor" because the illiterate peasant could "read" those pictures.

L. L. asked a couple of the students from the nearby villages to bring icons and in class explained their meaning and their artistic qualities. I was elated, thinking I'd be able to explain it to my *babunia*. The Russian icon was a combination of the original Byzantine style of icon paintings and the originality of Russian cultural development. A picture of Jesus, Mary, or the saints is painted in tempura on a specifically prepared wooden board. Each saint is presented in a prescribed form. The main rules were: the figures must be dematerialized, flat, two-dimensional to represent the soul in emotional intensity, and it must be artistically rich in details and coloring. Since the Renaissance in Europe, religious icons had become extremely embellished, almost realistic portraits. For example, a beautiful lady with a child would represent Mary with the Christ-child. The Russian church, especially the old believers, rejected this kind of representation of the holy spirits in materialistic form. In the church, a believer was seduced by the immense effect of the different aesthetic media enhancing his belief.

All this talk about iconography considerably eased our prejudice against the church and strengthened our admiration for church beauty. Vania, Secretary of our Komsomol, made a report to the District Party Committee that the icons were brought to class and religion was praised. L. L. was called to the Committee for explanation. It looked as if she had given a good historical lecture and Shcherbina supported her. But Vania received from us a new name: *donoshchik*—informer, squealer.

L. L. specifically liked talking about the character of the Russians and knew the subject perfectly. Russian Orthodoxy inspired the Russians to renounce their attachment to earthly things and to strive instead for God's kingdom. Orthodoxy promoted an ascetic, modest life and demanded sacrifice. Russians didn't feel chained to their private possessions or to their personal rights. This belief formed a psychological base for Russian collectivism and compassion. On the other hand, this idealistic belief was instrumental in creating a kind of duality in the Russians' character—an idealism against the needs of practical life. Orthodoxy inculcated in people first and foremost an idea of obligation for church and country instead of rights, and the necessity for humility and help to others which became the principle form of relationship in Old Russia. Congregationality in religion was the essence of Orthodoxy. They believed because they were meeting in the church and observing the holy ritual of praying, they could feel the divine spirit among them.

From the time of early Muscovy, there developed a strong monastic movement with a notion of personal purification as its main aim. Monasteries played an important role in the expansion of the Orthodox faith and Russian culture and also in the fight against the Mongols. The selfless, educated monks who were beatified were known as the "builders of Russia." Many of them, like Stephen of Perm, a learned ascetic figure, carried Christianity seven hundred and fifty miles east of Moscow to the pagan Comi people. He invented an alphabet for their language and translated holy scripture into it in order to help Christianize them. The ideology of Muscovite tsardom, which took shape in the early sixteenth century, was a creation of the strong and educated leaders of monasticism—mainly, Nil Sorsky and Joseph Sanin.

The more we learned, the more we were fascinated by our history. We were looking in the school's libraries and in private homes for any historical story. Further on, we learned that Ivan III the "Great" (1462–1505) was a strong and ambitious character who finished the unification of the land. He was the first to be called *tsar*. Byzantium collapsed in 1453 under the Turks' assault and left empty the role of leader of the Christian Orthodoxy world. To dramatize the idea of continuity, Ivan III married Sophia Paleoloqus, niece of the last Byzantine emperor, in an elaborate new style. A few years later, the Byzantine Imperial seal, consisting of the two-headed eagle and other symbols of the emperor's power, was brought to Moscow as a sign of continuity. In 1480, the Mongols' two hundred and forty year rule over Russia came to a complete end. In a real sense, Russia had saved Europe, protecting her from Mongol invasion by fighting the Mongols unceasingly. The Russians accepted it as their mission and historical destiny to help in this way.

Miracle of Love

L. L. told us that a few graduate students from the Leningrad University were coming to present a new method of teaching and learning, so-called "The Method of Projects." A few days later, L. L. introduced two young, good looking fellows. Lively discussion developed immediately.

Soon we noticed that the eyes of one were fixed on Nina, and the eyes of the other on Lena. After class L. L. introduced them, and before our eyes was developing a simply unusual scene. I looked at Nina, that cold beautiful marble statue became sparkling with life and beauty. Their eyes were telling all and saw only each other. Lena, who was vivacious, was even more so. It was a real "miracle of love."

We had all students meetings in the evening, discussing the new "Method of Projects." We liked it. Then they sang solos—both of our guests had good voices—and all of us were singing, telling stories and reciting poetry, and the music of our orchestra, as we called it, the "orchestra of cultural and uncultural instruments." And finally we were dancing. It was a most enjoyable evening!

Nina and Lena took their "loved one" to see their parents. Their fathers were directors of the schools in different towns. They grew up together and didn't want to part. Now both of them would go to Leningrad. It was a miracle.

Idea of the Third Rome

Our study of Russian history continued.

United Russia emerged as a backward but powerful religious civilization after 140 years of the tartar-mongols occupation and then one hundred years of their raids on the Russian territory for taking "tribute." At this time a teaching of Holy Russia, or the Third Rome, had just developed. The essence of this teaching was that the two previous Romes—Rome itself and Constantinople—had fallen because of their sins, that Western Christianity had become corrupted. This teaching held that only Russian Orthodoxy had remained pure, encouraging people to practice brotherhood and right living. Moscow had now become the Third Rome and the mission of Russia was to purify Christianity in the world by restoring its original spirituality of the Apostolic Church and way of life. This was the Messianic idea of Holy Russia which took deep roots in the people's conscience. What was the purpose of the Russian people in the world? Messianism gave the answer. The Russian idea was not of a flowering culture or of a powerful monarchy. It was the idea of the Kingdom of God on Earth, as Nikolai Berdyaev writes in his book *The Russian Idea*. Some historians have considered it natural that in the twentieth century Russia found an expression of her mission in the form of communism, a society of brotherhood.

As we were sudying the period of Ivan IV the Terrible (Grozny), we did not know yet about Stalin's sense of identification with him. Reading about Ivan IV's rule, the apologist Ivan Peresvetov cropped up in our minds as a natural comparison with Stalin. Peresvetov wrote if a Tsar is wise and feared, his realm will be enlarged and his name praised. Like Ivan, Stalin was terrible; his authority over the State was limitless. Like Ivan, who crushed the Boyars' independence, creating a centralized autocratic power, Stalin crushed any opposition to his rule. In the end, both vastly increased the power of Russia. Ivan's *oprichnina* and Stalin's NKVD had similar aims and deeds. Ivan created his image as a tsar, as a leader of the Christian Empire, while Stalin created his image as a leader of the just Communist State. But, both profoundly damaged their own images because they terrorized their own citizens.

Historical paintings of Ilia Repin—the red blood-soaked canvases depicting Ivan's murder of his son—made an everlasting impression on us. Ivan the Terrible was succeeded by his feeble-minded son, Fedor, and after his death in 1598 the old dynasty of Ruriks (founders of the Kieven Rus') came to an end. Boris Godunov, a regent who was partly Tartar, was elected. He was married to Ivan's daughter. We read in class excerpts from Pushkin's *Boris Godunov* and listened to the music teacher play from Mussourgsky's opera *Boris Godunov*.

After the death of the ill-fated Boris Godunov, there began a nine-year period of chaos, civil strife, starvation and confusion called the Time of Troubles (1604–1613). Swedes attacked in the north and Poles occupied Moscow. The invaders were thrown out and in 1613, the *Zemsky Sobor* met in Moscow and elected a new tsar, seventeen-year-old Mikhael Romanov, son of the powerful new patriarch Filaret, who was at the time in Polish captivity. We were surprised to learn the *Zemsky Sobor* was a Popular Parliament representing every social group except serfs (at the time there weren't many of them) and was practically the supreme political authority for almost a quarter of a century. We had never heard of such a thing in Russia at that time, or even later abroad. Russia's image was always of an endless autocracy. Even more striking was the fact that it was a defender of total autocracy, Ivan IV, who first summoned a representative National Assembly—the *Zemsky Sobor*—in 1566.

After L. L. summarized the plot, our music teacher played parts of the opera *Life for the Tsar or Ivan Susanin* by Mikhael Glinka on the piano. It is accepted as historical fact, but seems to be of questionable proof, that the Poles' military detachment was on its way to kill the young Russian Tsar who was hiding in a monastery outside of Moscow. Their Russian guide, a peasant named Ivan Susanin, took them in the opposite direction into the deep snow of a dense forest. The Poles killed Susanin, but they perished in the forest, unable to find their way out. As a music critic, Prince Odoevsky wrote that this opera started a new period in the history of music: a period of Russian music. Mikhael Glinka, as father of Russian classical music, began the use of nationalism in Russian music—glorifying the masses, using folkloric songs, making heroes out of patriotic peasants, and giving the spectacle an epic scope. The aristocracy was critical of this endeavor, calling it a *muzhiks* opera.

Tekhnikum's Theatre

We had quite a big group who were called "actors" for fun's sake. They were those who were in the *Agit Brigada* and who took part in other small performances in our dining hall fun. The majority of these "actors" were from our class and we thought we should prepare a full-production play. All our teachers were happy to help us and advised us to take a classic play called *The Thunderstorm—Grosa*. It was the masterpiece of Alexander Ostrovsky (1823–1886), the famous playwright who depicted the life of the merchant class, office workers, and clerks in provincial towns like Grayvoron of Old Russia. We planned to stage the play in the following semester, but organizational preparation had to be done immediately—the reading of the play, explanation of the period and characters, and assigning parts to be memorized over the summer. I got a leading female role as Katerina.

Our minds in general were set on social, political, and cultural issues which absorbed all our interest. In both classes, History of Russia and Cultural History of Russia, we came to an important period in Russian history—the *Raskol* schism.

The Last Time in Krasnaya-Yaruga

The semester was over. I was glad to be at home and to have a rest; the academic year had been very demanding, both socially and academically. At home, I also found changes. I hadn't seen Papa for close to a year and I painfully noticed an observable change in his face. It was older and not as sparkling as before.

He explained to me what was happening. The plant needed overhaul repairs; the machinery and equipment were completely worn out. But to get either new or used equipment in good condition was an impossible task. That year Papa had traveled to factory-plants all over Russia, only to meet other engineers like himself who were looking for machinery. Everything was for the new industrial plants. The director told Papa, "You get machinery, or you will be in Siberia."

My wise Mama demanded to leave the plant. Despite the fact that the workers held a meeting and asked Papa to stay, demanding that the director, the Bureau of the Communist Party, and the Plant Council not let him go, Papa's notice of leaving was accepted by the director—their relationship was not friendly. Then Mama took action. She, who was highly respected in our community, spoke to the workers and to all the bosses, saying she preferred to live in one little stinky room, but to have her good husband home and not in Siberia.

Finally, Papa's resignation was accepted. He easily got a job in Kharkov, but there was no place to live. Dedia's family already was squeezed to the limit with five of them living in two rooms. Now, Mama and Papa were preoccupied with moving to Kharkov.

I wholeheartedly agreed with Mama, although I imagined the dreadful living conditions in Kharkov compared to our little palace where we were living at the time. This did not disturb Mama. But I knew Papa felt embarrassed and guilty. After this unpleasant news, I saw their faces change—they burst into smiles. Dedia and the aunts were coming and then the Astapchuks would arrive, and guess what? My heart pumped violently as they told me Misha would come for a few days.

Dedia, *Krestnaia*, and Aunt Ania came and brought me some fabrics for clothes, shoes, and other articles. Recently, Mama had traveled several times to Kharkov, bringing food which Krestnaia bartered for what we needed, mainly for the future as well as for the family. The shortages in clothing, shoes, and house items had joined the worsening food shortages, and the prosperity for the black market. Mama was preparing a lot of canned, non-perishable food to take with us when we moved at the end of September. All of us were busy with these many chores. Besides, they gave us a lot of fun, especially going into the forest for mushrooms and berries to be dried or canned.

The Astapchuks arrived. Our families became close friends, visiting each other quite often. Misha came a few hours later from Voronehz. For a few days, it was a continuous banquet. *Babunia*, Aunt Katia, Volodia, a cousin, and several close friends were with us. In spite of our having a good time, it wasn't really a celebration. *Babunia* cried and sang her sorrowful farewell songs. Sometimes Papa, myself, and others joined her. Then Dedia, Mama, and I sang the Ukrainian folklore songs. Then Mama Rosa sang a Jewish song solo, and Misha and Papa Peter made background sounds without words. *Babunia* kept repeating that she wouldn't see her son again after he left and he would die in Siberia because he was honest and spoke the truth. Her feeling happened to be providential. I asked her not to say that anymore and she stopped.

Only two of us—Misha and myself—were really happy. Misha started preparation for the University entrance exams. In the spring he would be relieved from his job and take tutors in math, geometry, physics, and chemistry. He was looking for a private room for studying to move into from the hotel room he was sharing with two other coworkers at the Obcom.

Before leaving for the tekhnikum, I visited the teachers to say good-bye. My friends gave me a farewell party. I cried on Kolia's grave, asking him not to feel lonesome, saying I would always think about him and would come to talk with him. I came back twelve years later, walking in the winter from Kharkov to Krasnaya-Yaruga, over two hundred kilometers. I was leaving Krasnaya-Yaruga with a heavy heart, understanding that my happy childhood and early youth had become memories.

The Senior Year

As proud seniors at tekhnikum, we were in a super mood. Classes started and we had a heavy academic load. In two months of working hard, we were ready for the production of the play, *The Thunderstorm*, which was scheduled for the beginning of November before the finals. It was a huge project. The play depicted a despotic family pattern in a backward provincial town like Grayvoron. Katerina was a sensitive and poetic young woman married to Tikhon, the obedient son of Kabanikha, the cruelest specimen of the small town merchants' *samodur* (absurdly despotic). Her oppressive family environment pushed her during her husband's absence to a short affair with Boris Nikolaevich, a handsome and quite educated fellow from a big city who was also badly oppressed by his uncle, a rich merchant named Dikoy. Boris fell in love with Katerina but tried not to show his feelings because she was a married woman. It didn't work; the strong feeling was mutual. Katerina, a sincere believer in God, was tormented for her "sin" and during a storm, her nerves gave out and she made a public confession. It doomed her. She could not endure the life of misery in the family any longer and committed suicide by throwing herself into the river. Boris was sent to Siberia at the insistence of his uncle Dikoy, so that he wouldn't have to pay Boris the money he owed to Boris' deceased father.

It was an excellent learning process for us about time, life, and the behavior patterns of different social groups in Old Russia. We learned how to build and project the character one plays. Grayvoron had just one very small movie theater, nothing else. So a small stage was built in our hall, and we were planning for not more than four performances. But when the newspaper praised us high to the sky, specifically my performance, then all the people of the town wanted to see it, and the villagers even more so. *Kolkhoses* from around the district asked for tickets. People's reaction to the play was highly emotional; many of them were seeing a play on stage for the first time in their lives and they reacted as though they were seeing real life unfolding. They treated me with great respect—women brought presents like embroidered towels or baked *pirozhki* and other things for poor Katerina.

We had at least fourteen performances and demands for more were not yet exhausted, but the finals started and we had to stop. What I would do now with my life was unalterable to me—first going to the Theatre Institute and then acting in dramatic theatre. I knew I would do well. Director Scherbina, L. L., the teachers, and we as a group received letters from the District leaders, people, and even from the Voronehz Oblast Department of Education, praising the tekhnikum's excellent cultural-educational works in the district.

In our General History classes, we came to the period which deeply affected the Russian people and the development of the country. From the time of the reign of the Tsar Alexis (the second Romanov, 1645–76) to the early eighteenth century, a profound conflict developed between the country's needs for modernization and cultural progress on one side and those who stood for the religious traditions and the way of life of the Old Moscovy on the other. Western Europe of the seventeenth century was in strife—with the religious wars between countries and the Reformation. Some, mainly Catholics, found refuge in Russia.

Foreign refugees had snubbed Russians for their low culture, and Russians didn't trust them, being suspicious of their deceitful behavior. Regardless, the process of absorbing Western culture, not of technology but of ideas, was progressing.

There occurred a split or schism within Russia's two religious parties. Both the "Black" and "White" clergy were against the Latin church, which they viewed as corrupt and selfish. Patriarch Nikon, a leader of the "Black" monastic clergy, an ascete of immense spiritual intensity and physical presence, ordered the revision of the church books which had many errors and even serious nonsensical mistakes from being copied for hundreds of years by the monks. He introduced some changes into church rituals based on the Orthodox Holy Scriptures edited by Western Orthodox scholars, mainly Greeks. In essence, the two-finger cross, a symbol of the dual nature of Christ as both God and Man, was changed to the three-fingered cross, a symbol of the Trinity, the dogma of Christian belief. Likewise, the two *Alliluya* were changed to three. Changes were also made in icon painting.

The other religious party was the Fundamentalists. Their leader, the passionate Archpriest Avvacum, was determined to keep unchanged the Orthodox faith and rituals which had become a way of life. "White" clergy were the bone of this party. Soon, bitter resentment and uprising against Nikon's changes erupted in the country.

The Church Council in 1667 was the turning point in the religious crisis. Nikon's changes were upheld, but Nikon himself was deposed and exiled. The Fundamentalists were excommunicated. The *Raskol*, the schism, was completed. About one third of parishioners left the official church and became so-called "Old Believers." The majority of them left their possessions, went to Siberia's tayga or northern Russia and lived there in the communes. The others went to the southwest and eventually abroad to places like Canada. The most fanatical groups burned themselves up in their churches. The last scene of the opera *Khovanshchina* by Modest Mussorgsky shows the congregation kneeling and praying inside the church in which they've locked themselves and set on fire.

Why did they go to such an extreme? Russians were spiritual and passionate people; they placed beliefs and ideas over material matters. Fundamentalists could not accept the idea that Russian Orthodoxy was not the pure, original Apostolic Christianity, and had to be adjusted to Western practice which they considered corrupted. The Messianic idea of Russia was shattered. One significant cause of this tragic event was the low cultural-education level even among some of the nobility. Nobody was capable of generating any new concepts; devotion to traditional norms and ideals was unchangeable. The lack of knowledge of Latin or Greek, even among the high clergy, certainly affected the intellectual level of the whole society. The results of over two centuries of Tartar-Mongol rule were not easy to overcome.

The most important point in understanding Russian Orthodoxy is that Russia accepted the Byzantine view that the kingdom of God would be achieved through the Orthodox Christiandom. That's why the Fundamentalists took the changes in the Holy Books by the Patriarch Nikon as an indication of the Latinization of Orthodoxy, which meant in their view the imminent coming of the Antichrist, and they were preaching the coming of the end, the Apocalypse.

We studied the historical painting, *The Boyarinia Morossova* by Vasiliy Surikov (1887), his masterpiece. It's enormous in size and reminds one of great Italian monumental paintings, like those closest to the Veronese. It depicts an "Old Believer," wealthy Boyarinia Morosova, being driven on a sleigh through Moscow streets to her execution. Along with her younger sister, she was thrown into a deep pit for a prolonged death. In the dynamics of the picture, different groups of people were recreating the mood and tensions of that period. In the center on a sleigh was the defiant Boyarinia with her dramatically uplifted hand giving the two-finger blessing.

The schism dealt a profound blow to Orthodoxy, after which its authority and role were in the process of diminishing. That was a big help for the Revolution's success in 1917.

Our life. Students from a town and villages not far away often invited their student friends to their homes. I walked with Galia to her village a few times, and her parents spoiled us tremendously with their good food and sincere love.

Galia invited me to the wedding of her cousin, a junior student at the Agriculture College along with her husband to be who was a senior. He already received his assignment as an agronomist to the North Caucasus region. The next year, as a wife, she would be sent to the same region.

At their wedding, I noticed that the general mood of the people was subdued, not happy. The prospects for the next year's living conditions was not promising, although it was served still enough plain food.

But we, the youth, many of us students, had a lot of fun. I taught girls to dance the bride wedding dance. Parents and grandparents wiping their tears thanked me for teaching their girls an old custom, which they don't want to learn, saying "It's old-fashioned."

"But they learned it from you, a city girl!"

Our fascinating studies continued. In this period of profound crisis, the reign of Peter the Great began (1688–1725). He rejected all religious solutions and turned toward the west for secular and political solutions. Russia had three radical innovators in her history: St.

Vladimir, Tsar Peter and Vladimir Lenin. They accomplished their reforms with a lot of suddenness and ruthlessness. The slow process of change in all three occurrences had started long ago. Peter's reign brought new ideas and a new spirit. Consequently, he put Old Russia on her way to changing into the European Great Empire.

Peter was an extraordinary human. He was about seven feet tall with abundant energy and a largely self-taught intelligence. Peter spent some time incognito in Germany and Holland, working in shipbuilding yards as an apprentice learning shipbuilding as well as about the states' organization and ways of life. He realized it was an absolute necessity for Russia to have an exit to sea—in the south, the Black Sea was under the Turks' control, while in the north, the Baltic Sea was under the Swede's control. Meanwhile in Moscow, a new uprising of the *streltsy,* the Tsar's guard, was being directed by Sophia, his half-sister, and the boyars. Peter hurried home and dealt ruthlessly with the uprisers—hundreds of heads were chopped off and others were hanged in rows of gallows on the Red Square.

We discussed a historical painting called *A Morning of the Strelets' Execution* by Surikov, which left us feeling gloomy. The setting is the Red Square. The *streltsy* were the Old Army, created by Ivan IV and abolished by Peter. They were the Old Believers, against Peter, representing the passing Old Russia. They were depicted against the background of St. Basiel's Cathedral, being brought for execution. The New Russia was represented by Peter who was proudly mounted on a white horse, watching the execution. Behind him was his new army, all against the background of the Kremlin, which meant power, and by his side were foreign ambassadors with their carriage. The picture is colorful, although gloomy and tragic. The story says that Peter went up to the *lobnoye mesto,* the place where the executioner had chopped off the heads. A *streletz* brought up for execution said to Peter, "Step aside, Tsar. Here is my place."

The general conservatism and primitivism of Russia involved Peter in a clash with all forms of tradition, including the dress of the people and the appearance of their faces. He ordered them to adopt European dress in place of the long flowing robes and to cut their beards. The last demand was against the Church's teaching that a man is a reflection of God. Peter himself snipped off many beards as well as cutting off the long robes. The Old Muscovy proclaimed that Peter was the Antichrist and discontent grew all over.

Peter the Great excited our imaginations. Someone obtained a little book of funny stories about him. Here is one story, *The Beards*:

Peter called several boyars who didn't want to cut off their beards. He ordered his men to cut them. The boyars simply went crazy; they fell down on their knees, crying and begging Peter.

"Don't make us look like we are not God's creatures," they said.

Peter got angry. "Get up," he demanded. "It's not a beard that makes you God's creature, but your mind and your good deeds."

Their beards were cut off. Some of them ran away screaming and covering their faces; others were walking on all fours, saying they were animals now. One boyar asked Peter for permission to pay for the privilege to wear a beard. So Peter established the "beard tax." Some boyars proudly wore their beards. After a few years of paying the tax, they realized that half of their wealth was gone. They had to reject this pleasure, much to the disappointment of Peter, for the "beard tax" had helped him to build a few ships.

Many foreigners who were knowledgeable (even slightly so) were brought to Russia to teach economy and business development in all kinds of capacities—from shipbuilders, scholars for the Academy, officers for his military training schools, architects, down to actors and dancers. In an unbelievably short time, a modern armada was built at Voronezh shipyard and crushed the Turks, taking the sea port of Asov. It was Peter's first victory. The next was on the Baltic Sea against the Swedes where St. Petersburg is now. As I mentioned before, the mighty Swedish army was defeated at Poltava field in 1709, and much later, Pushkin's great-grandfather, Admiral Ghanibal, destroyed the Swedish fleet. Russia became a power in Europe.

Many administrative reforms and a utilitarian "table of ranks" which required permanent state service of each social class had been established. Peter abolished the Patriarkhat and created in its stead a new synodal pattern of church administration under state control, diminishing church authority. He launched secular comprehensive schools, linguistic reform, and developed a new alphabet. The first periodical and secular books were published in the country, and many other reforms took place. In 1703 he started to build St. Petersburg, a city of European planning and architecture, as its nickname, "window to Europe," implies.

106

He ordered the organization of the Academy of Sciences. At the beginning of the Academy, all the professors were foreigners, but it became a seedbed for native teachers and scholars and the developing system of education. The most important outcome of these reforms was that Peter had created the conditions for the birth of the Russian cosmopolitan liberal intelligentsia from nobility and, instead of a religious preoccupation, philosophy, literature and classical art dominated this aristocratic culture. Since the middle of the nineteenth century, the Radical intelligentsia started to occupy the Russian mind, preparing the way for the Revolution of 1917.

Once, in our after-dinner conversation, a very honest boy from the village told us that his mother compared us to small babies. She said that if one baby starts crying, all of the babies around answer that call. And we, the youth, have been "crying" and don't even know why. She asked him to explain what was happening: for many centuries, peasants lived in their traditional ways, and now in just several weeks, the lives of all peasants had changed, and were broken. One big "baby" in the Kremlin started to "cry," wanted change, and then all of you are following him instinctively, his mother said. The reaction of our Komsomol "active" was swift. The next day a Komsomol meeting was held and the "active" demanded the expulsion of the boy from tekhnikum for anti-Soviet propaganda. But Shcherbina rejected this demand, although we understood it was a political risk for him.

Studying the past helped us make connections with the present. The rapid changes were all around us. We understood and upheld the general aim—a building of the socialist society. But the importance of and specific implications for the future of many of those changes we did not comprehend.

Many changes in the progress made by Stalin's revolution were as anything in the past. It expanded and changed the function of the State. Hence bureaucracy's importance. The State became not only the monopolist in the production of everything, but also a distributor. The allocation of consumer goods became one of its most important functions, a system that became political and graded with time. The highest grade was for the Party elite, down to a zero for the "enemies of the Soviet folks." We saw a beginning of this system and certainly did not imagine its implication.

There were more studies after Peter. A well-known saying is that if Peter had opened a window to Europe, his daughter Elizabeth had decorated it in Rococo style and Catherine the Great had widely opened all doors and windows, trying to remodel the house itself. Instead of the practical Germanic and Swedish influences of the Petrian era, during this period French philosophy, culture, and language took strong roots. The Russian aristocracy now spoke French instead of Russian, isolating themselves from their own countrymen in general and from their serfs specifically, but fitting well into the mainstream of European culture. Voltaire soon became like a patron saint of the Russian secular aristocracy, followed among others by the "Encyclopedists," the English economist Adam Smith, and finally Rousseau. Catherine was an "enlightened despot on the throne," with the conflict between her enlightenment and liberalism on one hand and her despotism in practical governing on the other hand. She greatly increased the number of peasants in serfdom, creating intolerable conditions—absolute serfdom.

We were interested in the many stories known among the people of the love exploits of Catherine and some of Elizabeth. Naturally, they are not presented in the official history, except for a few. For instance, Elizabeth, who led a very elaborate social life, at one time owned fifteen thousand dresses. Another, a joke, also was known in Europe. In the Russian court, Zarina Elizabeth received, as was the norm, the announcement of the birth of a prince in one of the German Principalities. The congratulations were not sent until the prince was seven years old, because Elizabeth had no time to read and sign the letter.

We were really amazed at the proliferation of Catherine's cultural reforms: the first university was founded in 1755 in Moscow, as was the first theater, Moscow Drama. There was the emergence of scientific scholars, the first among them being Mikhael Lomonosov, a universal genius who made Russia a contributor to European science. Writers, poets, and historians also began to contribute to European culture. Neo-classical architecture and planning changed the appearance of the cities. Squares and plazas were now being provided for military parades, rather than for the practical needs of trade and industry. Catherine continued to create an elegant Capitol, with splendid palaces and buildings built by Italians, first of all Rastrelly, Scottish and Russian architects. The Hermitage Art Gallery became a rival to Peter's Armory at Kremlin.

The more sensitive minds among the elite were tormented by the contrast between their lives and that of the rest of the people. They began to feel alienated from the existing order and from the Reformed Despot as its keeper. The French Revolution in 1789 scared all the crowned heads of Europe, including Catherine. Her game in liberalism was over. Brilliant men such as Alexander Radishchev and Nikolai Novikov illustrated the seriousness of aristocrat's alienation. Radishchev wrote his famous *Journey from St. Petersburg to Moscow*, criticizing the nobility. His criticism of the institution of serfdom was novel and unacceptable. Catherine ordered his arrest for treason and sentenced him to death, which she later commuted to exile in Siberia. Novikov, a member of the exclusive Ismailovsky regiment and of Catherine's legislative commission, was a publisher of satirical journals which criticized Russian nobility, Catherine's close imitation of French life, and her stone-deafness to social injustice. Novikov's journals were the first in Russian history to be critical of social problems. Catherine exiled him to Moscow. He soon transformed Moscow University into a center of intellectual ferment: emphasizing German classical philosophy rather than French, publishing voluminous documents on early Russian history, like *History of Russia* by Prince Shcherbatov, and glorifying Russian ways. The struggle between Catherine's St. Petersburg Enlightenment and Moscow's patriotic anti-Enlightenment aristocracy continued in the Decembrist uprising of the progressive aristocracy in 1825, then in the Slavophile-Westernizers controversy which with time developed into radical ferments and socialist ideas.

Peter and Catherine created a new powerful Russia, a part of Europe, out of a formerly backward country. But that former country had inner unity: a boyar and a peasant spoke the same language, had the same beliefs, followed the same traditions and customs, sang the same songs, and danced the same dances. As a consequence of the reforms, the first to be alienated from the other classes was the nobility and then, through education, the "third rank" of citizens appeared. These were the educated, enlightened *intelligentsia* who formed a new class, a new rank, between the nobility and the servile peasantry. They were a new race of man; their solidarity was not professional as in Europe, but ideological. They, along with a part of the nobility, became alienated from the Tsarist regime, making revolutionary changes inevitable.

Kharkov Is Now My Parents' Home

The semester was over and I went home to Kharkov. My parents met me at the railroad station and we took the tramway through to the other side of the city. Then we took a bus to the city line and walked about three kilometers until we finally reached a small hamlet of about ten houses situated among the trees. Our small house had three rooms, a kitchen, and a utility room. The owner, a recent widow, occupied one room. The other two small rooms she rented to my parents along with the shared kitchen. My parents considered themselves very lucky to have such a paradise instead of communal living in one room and sharing a kitchen with up to ten families, and only one or two bathrooms. My *Krestnaia* used her black market connections to find it. Here, each house had a vegetable garden and fruit trees. Papa had a good job as head engineer of the large department at the biggest plant of the city, Kharkov's Railroad Engine Building Plant. Already at the beginning of the thirties the plant produced tanks and other heavy military equipment, although it was an absolute secret.

I spent my time mainly attending theaters, movies, and concerts with my *Krestnaia*. Misha was allowed to quit his job and fully immersed himself in preparation for the entrance exams to Moscow University. I contemplated where to continue my further education. Grandpa and his family advised applying to the Theater Institute, but Mama and Papa were for the University. I decided to apply to the History and Philosophy department at Kharkov State University. I wanted to get a good education in humanities and then in a year enroll in evening classes at the Theater Institute.

Food shortages were getting worse. Even with ration cards people stood in line for hours and sometimes went away empty-handed. *Babunia* was not used to having shortages, because of our help. But now a miracle happened. As I mentioned, my Grandpa had worked all his life as a doctor at the Policlinic in the workers' region. At that time, doctors went to people's homes to see sick patients. The following scene was not unusual:

"Doctor, please take this—that's all we have."

"That will do for your bread and milk. Do you have money for the medication?"

"That is all we have."

"Well, take these fifteen (or twenty) *kopeks* for the medicine. Pay me when you have the money."

The family would never have had a comfortable life only on Grandpa's Policlinic salary, because the money from house calls would have amounted to a trifle if it hadn't been for Grandma's substantial dowry. Now the Russian souls remembered a kind-hearted doctor who helped them in their life's hardship. There would be a knock at the door and the caller would say something like: "When I was a child, I was very sick. Dr. Bilyk-Pichka came more than once and saved my life. My parents were poor and couldn't pay him. Now I'm an officer in the Red Army and I've brought you some flour." It may have been sugar, butter, sausage, meat, or anything. Those visits sometimes happened quite often during bad food shortages. *Babunia* even helped us.

In 1934, Grandpa died and about a thousand people came walking behind his coffin at the funeral. Some were crying, saying "he saved my life" or "he saved the life of my son." This picture was characteristic not exclusively of my grandfather but probably the majority of old-type Russian doctors who believed in their calling to save human life regardless of rewards.

The Last Semester

The last semester we realized we were crossing the Rubicon; we were adults. In seven to eight months, many of us would be teachers, performing the most responsible job in society—forming good human beings. On the funny side, we changed in our behavior—trying to walk with dignity, some even with lofty bearing, talking clearly and using correct sentence structure. We looked like inflated turkeys. It all became a good target for ridicule and hearty laughing at ourselves. During after-dinner conversations, we exchanged thoughts about our futures. The majority, mainly students from villages, planned to take teaching positions. Others had hopes of enrolling in the colleges or university in Voronehz. Our attitude was very serious and responsible as we realized that we were the avant-garde of the builders of socialism, and the schools were in great need of new teachers with the communist ideology. We still believed that communism was the truth and it would prevail when it was practiced according to the Marxist teaching by people and the Party. We didn't think about money. The important thing was to take a job where we were most needed. L. L. and P. P. were the guiding examples for us.

The shortages in 1931 were getting worse than before. Sometimes, students complained about the food. But they were met with indignation from all of us.

"Complain? Look, our country is only fourteen-years-old, but it has accomplished more than Old Russia did in hundreds of years."

"That's right! We are children of workers and peasants. Our studies, our dorms, our food—all of this is paid for by our government."

"Fourteen years before it would have sounded like a fantasy. We couldn't find another country in the world which fully provided its working people with an education, housing, and medical care like our own country did."

Once we had a menu of a normal Tsar's dinner. It was about a page long. We understood just a few of the names of the dishes, like soup and bread, but it did not confuse us or make us envious. We just laughed at the joke that the Russian *zar* and *zariza* (Nikolai and Alexandra) had German and French stomachs.

On February 4, 1931, Stalin delivered his famous speech to the industrial executives. He kindled high enthusiasm and pride in the workers and people of the country. He talked about great achievements and great difficulties. In the end, with great emotion, he said we couldn't slacken our pace of industrialization. On the contrary, it had to quicken because those who lagged behind would be beaten. The Old Russia had always been beaten because of her backwardness—beaten by the Tartar Khans, the Turks, the Swedes, the Poles, the Germans, the Japanese, and by the Anglo-French capitalists. This happened because to beat her was profitable and went unpunished. He said we were fifty or one hundred years behind the advanced countries and must make up for this lagging in ten years' time. Either this would be accomplished or we would be crushed.

Director Shcherbina called the students' meeting and informed us about the speech, mainly reading excerpts from it. We were hypnotized; tears were in our eyes; goose-bumps covered our skin. Many made short speeches. As I remember, our resolution was strong. We thanked our beloved leader Stalin for his leadership and promised we would be ready for any of his calls, for anything that was needed for our Motherland.

The country was in a gigantic build-up. The First Five Year Plan (1928–32) had to be fulfilled in four years. Industry would increase production up to fifty percent per year. But the agrarian revolution from 1928–33 had catastrophic consequences—horses and cattle were slaughtered or sold. The country had only seven thousand tractors. An accelerated mechanization of agriculture became a matter of life or death. The production of coal, iron, steel, and electricity had been given priority. Many new gigantic plants were built. The railroads, and inland waterways (the White Sea Canal and the eighty miles long Moscow-Volga Canal) were expanded or built. Military considerations were behind the huge expansion of the transport system. We knew by heart and repeated with pride the two numbers: five hundred eighteen new plants, huge combines, railroads and canals, and one thousand-forty new machine-tractor stations must be built in the First Five Year Plan.

As a result of collectivization, the peasants lost their initiative and their eternal love of the land, which wasn't theirs anymore. The last had a catastrophic effect. Their reward was regardless of their industry and output—the same misery pay. General dissatisfaction led to a considerable drop in production. Even worse, many went on strike and left the fields untilled. The result of all these factors was a great famine in 1931–33 which ravaged the land. The number of victims was estimated at between four and six million.

The government began to make some concessions to *kolkhozes* and *kolkhozniks*. They were allowed to cultivate a small piece of land for themselves, to keep poultry, goats or sheep, pigs, and even cows. A peasant was to share in the net profit of the *kolkhoz*. Industry was sending in agricultural machinery and tractors in larger quantities.

The country was involved in a frontal attack on everything "old," everything from the pre-Revolutionary time. Director Shcherbina was instructed to graduate good students at the end of junior year, in two years instead of the normal three. The Party wanted to replace the old school teachers with new ones who held to the communist ideology, but in doing so they were replacing professionally well-prepared teachers with rather poorly-prepared ones. So several juniors were simultaneously taking junior and some senior classes. Specifically, they had to take a class on pedagogy along with us. It happened to be a quite fascinating subject, in spite of a dull teacher. We read and discussed Makarenko's writings about his experience as a Director of the Children's Commune in the name of Dzerzhinsky near Moscow. Later, in 1934, he published a book on his experience, the famous *Pedagogical Poem.*

At the end of the Civil War in 1921, thousands of homeless orphans were populating the cities. They often terrorized people, but their first victims were food markets and stores. These *bessprizorniki* (neglected orphans) organized in big groups and by using foxy schemes could steal everything that they needed. Dzerzhinsky, as head of the GPU (State Political Administration), often by force gathered these children into the commune, colonies, and orphan homes. Makarenko, a gifted pedagogue, invented and used an absolutely new pedagogical approach to bring up these children hardened by a cruel life. Pasternak in *Doctor Zhivago* wrote a story told by Zhivago's daughter Tania who became an orphan in the tragic circumstances of war: "Then I traveled with *bessprizornics,* half of our own country and half of foreign countries—we were all over. It was freedom and happiness and a lot of plight and evil" (Boris Pasternak, *Doctor Zhivago*, p. 529, Russian Edition, Ann Arbor University Press, 1959).

Makarenko's writings and his later *Pedagogical Poem* enchanted all of us. It proved that man could be regenerated and perfected. Most of the juvenile delinquents gradually developed into good conscientious citizens. His approach was based on children's self-management; the leaders being elected by all members of the commune; confidence in them; demand for truthfulness and sincerity; and on open discussions with a group or with an individual child. They studied in their school and did manual labor in their factory. The commune had its own theater where various productions played by the kids were staged. But the most popular things were the "self-entertainment evenings." The children had a choir, an orchestra, an art studio and movies. There were exhibits of their paintings and drawings. Our students wanted to learn how to prepare an amateur evening, so with the help of our teachers we prepared and staged it. It was a good learning experience and fun.

Our most interesting studies were those about the cultural explosion in the first quarter of the twentieth century—Russian cultural modernism in literature, art, music, and theatre. The young Soviet literature and arts were already prolific. We had read some of the new work before, but now L. L. made us understand the essence of the new Soviet literature. The main distinguishing characteristic was its heroic base. The question about the principles of creating a hero was widely discussed in our literature as well as in the literature abroad. Some of our writers were for the creation of an "ideal hero" as an icon to follow. Others were for simply a normal positive human who performed heroic deeds. Anti-socialist criticism considered the Soviet hero to be an artificial flower, that is, not a fair presentation of the Soviet reality. Blok, in his famous poem *Twelve* symbolically identified the Revolution and its leaders with Christ. In wintry St. Petersburg, a Revolutionary band of twelve marched through the streets and saw the pictures of Revolution and destuctions. Then, in the end, the image of Christ wearing a crown of white roses was leading them, no destructions any more.

L. L. was somehow able to obtain a couple of the new heroic movies, including Eisenstein's *Battleship Potemkin*, one of the first examples of the Revolution's realistic passion. All of them made a deep impression on us.

Club of the Young Pioneers

The Secretary of the District Komsomol Committee called me to his office and told me that the Bureau of the Komsomol Committee appointed me to be the Chairman of the Board for organizing the town's club of young pioneers and school children. They appointed me without asking me beforehand.

"I like the idea, but I can't," I said. "There are only about five months left before graduation and I have a lot of studying to do."

"Don't worry about studies. I'll tell Shcherbina and he'll graduate you anyway."

"No. I want to study and learn those interesting subjects."

"Listen. We are not asking you about your wish. We gave you the shock task and you have to carry it out. Your name is well-known in the town and that certainly will help you and all of us. You don't understand the importance of your task, to take children out of the often unhealthy political influence of their families, especially of the grandparents who still like the old times better with their Church, small shops, and hypocrisy. Our aim is to keep the children under our influence for the most part of every day. This is the political aim of your task. Now go to the Director of the High School who wants you to be the Chairman. He knows what should be done. Make the plans together and start working."

On the bank of the river stood an old empty mansion on a huge lot of land. The Komsomol Committee and the Department of Education decided to rehabilitate the house and equip it for children's after-school activities. In the frontal attack on pre-Revolutionary ideology and customs, the Communist Party emphasized the education of all children and youth in the Communist ideology. The opening of clubs, houses, theaters, and palaces for children started to be a political fashion all over the country. The Director of the High School, a few other teachers, and I made a plan, although I had no idea what to do and how to accomplish it. But the director kept telling me we would work together, the town people liked me because for them my image was of the beautiful Katerina who had unjustly suffered.

First, we composed a list of members of the board and wrote a letter to them. Then came a flood of activities: meetings of the board, discussions of plans, making a list of those who could and would want to work on renovating the house—mainly carpenters, bricklayers, painters, and others. Each board member was a brigade leader.

At a town meeting all "bosses" of the district—Party, Soviet (government), Komsomol, and Education Department were present and talked. I agreed to open the meeting but I didn't know how to conduct it, so my vice-chairman, the High School Director, had to take over. All the needed materials, like wooden boards, windows, bricks, roofing materials, and many more things were the responsibility of the town's Soviet (Council) and the District Department of Education. Of course, everything, including people's work, was free.

In the early spring, amazingly enthusiastic work started on the building. Usually people came after work and each labored in his profession's brigade. Even the "big bosses" worked on jobs from time to time. Practically the whole town was involved. The largest and most enthusiastic group was the Komsomol brigade. The newspaper regularly informed the community about the progress, presenting pictures of the *udarniks* (shock workers). Every day after classes I was there. The brigade's leaders or chief builder told me what was needed and I

116

in turn demanded it from the district and town "bosses." Now I understood why the High School Director wanted me to be chairman: because he would not be in a position to make straight demands the way I could.

A few times, I was working with the outside brigade, clearing bushes, organizing a yard for sports games like football, basketball, volleyball, archery, and for the vegetable and flower gardens. Once a Party boss saw me working and he told me, "Go home and study. Physical work will be done without your help." The workers agreed with the boss. They usually made jokes at me: "Our Ninochka is a *molodets* (good girl). She can even hammer in a nail."

We assigned each room in the building to certain activities: for mechanics, learning machinery, making mechanical toys; for sewing and modeling clothes; for naturalist learning, making collections; for theatre, drama, comedy; for music and singing; for folklore and collecting it in villages; for art, and many others. The first floor was to hold a big hall. The hardest task was to get at least the minimum of needed equipment and materials for each activity room. We sent several teachers to big cities like Kharkov and Voronezh, but their success was negligible. The situation was partially saved by the town's supply department and local craftsmen who proudly presented their skillful work pieces as models. The last important task of the board was to assign the appropriate people to be instructors for each activity room and for outside sport. The Department of Education had affirmed them.

Finally, on the first of May after a public parade, all the townspeople moved to the Club: the young pioneers, schools, Komsomol, working brigades, proud *udarniki*, and orchestras all marching smartly to celebrate the colorful opening of the Young Pioneers' and School Children's Club. It was really an unbelievable achievement in an remarkably short time. Many people received commendations, myself included. People called me *Nasha Ninochka* (our *Ninochka*). The Regional Voronezh newspaper wrote quite a bit about us. I sent the newspaper clippings with my pictures and other materials to my and Misha's family, and of course to Misha. They were impressed.

I made a formal report to the Bureau of the Komsomol Committee about the accomplished Club Project and asked to be relieved of the assignment as it had been carried out.

"No!" the Secretary said. "The District Department of Education decided to hire you as the Department's Inspector of after school education and the Komsomol Committee affirmed it. You are already acquainted with this job."

"Oh, no. I can't," I insisted. "I applied for admission to Kharkov's State University."

"Okay. Let's make an agreement. If you work well, we'll let you go in two years."

I was completely devastated. My dreams of being home for good in a month all were crushed. Like all of us, I was accustomed to the idea that one's first duty was to society and personal interests and needs were secondary. Moreover, I felt deep fulfillment and pride. Many praised me for being able to keep the main threads of the project in my hands. Now, looking from far away, at a distance of close to seventy years, I like three of my accomplishments most, specifically my acting, which unfortunately was not developed into a ripe profession; the Club project; and the Olympiad in Kharkov. To me, they were monumental and exciting achievements.

<u>Summarizing our study and life</u>. We had no new textbooks. If I'm not mistaken, we had a new textbook for geography, chemistry, and the history of Russia by Professor Pokrovsky with his new sociological approach. One of the popular anecdotes about it:

A history teacher asked a student: "Who was Ekaterina the II?"

"She was a product of her aristocratic society," the student answered.

"Good! But who was she?"

"She was a product of her aristocratic society."

"Good! But what was her occupation?"

"She was a product . . . "

We wrote "conspects"—word by word transcripts of teachers' lectures. It wasn't difficult because all the lectures were informal— talk, questions, and explanations. For classes in literature, culture, and history, we received assignments to read the original works. But we found just a few of them. We had to read aloud in groups. We studied diligently and a lot, helping each other and having fun.

A focal point of our self-critical humor was our bi-weekly or so "wall newspaper," which made fun of any one of us or of general conditions. We invented a funny game: to a written question or statement, anyone could insert an answer or comment. This part of the newspaper was the most popular and humorous. Practically all the

118

students wrote something. Once we made up an anecdote: "Do we need the letter 'M'? Look, there's no m*iaso* (beef), no m*aslo* (butter), no m*uka* (flour), no m*oloko* (milk), no m*ilo* (soap)." The editorial staff had taken a lot of "teaching," first from Shcherbina, then from the Komosomol Committee which reprimanded the staff; I was a member. Finally, in a general meeting all students were accused of a loss of class vigilance. It was hard for us to swallow this bitter pill; as we understood it, we had only written an innocent joke on real existing conditions.

Our value system was based on our mutuality. We felt responsible for each other, for the school, and for the country. Hatred among us or little *cliques* were not practiced; normally each of us had several close friends. Selfishness was regarded as anti-social behavior, but self-respect as part of human dignity. Collectivism became a blend of natural behavior and social self-control. Some traits in the Russian character are rather anti-collectivist, like melancholy and anarchical independence. Like many of us, I didn't want to look and behave like everybody; I tried to expose my individuality. We enjoyed what we were doing and we enjoyed life. All of these things were possible because we had great belief in ourselves and in the aim the whole country was struggling toward. Our relations with the teachers were friendly.

As I understood later in my life, our psychological stability was helped by our social content. The majority of students were of peasant stock. They were stable, easily satisfied, optimistic and resilient, industrious, with a strong sense of moderation. Sometimes, they acted according to the centuries-old peasants' common law of judging strictly—what is good and what is bad. In all respects they were a healthy bunch. We realized success could only be attained by self-discipline.

Belief in our ideology gave meaning to our lives. It was not greed for more material things; we led a normal existence with few of them. Could having more of them provide a happier life? We doubted it. Certainly, we would have liked to have had nicer clothes and shoes. But, in this sense, we lived in happy simplicity. Our aim was to acquire knowledge, to make our minds open and our hearts kind, to be able to help fellow humans, and in doing it, we also had much fun.

Graduation from Tekhnicum

Finals were behind us. A few days later we were gathered in our hall for the last time. Director Shcherbina congratulated us and spoke about our duties in building a socialist society. The best graduates were recognized, I among them. Teachers gave us some warm advice. A music teacher played some pieces on the piano, including *Gaudeamus Igitur*. Then the secretary of the school distributed our diplomas. No parents were present except mine and Misha's mothers.

They came because I had to start my work right away and have my vacation later, although it was unclear when. They knew I would feel very lonesome. Why was there such urgency to start my job? The several villages had quite a number of orphans, parents had died and there was no one to take care of them. The District Party Committee adopted a resolution that each *kolkhoz* had to open and support an orphanage. The District Department of Education had to follow up on this directive. That was my work assignment.

With the help of my two mothers, my new life was organized. I rented a nice room with board from a pleasant house lady. My mothers were impressed with "my" young pioneers' club. Director Shcherbina invited us for tea. We brought a couple of pies. It was utterly painful to watch how Shcherbina's kids devoured them. They had practically the same food as all of us in the school. Director Shcherbina was in a depressed mood.

"Every day, all my energy is spent in getting supplies, food for the school," he said. "I am afraid that next year is going to be even harder." He thanked my mothers for giving the school the two best graduates ever.

My mother and myself in 1931, at my graduation from
Tekhnicum, Grayvoron.

5

Adult: An Important Job

Work at the District Department of Education

Now at seventeen, I felt totally a mature adult on my own. On June 15, 1931, I started my lifelong work. The head of the Department of Education was a woman, a smart and fair career-oriented Party *apparatchik*. I knew her quite well. She welcomed me, explained my duties and the general rules.

"Remember, you are not Nina anymore. People have to call you Nina Mikhailovna." It meant Nina, daughter of Mikhael. This was according to a Russian custom showing respect for adults and authority.

She told me that the Department had some clothes, shoes, and blankets for the orphans, but only a last resort addition if the *kolkhoz* really couldn't provide them.

I was in a big village, though it was the poorest in the district. There was an orphanage in a big house formerly belonging to a *kulak*. The picture of the orphans' existence was depressing: two empty rooms and a kitchen with a table and benches; one room for girls, another for boys. They slept on straw in the big stationary bed, or on the floor—no pillows, sheets, or covers. They had their parents' worn clothes, and no shoes for winter. An older *kolkhoznitsa* (*kolkhoz* woman) prepared food for them—soup three times a day, some vegetables and bread. They still were undernourished and anemic even with having summer vegetables. The parents of some had died; the others were left behind during a family (*kulak*) expropriation. Their deep psychological scars were evident—they looked at me with wide-open, unblinking eyes, in which shone the despair of hard times.

It took some time and warm persuasion before they trusted me,

122

opened up, and started answering my questions. The next day they met me with sincere child's trust. We played uncertainly, sang with shyness, spoke a few words, and even looked as if we were smiling. I hugged them and now each of them wanted my attention, to be close to me.

Meanwhile, the Chairman of the Village Council sent Komsomol activists to the poor peasant families living now at the *kulaks'* homes to bring back things useful to the orphanage. But what can be collected from a poor family with many children? A few worn things and a table and a bench. The village store was empty. I asked and the Komsomol appointed a member to be responsible for the well-being of the orphans. Before I left, I had a talk with the Chairmen of the Village Council and the *Kolkhoz* and the Komsomol Secretary. When I told we helped them, they merely disbelieved me.

"Nobody gave anything to us. They just took from us. Our villagers are very poor. We are situated on poor land with no meadows for hay. Thanks to the M. T. S. (Machine-Tractors Station) for plowing and sowing about half our fields. We don't have horses or oxen to plow the rest of our fields. How will we pay the M. T. S.? Last winter, more than a dozen people died from malnutrition. Please don't tell that to anyone."

They promised to do for the orphans as much as possible. The man who brought me home, a *kolkhoz* cabby, received things: blankets, sheets, pillows, some clothes and boots. Later I received a letter from the orphans, written by an older boy and signed in different fashion by each of them. I read it and almost cried. I kept a number of those heartbreaking letters, but they were lost in the flames of WWII.

I probably visited more than a dozen villages. In each of them, I faced more or less the same situation. I applied the same steps and measures to solve the problems.

Deportations continued and it was already reported about 400,000 *kulaks'* households, close to two million people were forced to leave. They lived in special settlements which they had to build, working as laborers at construction sites, or were sent to new, uncultivated land. Many of the deportees had run away and "masked," changing their past. Establishment of the passport system for each citizen helped government to "unmask" those unfortunate "socially dangerous elements." They were again sent to Gulags or special settlements. More children were left homeless.

Vacation. Visiting the Ostapchuks

It was the middle of August and I was at home. Papa and Mama were beaming with joy and laughingly addressed me as Nina Mikhailovna. Sincere, simple happiness, but Papa seemed tired. Because of the socialist competitions they often worked additional hours, certainly without pay.

"All my workers are good enthusiastic men. Our *zekh* (department) is going to win the socialist competition this time."

Unfortunately, our living space now couldn't accommodate guests, so we visited the Ostapchuks, and my *Krestnaia* went with us. She and Mama baked a lot of good food we took with us.

It was an incredible reunion! Misha, only a student of Moscow State University. And me, an important employee of the District Department of Education, not Ninok, but Nina Mikhailovna, and don't forget to make a low bow while addressing me. They were all laughing and joking with us. Misha was deeply satisfied, now on the road to being a scholar-physicist. For two days, our company sat around the table, drinking, eating, and talking politics; but Misha and I were only sometimes a part of that.

Misha's father was almost an "Old Bolshevik," having joined the Party at the beginning of the 1920s, and was better informed about politics and policy in the country. He said many scholars and well-known specialists were arrested as "wreckers" of the economy and education. Among them were academicians P. P. Lazarev, Yevgeniy Tarle, V. V. Vinogradov, and many more; the Czarists military specialists who came to the service of the Revolution and helped build the Red Army; known biologists and agronomists; scholars in the humanities and sciences. It ran into many thousands. The political and economic trials of 1928–30 were widely publicized, but these arrests were not made public. Why? Probably there were already too many repressions. He said that the last winter had been brutal, our transport system not able to handle all the peasants running from hungry villages. Numbers of them died on the floor in the railroad stations and the police took the bodies for disposal.

Misha was very funny and liked to make me laugh. Usually when we met, he asked me with a strict facial expression, but laughing, tender eyes: "Did you fall in love with somebody else?"

"No! My word of honor," and I gave the Young Pioneer salute. Then I asked the same: "Did you fall in love with someone?"

"No!" and he saluted.

"Did someone fall in love with you?"

"Yes!"

"Oh, tell me!"

Misha wanted to tell this to everyone.

"A girl came to my room. She was a real picture of the Komsomol girl: a red kerchief and an old leather army jacket. She said, 'I will be to the point. I am a Komsomol member and I believe in equality between man and woman. You don't know me, but I know you, and . . . I have fallen in love with you. I would like to be your wife. If you are interested, then let us date, and get to know each other.'

"I behaved in the same way as Eugene Onegin toward Tatiana (from the opera *Eugene Onegin* by Tchaikovsky). I said, 'I am answering you in the same way, straightforwardly and sincerely. Sorry, I am engaged to a nice girl and soon will be married.' She said, 'Excuse me,' and left. Who was she, her name? I don't know."

The ladies of our company were shocked and talked about the new, amoral, shameless behavior of the young generation.

The question was raised again why Misha decided to be a student for seven years when his future was already bright without any doubts. In a few years, he would be Komsomol secretary of the Voronezh Oblast Committee. Then in another several years, possibly he would be secretary of the Central Committee of Komsomol of the Soviet Union and a member of the Party Central Committee. Who knew how high up the Party ladder he could climb.

"Yes, it's a very probable assumption," Misha said. "But I want to be a scholar. The scientific and technological progress of the twentieth century will be breathtaking. Just think about atomic energy! That's what I'm going to work on: splitting the atom. We can't imagine now how the whole world will change, how people's lives will get better. Wars won't be fought because this would lead to the destruction of the world, victors and losers both gone. I believe my mission in life is science for the good of humanity. I am a little dissatisfied with our country's political development. The democratic form of the State is giving way to the domination over people by the Party bureaucracy. I want to have love in my family and use my personal power and talent for the good of people, not for domination over them as if they were not able to build their own good life. In this way, people's thinking can be divorced from reality and depend upon the dictates of the authorities. If it continues, it could bring many difficulties to our Revolution and progress."

Soon Papa and Mama left. *Krestnaia* stayed, having fun with Mama Rosa and us. We had a whirl of activities until Misha departed for Moscow. As always when we parted, I became melancholy for weeks.

At home, I wanted to acquaint myself with Kharkov's cultural news. We attended Tchaikovsky's opera *Cherevichki* (*The Shoes*). It is a comic-fantasy which takes place near my mother's birthplace. Against a background of beautiful Ukrainian nature and the people's colorful customs, a love story and funny situations unfold. Similar to Goethe's *Faust*, a devil is involved, but a smart, young Ukrainian blacksmith used him and sent him away, preserving his own soul and winning the love of the beautiful Oksana. The music was permeated by Ukrainian melodies and rhythms.

Back to Work: Schools

We decided to target several seven-year schools in the better *kolkhozes* with the purpose of organizing some more permanent after-school activities in the school or the village hall. But my "child," a club, had many difficulties and I had to stay to work them out. Only at the end of December was I free to drive to the presumably rich village. What a difference since I was there six months previously. The people looked like shadows, with white or brownish faces and watery eyes, and moved slowly. All vigor and energy was gone. I stayed with the Director of the school, Yelena, a single woman in her thirties, a graduate from Voronezh Pedagogical Institute (College), very strong physically and morally, a really nice person. We became friends and she visited me a few times in Grayvoron. I visited classes and watched the children. The majority were malnourished and behaved in a serious, somber manner like adults. They didn't run or play during breaks and one didn't hear children's loud laughter. They just smiled timidly as if this unhappy situation was somehow their fault. Their academic performance had plummeted. For a few evenings Yelena and I talked openly and honestly.

She thought that this was not the right time for organizing after-school activities. The majority of children were too weak. She asked parents to spare the energy of the children if possible, not to ask them to work at home. She hoped not many people would die. Others would survive the coming critical three months until April when the good weeds and tree leaves could be used as food. We both believed in a future socialist society. But how were we to understand the present time?

Yelena asked me not to tell anyone, but she thought it was a *thermidor* (as it had happened in the French Revolution of 1789) of the Russian Revolution that Stalin was carrying out with the help of some members of the Politiboro. Stalin represented both Robespierre and the reactionary movement of the French Revolution. There was no other explanation for having killed millions of the best peasants and now to have a famine approaching. The peasants didn't believe Stalin anymore, and didn't see a way out because revolt would not work. Their villages would be erased and those who survived would be sent to Siberia for hard labor and death.

Yelena's thinking crushed me; my thinking was divided. On one side I thought that Stalin, in his recent emotional speech, said in ten years our country had to be industrialized, economically and militarily strong or history wouldn't remember us and Russia as a power. Now the majority in the country enthusiastically worked to achieve this aim. On the other hand, why destroy peasants? Without them and their products, our country could not survive. Why repress scholars, even the Old Bolsheviks?

Since this conversation with Yelena, double thinking occupied my mind. It was heartbreaking because I couldn't talk even half openly any more, although all my life I had been open and sincere. Now, double thinking and talking became the norm. It changed me more. I didn't want to talk politics because I couldn't bring myself to sing dithyrambs to Stalin, and yes it was unthinkable to accuse him of any crime against the Revolution and the Russian people. So I became even more careful in my political expression. The best way was to be silent, as many did. The youthful, open-hearted attitude was gone, but the belief in a socialist society built by all of us was not yet diminished.

"Stalin is not forever, but Russia and its people are. Why are Russia and its good people so unlucky as to have despotic or incapable leaders? Whose fault is it? Where are our Peters and Lenins?"

We celebrated the New Year in the Club. Children celebrated in the afternoon and it was great: performances, singing, dancing around *yolka*. They even each received a few candies. In the evening, it was a joyful adults celebration; they brought food and vodka. They were really joyful and even had spontaneous dance competitions. When villages and big cities were suffering from hunger, the small towns like Grayvoron were not in bad condition because people had vegetable gardens and fruit trees in their back yard or gardens along the river, and many had chickens, geese, pigs, and even cows.

I did not visit villages. In March, I had to see several schools and to check a couple orphanages. One village where I had been with the tekhnikum's Agit. brigade and had performed about two and a half years ago and where I had seen hundreds of healthy laughing peasants, was now a village that looked dead. The chairman of the Village Council was really happy to see me. We went to the orphanage and, taking into account the general situation of the villagers, the children were not in desperate condition. Then the chairman took me home for supper. His wife, a kind, middle-aged woman, embraced and kissed me like an old friend.

"Oh, people remember you," she said. "No one before had said such nice, truthful words about us as you did. You have a kind heart and love for the simple people."

We talked a lot. I asked the chairman about the people's condition in the village, and he opened his heart.

"We will survive until May. Some old people have died. More small, weak children and old weak people will have died. But I am afraid that next winter many people will not survive. Look, people are too weak to sow all their acreage under crop in the spring. Our young people have left for industrial building work in the Urals. We will get a tractor for only a few days. This means a part of our fields won't be cultivated. But we have already received the grain and beets procurement quotas from the government based on all the acreage and they would take almost all of our harvest. If we don't deliver it, they will come and take by force completely everything. Do you know Stalin continued to export grain to European countries in spite of the famine? Now in the Ukraine and the Northern Caucasus a lot of people are dying. Europe can't help us as in 1921 during the Civil War, because now any reference to famine is prohibited. Nobody knows about our tragedy. If you were to tell someone in power what I am saying, they would arrest me as a 'counterrevolutionary agitator.' I know you won't tell."

The next day, I went home again with a heavy heart. I entered and my *khoziayka* joyfully embraced me. "Happy birthday! Happy eighteenth birthday!"

Oh, my God! I forgot. It was the 15th of March—my birthday. I started to cry bitterly and my *Khoziayka* calmed me down. "I am preparing a festive dinner. *Khoziain* (her husband) brought good wine."

She opened the door to my room. "Look, you received four telegrams and three packages."

I opened the telegrams from Misha, my and Misha's parents, and Grandpa's family. Now I was so happy. I washed, changed clothes, and shared a festive dinner with my hosts. Life was still wonderful!

It was May and the Secretary of the Party's District Committee called me to his office.

"I was in Voronezh for a meeting of the District Secretaries of the Party," he said. "Comrad Nikiforov made a report about the schools and after-school education. (Nikiforov was the head of the Oblast Department of Education and very influential.) In his report, he mentioned our positive work of opening a good club for children's activities. He asked me to tell our experience at the Secretaries meeting, and they were impressed. He wanted to see me, and guess what? He asked me to send you to work in his department. I told him you are a dependable and intelligent girl with a bright future as an actress. So you are leaving for Voronezh. It's better for you to live in a good cultural environment."

Transfer to Voronezh

Several weeks later, I was on my way to Voronezh. I received excellent recommendations from my Department and the Komsomol Committee that were always very important to have.

Nikiforov himself received me with a fatherly smile. He asked me about my family, my plans for the future, and told me that his son Yura was two years older than I. I held my tears when I told him about my brother Kolia. He called the head of the department where

I would work as an inspector of after-school education. They gave me several days to settle down and sent me to a hotel to live.

The three girls who worked in the Oblast Komsomol Committee occupied a huge room. I was to be the fourth. They greeted me in a friendly fashion. Nadia (Nadezhda means hope) was my work counterpart at the Komsomol. She was a phenomenal girl, full of energy, friendly, who liked to play guitar and sing. We became close friends.

The "Mother-witch" was Tamara, head of the Culture and Propaganda Department. She was much older than Nadia and I and constantly taught us the proper behavior for Komsomol members, using stale tags from newspapers. We were really afraid of her because she could easily make a political "case" against anyone. She wouldn't mind ruining the life of anyone and presented herself as a class vigilante against enemies of the Party line.

The third girl was Valia, a spent, but good human. She was Komsomol Secretary of the big District. For several years, she carried on a love affair with the District Party Secretary, a very powerful man. She had had many abortions until her health was seriously damaged. She was sick and unhappy. He had to get rid of her and arranged for her promotion to the Oblast Komsomol Committee. Quite a lot of the time she was in bed or in the hospital. It was a pity, because she was a smart, good-looking, and a kind person. Nadia and I helped her a lot.

We were assigned to the "closed" (only for members) restaurant, which had good food three times a day and was very inexpensive. In 1932 a system of "closed" stores and restaurants was already much used. In addition, the system was graded. All of us, except Tamara, belonged to the lowest third grade.

At work as real bureaucrats we wrote instructions for the District's Department of Education on how to organize after-school activities. But a more practical approach was to target several cities like Voronezh, Kursk, Orel, Tambov and more for organizing the Young Pioneers Clubs. Nadia (Komsomol) and I (Education) started to put permanent pressure on our targets, including visiting. I knew it was not the right time for these activities, but it was the Party directive. Although the main task now was to send children to summer Pioneer camps, practically each plant, factory, institute, and government institution had a stationary camp in the forest. Even in these hardship years of 1932–33, food and services in the camps were quite good. The Department of Education provided additional food and money for the poorest of the camps (organizations).

It was summer 1932 and I hadn't seen Misha and my parents since August 1931. During winter vacation, the Central Committee of Komsomol sent Misha to Belorussia's Central Committee to tackle some problems. As a former professional Komsomol functionary, Misha was still in the Central Committee file and they could use him as they pleased. The poet Mayakovsky wrote that "All of us are walking (living) under the Central Committee and without C. C. permission no one would even sit down."

At the end of the 1932 school year, Misha couldn't come home again. For several years, the whole Komsomol organization and the majority of the student body of Moscow University had spent summer vacations on construction projects all over the country, mainly in the Urals and in the region beyond. Students were enthusiastic about this work because, in addition to having socialist conscience and a strong feeling of duty, they received high pay. Misha was a *brigadier* (leader) of his class. After exams, they immediately left for the southern Ural region.

August 1932 Vacation: Misha's Stories

In August, I went home and brought about twenty pounds of flour with me. Although my parents had enough vegetables and were not suffering, Mama went several times to Krasnaia-Yaruga and bartered household goods and clothes for food. It was a hardship to get bread in the store across the city line where they lived.

As usual, I was busy culturally. My parents and all the relatives noticed I had changed—the childlike, happy expression in my eyes was gone. Instead, concentration, even some pain now showed in my eyes.

At the end of August, we visited the Ostapchuks. Misha was expected to come for a few days on his way to Moscow from Central Asia. We were at the station when a train pulled in and a worker in dirty clothes got off; he had on a funny cap, shoes falling apart with his dirty toes openly looking at the world, was well-tanned, and looked healthy and happy. It was Misha. During those few days he told us about their enthusiastic good work, about the people and environment. They had driven to Kazakhstan several

131

times to meet and talk with people.

I vividly remember one story Misha told and several decades later I read quite a similar story by the great Kazakh writer Chingis Aitmatov. Kazakh people have a lot of horses, cattle, and sheep. Their men and women are unbelievably skilled horsemen, better than circus performers. The winners of competitions received widespread fame.

Peasants were driving their herds from used pasture to fresh pasture. Once the herdsmen found a wolf-pit with the wolf cubs alone. They brought them to the village. It was a terrible mistake. An elder (usually an older, wise, respected man) told them to take the cubs back to the pit immediately. But it wasn't done. At night a wolf pack attacked the herds, killing sheep but not taking the kill for food. It was clear revenge.

Several wolves were killed by herdsmen. Among them was the largest and strongest one, a partner (mate) of a famous green-eyed she-wolf, who was a pack leader. That meant they should expect more revenge attacks. At night in the village, the green-eyed wolf, mother of the stolen cubs, walked around and around the shed where her cubs were, trying to get at them. The entire wolf-pack was there, chasing barking dogs.

The herdsman who kept the cubs had a baby son about six months old who played outside in the morning. He heard the baby scream and saw a wolf running slowly away holding the baby. The father took a risk and fired at the wolf. She fell. When he and the others got to her, they saw a dying wolf and the baby sitting by without a scratch. The she-wolf opened her green eyes and looked at the people accusingly. An elder said, "Now you have seen a humanly kind mother beast and beastly cruel humans."

Hardship in Villages

It was the end of 1932. We didn't know if there was starvation in the villages because those who knew would not tell the truth. Fear of repression affected people's behavior.

The Department of Education was receiving reports from some Districts of more orphans and no means to take care of them. Nikiforov was fighting for food and funds for the orphanages. What little he received was sent to the most hunger-stricken Districts. In Voronezh we did not see any serious signs of starvation. On the cities' borders, police were assigned to keep hungry peasants from getting into the city. Some of the peasants died, the corpses were collected by trucks and taken to mass graves. We knew Stalin's sharp answer to Terekhov, a Secretary of the Unkrainian Communist Party Central Committee who reported on the terrible situation in the villages of Kharkov Oblast.

"You have made quite a fable about famine. It won't work." Stalin's advice to him was to quit his post and write his fables, for some fools would read them.

We led a normal life, unaware of the scope of the tragedy around us, since it was taboo for newspapers to write about the starvation. Nadia and I liked to attend the City Drama Theatre or concerts or movies. Sometimes our colleagues, boys and girls, joined us and we had so-called *cult-pokhod*, cultural group attendance.

I was not happy with my job. It was mainly shuffling papers, asking District Departments for information and summarizing it. Quite often I did not believe in the numbers or facts given by them. We called it *tufta*, augmentation of successes and leaving negatives unsaid. This process brought a distorting mirror into politics and the whole life of the country. The Komsomol Committee's work performance was even worse than ours. They were very busy having meetings, writing directives to the District Committees strictly demanding they do this or that, and talking politics, calling for class vigilance because enemies were all around.

On November 11 or 12, *Pravda* and the other newspapers published notice of the death of Nadezhda Alliluyeva, Stalin's wife. There was no explanation as to what happened. At the same time, rumors started to circulate that Stalin killed her because of her disagreement with his policy, specifically the repressions, his one-person dictatorship, collectivization and famine. Roy Medvedev, in his excellently researched book, *Let History Judge*, gave a full account. Nadezhda committed suicide—her life with Stalin had become increasingly difficult, for both personal and political causes. Her death brought more gloom and questions.

I received a long letter from Misha. He wrote, in spite of being busy all the time and studying a lot, he felt lonely. He wanted to have a permanent station and anchor in his life, that is, a marriage. He promised we wouldn't have a baby until I finished my studies. Even if it did happen, the two grandmas would be happy to take care of the baby and he would provide economically. He wanted to come on March 15, my nineteenth birthday, and we would be married. The "brother" role had to be over. In my letter to Misha, I expressed the same feeling of loneliness. I didn't want to date anyone and was thinking about him all the time. Across the first page I wrote in red pencil "*Uhu,*" which we understood was "I agree."

I received a very disturbing letter from Mama. She wrote: "It's hard to get bread even with a ration card. We have to go to the city at dawn and stand in line not less than an hour. To go later means staying in line for at least two hours and the possibility they will run out of bread. People are cold, angry, go home empty-handed. For men and women equally, it is dangerous to walk alone or even in twos because the hungry peasants from the villages were all over trying to sneak into the city at night unnoticed by the police. Recently at dawn, a group of peasants knocked down two women from our hamlet. Luckily, they didn't hurt them, just took their ration cards and money. Besides, they asked the women to forgive them. Now every home has a dog outside on a leash; the police even provide a rifle for defense."

I wanted Mama to come and I would give her a small sack of white flour. But my department boss said it was a bad idea because all the railroad trains were crammed with peasants going either to the cities, or out of cities with some food, usually for their children who had been left behind. The police were taking away even those little food supplies from them. One could see the heartbreaking tragedies on the trains. They probably would take the flour from your mother. He had a better idea. He had a friend in Kharkov, the director of a school, who had graduated with him from Voronezh University.

"We can send two parcels from the Voronezh Department of Education to the school as school supplies so that they won't be confiscated."

I wrote to my parents and he wrote to his friend. The next day we made two parcels—one to my parents weighing forty pounds and the other to his friend weighing twenty pounds—and sent them. It was the middle of December. Later, after Orthodox Christmas, I received a wonderful letter written by Mama, Grandpa, and *Krestnaia* telling me what an amazing Christmas celebration they had. I was especially struck by my Grandpa, the kind doctor. He wrote, more or less, something like:

This was, I think, my last Christmas. I am really happy—my whole family, even my grandchildren, were here with me; our table was covered with rich fine food unusual for our time, like white flour *pirozhki*, white flour pies, sausages, chicken and more. You, my beloved granddaughter, helped to make my last Christmas happy.

As I read the letter, tears of happiness and sorrow ran down my cheeks. I realized that Grandpa would die soon. He knew and asked me to come to see him. I had to find time to do that.

Nikiforov decided to take some food from the food fund for the summer children's camps and send it to the orphanages in the worst starving Districts. Nadia and I had to go to the Districts immediately and decide which orphanages were most in need. I visited several Districts, and many orphanages. It was bad, but not as awful as it was in the Ukraine. I didn't see any dead bodies on the streets; they were collected from the homes every morning. Mainly the old, people in poor health, or small children were dying. Some orphanages were in catastrophic conditions. The orphans had some watery vegetable soup with a few potatoes or cabbage, beans or grains. They were weak and looked like little skeletons, sitting or lying with big fixed eyes. No school for them. They slept on the straw on the floor or in big stationary wooden beds. Only some had old dirty blankets or wearable winter clothes. Each time before leaving for a district, I asked Tamara to buy a few pounds of candies for me. She belonged to the better *nomenklatura* store for high Party bureaucrats. Usually I gave a piece or two to each child.

The children's reactions were unusual. They didn't display any joy—just the opposite: more tension. They grabbed the candy, holding it firmly, and put it in their mouth. Only then did they relax and maybe even something like a happy expression lit up their faces. It looked as if they finally believed it was really happening to them. As I talked with them, sometimes I told a funny story. Seldom did they smile and never did they laugh. When I selected the orphanage to be helped, I immediately called my Department and asked for food and blankets to be sent as soon as possible. I selected many orphanages.

Marriage

March 15, 1933 was approaching and I became very excited. Only Nadia knew about my coming event. It was the morning and all the girls went to work. I was dressed in my best and even put a little rouge on my cheeks. About ten o'clock, Misha appeared, smiling happily. I had never seen him so dressed up. He wore a new modern coat, a new suit, new shoes, and even a necktie which he laughingly admitted had never worn before.

"For my once-in-a-lifetime occasion, I want to look like never before, my best." We were in ecstacy.

I told Misha that the city's Office of Registration was closed for several days and we couldn't be married. Misha said nothing. He asked to refresh himself and changed his shirt. After that, he asked me if it was important for me to have that registration, that piece of paper, now.

"Of course not," I said.

Then he put two chairs facing each other and we sat down. He took my hands and said: "I, Michail Ostapchuk, take you as my wife forever. I promise you sincere love and respect, to take care of you in good and bad times. You are my wife. The official paper we will get at the first reasonable moment."

I held back my tears and said: "I, Nina Shuliak, take you as my husband for life. I promise to you my sincere love, respect, and help in everything throughout our life. You are my husband."

Misha pinned on me an exquisite golden brooch with enameled white camellias. "It's an emblem of our marriage, like our parents had rings." I was so embarrassed that I hadn't prepared any gift for him. "You prepared yourself for me. I don't want anything else."

We were in a state of ecstasy and felt a solemn moment had occurred in our lives; something new had begun.

"Now you can kiss me on the lips," Misha said. "And, my *zhenushka* (endearing diminutive from *zhena*, wife), I propose a plan for today. First we are going to have breakfast, then we will go to the telegraph office and send telegrams to both our parents and to Grandpa's family. Then we will go to my closed food store; I have a card that will permit us to shop there. After that, we will go to the home of my former *khoziayka* for a dinner celebration. We will stay there in my former room. I wrote to her and they are waiting for us."

I took what I would need and we left. During breakfast, suddenly Misha took out his wallet, counted his money, and started laughing. "Here I am, a bridegroom come to get married and I forgot to take enough money. *Zhenushka*, do you have any money?"

We burst out laughing. Misha put a bank savings book in front of me and asked me to look through it. On the first page were written his name and mine as his wife. The book was over a year old, and he had quite a bit of money from his summer work in Central Asia and the Central Komsomol Committee assignments. At that time, we did not respect money too much, but that first page profoundly impressed me and emotion overcame me.

"My love, I don't deserve you. You are better than I."

Misha became serious. "No, I think you are a much better human being than I am. Look . . . " And he started to enumerate my character traits, real and imagined, mainly my sincerity, honesty, kindness, still unable to tell even a small lie. He considered me very talented and so on. Finally I stopped him and started to enumerate his traits of character, repeating those that he ascribed to me and adding more. Misha smiled. Then we laughed and decided we were the most perfect human beings on the face of the earth. These panegyrics to each other developed into a game. I kept a list of our plusses and minuses, which was constantly changing. Later, our Mamas also took an active part in the game and it gave us a lot of fun.

At the telegraph office, we sent our laconic telegrams. "Congratulate us. We got married, 3.15.1933. With love and respect, Nina and Misha." On the streets we drew quite a bit of attention. We were a happy, good-looking, laughing pair, fashionably dressed, unusual for that time of drab appearance. Russians like to make comments to people on the streets:

"Ah, Youth, looks like you just got married. Huh?"

"You are right," Misha answered.

"Then, happy life!"

Other comments were: "Ah! Looks like you just came from abroad." "Dressed up, just as in a picture! Ah, then good luck!"

Others would say: "Oh no! They are not ours. They are probably Germans, capitalists." "Ay, happy pair, have you something to sell?"

Finally we crept to Misha's *khoziayka* with lots of packages, definitely including vodka and wine. They were waiting for us. Quite a bit of food was prepared and the celebration continued for two days.

Misha and I had marvelous peace and tenderness for each other in our hearts, feeling that our life was now complete and a phenomenal future was waiting for us. Misha said I gave happiness and permanency to his life. Peace and love enveloped us.

In the morning, Misha was musing, talking dreamily. "I want to understand and explain my feeling—love—logically. If it is possible, then it makes this feeling the same as others. But true love is the only feeling without comparison. It is more spiritual, a state of enchantment, a state of idealization. When the subject of love is idealized, it does not look real but better than in reality. In love is the joy of discovery when the only incomparable miracle on the earth is born—the beautiful unity of two souls. This unity in love changes a human from an egoistic person concentrated on himself, and for himself, to a wholesome humane personality—husband, father, member of human society. Love inspires us in heroic, unselfish deeds."

"Do you remember," I asked Misha, "a Russian fairy tale *Snegurochka (The Snow Maiden)*? She existed for centuries, beautiful and cold. Then a human couple took her and a lad named Lel fell in love with her. She reciprocated with a feeling of admiration and warmth like she had never known. Spring came and Lel called her outside to dance. She knew it would be her death for she would melt. But she said, 'One short moment of love is more precious to me than centuries of cold anguish and tears.' Then she loved tenderly and melted. The loss of love or inability to love is a tragedy which has no comparison, no equivalent in wealth or power or anything."

"It happened more than once a girl showed some interest in me," Misha said. "I looked at her and thought, 'She is a wonderful girl, but she is silver and my Ninok is gold, or she is adamant and my Ninok is a diamond.' I don't know if I am right or it was my fantasy, but it does not matter, because you alone are my soul, my admiration. This is the greatest secret of human beings' existence. If we lose this secret, this true spiritual, emotional love, we humans will become as animals."

We decided that it would be better for me to move home to Kharkov. Sunday evening Misha brought me to my hotel. The girls prepared wine and snacks, congratulated us and sang folklore wedding songs. Misha left for Moscow. In my heart was both happiness and emptiness.

I asked the Head of the Department of Education, Nikiforov, to release me from my job. He and the head of my department asked me to stay until September to be sure the children's summer camps would be properly provided with food and other necessities.

About a week later, Misha's father stopped to see me on his way from Moscow, where he had been at a meeting in the Ministry of Transportation. I was so happy to see him and according to Russian tradition I called him Father, Papa Peter. He liked that and called me "my daughter." He informed me about the catastrophic food situation in Kharkov and the whole Ukraine. I asked him to take me with him. As a headmaster of the Belgorod's Junction Railways, he had the right to use the service compartment on any train on the Moscow-Kharkov-Belgorod and other lines. The next day, I received forty pounds of flour—twenty pounds for my parents and twenty pounds for the Ostapchuks—and a few pounds of candies from the special fund. At the Kharkov station, he asked the stationmaster on duty to hold my baggage.

Pictures of Famine

It was morning and I decided to go straight home. At the city line, a policeman advised me not to go over there, but I had to. Then he gave me something like a hammer in case I would need to defend myself. I will never forget that three kilometer walk. It was one more decisive drop in the bucket which made me lose faith in Stalin's socialism. Walking down the road, I saw on my right the city's garbage dumps. A little farther up was a gray mass of people, probably a few thousand of them—sitting, lying, walking in an unplowed field. Amid them was a small hut, a store for "commercial bread." Several weeks before, the government had opened these huts on the outskirts of the cities along the roadways full of hungry peasants trying to get into the cities. In these stores, bread was sold at twice higher than normal, but still inexpensive. Only one loaf to a person, they were in a permanent line.

Each morning a truck came with two workers to collect dead bodies. Sometimes they dumped them in the nearby city garbage dumps and put a lot of lime on them. Other times they took them elsewhere. Nobody knew where. There were not too many people on the road to this place. It was already too late in the morning or it was probably most important that some help—grain and bread—start to arrive in the worst starved villages.

To those whom I met on the road, I gave candy. The faces of some people were swollen, with glassy eyes. The others looked like skulls covered with yellow-brown skin. Some of them were in stupefied condition; the others' reaction was still not too bad. All of them wore sheepskin coats, warm and heavy. They walked very slowly. Usually they looked at the candy or at me and softly questioned with disbelief, "*Konfekty* (candy), for me?" I told them that the candy would give them energy. Those who were not stupefied tried to kiss my hand, wailing softly, repeating, "Why are they killing us?" No one said, "Thank you" to me but, "God save you."

I stopped a mother with two children about ten and eight years old who were quite weak. I talked to them and then gave all three quite a bit of candy. They didn't believe it was happening to them or didn't know what candy looked like. I told them to put one in their mouth and they didn't even bother to take off the paper wrapper. All the people did that. The mother told me that she already buried her husband and two other children.

"We know that God is punishing us, for we forgot Him and how to live together in brotherhood, as our forefathers lived. But God is going to show His mercy to us. You'll see. He even sent you to help and talk nicely to us. *Baryshnia* (city girl), God save you. God save you."

As I was ready to turn left to the hamlet, a big man stepped aside to let me pass. He was huge—about seven feet tall—with a sheepskin coat and a blanket on his back. I looked at him, his eyes already glassy and fixed. It was extremely painful to see such a strong man, a worker who had great power and wanted to survive. Maybe somehow he felt my thought. I gave him a handful of candy.

"Oh, kind *baryshnia*, I am a hard-working man with the strength of a horse. Why are they killing us?"

We talked a little. He put some candy in his mouth, and I gave him more. "God save you, a good human." He repeated it and repeated it.

I was already standing at the gate of my house. Dogs were barking. I looked back. The huge man was standing at the same spot looking at me and I felt him repeat, "God save you."

The image of that man stayed with me for many years. It came

140

back to me in 1944 as we were crossing a green border over the Tatra mountain from Poland to Slovakia; we were running from both the Red Army and the Germans, who snatched us like dogs and sent us to work in Germany. Finally we reached a village in the valley. People gave us some food and said that the Tatra and Karpathian mountains were full of partisans. They were killing not only Germans but Soviet people as well as whose direction was to the west, not the east. Our group wanted to go west immediately. At this moment, I heard in my mind "God save you" and it seemed that I saw in the air the image of that huge man. Certainly, I don't know what it was. Perhaps my excited psyche was seeking some consolation. I persuaded my husband not to go and we stayed in this village a few weeks longer until we had an occasion to follow the Slovak's horsecarts. Several days later, we heard the whole group of our friends who had gone on were massacred by partisans.

At home, the whole hamlet was encircled by a barbed wire fence, and each house had a chained dog. Mama and *khoziayka* Danilowna (patronymic) were running to the gate, happy to see me. We decided to meet Papa at the city line, then he and I would go to the railroad station for my baggage and join Mama and Danilowna at Grandpa's. Everybody in the family congratulated me. It was a real happiness to be back in the family.

Grandpa was weaker. He knew not more than a few months were left for him and asked me to come back the next day. He wanted to give me instruction about the family's pictorial history he was leaving in my care. Grandpa probably had cancer and knew, but he said it was a stomach ulcer. At that time, people hadn't heard or known about cancer as a terminal illness. Grandpa died in July.

6

Kharkov—My Home

In September 1933, I was at home in Kharkov, the city of my birth, which my parents left when I was about six months old. Papa's chance of receiving a small apartment or a room in the city was zero. The housing problem was getting worse. Many people were coming into the city because of industrialization, specifically the building of a huge tractor plant on the outskirts of the city. In order to get a room, I realized I would have to work at the Oblast Department of Education or the Oblast Komsomol Committee. I saw Novak, head of the Oblast Education Departments. We talked and he looked through my excellent personal papers. I gave him Nikiforov's telephone number if he needed more information. Then he was silent for some time.

I was preparing for the worst when suddenly he said, "I appoint you as an inspector of after-school education. We will try it for a few months."

Novak happened to be a wonderful man: smart, intelligent, and kind. People really admired him. Unfortunately, his life ended tragically, like so many people at the time.

It was a new beginning and my mood was high. The "Bread Huts" had disappeared. That made all the people feel relaxed and hopeful. In the spring, the peasants resumed work in *kolkhozes* and the fall produced an excellent harvest. Popular unrest was extinguished. The most important outcome was that Stalin gave the peasants a deadly lesson. On the other hand, Stalin realized that peasants organized in *kolkhozes* in certain circumstances could be a great danger to the government. So special political organs, "Political Detachments," were created throughout the country for effective control over the peasants. The Communists and Komsomol members had been sent from Moscow and Leningrad to those "Polit Detachments" in the Ukraine. The local members were not trustworthy enough. In

1932, the Second Five-Year Plan started, with the goal of achieving a high mechanization of labor and industrialization of the country. So-called socialist competition in industry and *kolkhozes* was rising. The level of labor production rose—at least that's what we read in the newspapers.

Kharkov, a city I loved, situated in the very northeast of the Ukraine, is European in its planning and architecture. Kiev-Kharkov is an exact parallel to Russia's well-known pair—Moscow, an old city with Russian character, and St. Petersburg, a new city of European character. In the Ukraine, Kiev is an old city of Slavic character, and old Capitol, the root of three Slavic nations—Russia, Ukraine, and Belorus—and Kharkov is a new more European city, the Capitol of the Ukraine until 1934, an industrial and cultural center, and an important railway and air juncture. That's why Hitler held Kharkov at any price. In spite of its belonging to the Ukraine, it was really a Russian city because the majority of the population, as well as the language and culture, was Russian.

Founded in 1801, Kharkov University is the third oldest university in Russia, after Tartu in Estonia, and Moscow in 1755, not counting Kiev's Religious Academy of the 16th century, the Slav-Greek-Latin Academy in Moscow, established in 1687, and St. Petersburg's Academy of 1727. The University library at Kharkov was known for its treasure of priceless antiquarian books. What happened to some of those books, which were not evacuated behind the Ural Mountains in 1941?

In the winter of 1941–1942 Kharkov was occupied by the Germans. The University stands on a hill and in winter, because the University street was slippery and difficult for transportation, a mixture of salt, carbide and sand was used to thaw the ice. Instead of a salt-sand mixture, the Germans used the books from the library, including the oldest and most valuable ones. Bravo to the Deutsche Culture!

Known as a city of workers and students, Kharkov had over a dozen Institutes of Higher Education and the Military Academy, first-class theaters, a few small museums and art galleries, and a philharmonic. Before World War II, the population was close to one million. It is hard to imagine that during the German occupation of 1941–43, a city of this size was left for a long period without electricity, running water, sewage treatment system, coal or wood for heating and, of course, no food. Kharkov was a green city, with many small and big parks and tree-lined streets.

Since I left the city in August 1943, I have been back only once in 1992, although I have been in the Soviet Union many times. But I was not allowed to go to Kharkov. Kharkov had been quite ruined by the war. Now it was rebuilt and spread out immensely. I had come in 1992 to take care of the family's graves. Before going, I had been writing to the cemetery office and sending money for their upkeep. At the railway station, I was met by tourist officials and asked them to take me straight to the city cemetery at the end of Pushkin's Street.

That cemetery doesn't exist anymore, I was told. The graves of those with living relatives who paid for moving them were relocated and the others were leveled. A park with trees and flowers was laid out. The next morning, I was walking around the park, maybe over the graves of my mother or Grandpa or other relatives. The pain in my heart was eased by watching little children playing; their angelic laughter or even their crying was comforting to hear.

I thought I knew the locations of three graves: Kolia's, Mama's, and Grandpa's. Now I don't know if Kolia's grave is still there. Tragic! Where do most of the family have their places of peace? I knew that Grandpa's family—Grandma and three aunts—were moved to Alma-Ata, Kazakhstan, just a few days before the war started in June 1941. Cousin Nina's theater played for a whole year in Alma-Ata. No one came back. Their fate is not known to me.

Are Doubts Justified?

I decided to start my new job on the first of September, after Misha's stop on his way from Siberia, where Moscow University students were working that summer. We traveled to Belgorod. Papa Peter knew the number of Misha's train, even the number of his car. So we were standing on the platform, waiting the appearance of a worker in shabby clothes. Instead, a gentleman came strolling along, elegantly dressed in a light summer suit, matching shoes, and even a straw hat. Behind him a porter carried his suitcases.

Misha's audacious grand entrance was in fun and he made a big splash. Even employees who knew Misha came out to greet him and we laughed together. In our curious strange time, a shabby appearance was normal and people were used to it. But an elegant person showing up was not usual; it aroused laughter or envy or sometimes mistrust because even for people with money it was difficult to get clothes and footwear. They were hardly available, even in Moscow; but they could be bought at the big industrial construction projects in the Ural region and in Central Siberia. Some merchandise was even of foreign origin and not too expensive.

The government policy was a logical way of tempting people to go to those places with severe climates. Misha used this occasion to the fullest. He dressed well himself and one of his suitcases was for me—mainly full of beautiful material for dresses, suits, and coats. He also brought a suitcase of things for our parents. The fathers were especially impressed with the leather for shoes and the boots for all of us. Once again I became a well-dressed young woman in the city.

All this was unique—we were excited and Misha happily watched over us. Since our marriage in March, we hadn't seen each other and now we felt that our happiness was irrepressible.

For a few days, we carried on an endless discussion about the situation in the country, things that people didn't express openly in public. Misha, with his wisdom and optimism, had tried to set hope in our minds.

"The people are serious about reaching our aim to make our Motherland strong," he said. "We have already built hundreds of new industrial projects: electric stations; huge plants; factories; railroads; canals and more. We have an ideal and are hurrying toward our goal, to have a society of equal citizens living well. Maybe this march is much too fast and brings unnecessary sufferings. I don't know. But mistakes were made; we know that. In principle, we don't have any other way to go."

Misha's point was that, "Doubts are entirely normal because our country's hard drive to build a completely new society is unknown in the history of humankind. There is no precedent. We have to try. Now, only dull dogmatists don't have any doubts. History has taught us that fanatics and dogmatists often turn out to be criminals against their own people. I recently read *The Magic Mountain* by Thomas Mann. The mountain was made from what looked like stones, but were actually the fossilized sufferings of mankind."

Our parents decided to give a wedding feast for us.

"What will we do if our parents ask us to show our papers of marriage?" Misha said.

"It's simple. Let us go now to the Office of Registration and get the papers." We did it.

Our parents invited their and Misha's friends. The tables displayed good food, vodka, and wine. By custom, guests playfully yelled *gorko*—it's bitter—a nuptial pair kissing made vodka sweeter. Misha invited more yelling by telling them that we had been married for six months but had only seen each other for three days in all that time. We sang and danced to the accordion. Misha and I were poor dancers; it is hard to believe, but we had never danced together before. We didn't have time for the dance parties. Both Mamas asked me to dance a wedding rite "bride dance," though it was not customary anymore. I was a good folk dancer and had danced the wedding ritual before.

I danced alone on the floor and Misha had to sit proudly in front of the guests as a Prince-Groom. Portraying the bride as a swan, I danced easily, smoothly, expressing emotions of sadness and happiness. Everybody was impressed with my performance although I was not the dancer type. Some people were seeing this ritual dance for the first time.

Work—More of the Same, Only Different

At the beginning, my job was similar to that in Voronezh—taking care of the orphanages—only here the number of orphans was much greater, in the thousands. But the final number for the whole of the Kharkov Oblast I didn't know because the information about each district was given straight to Novak's secretary. It was a secret.

I vividly remember one of my first visits to a village, whose name I don't remember. As usual, I was in a horse carriage. Approaching the village, I saw stretched over across the road a huge broad placard displaying Stalin's new slogan "Life has become better, life has become more joyful!" on a white sheet written in black letters. I had read and heard this slogan many times; it was not something new. But seeing it over there was the height of hypocrisy. This village had lost almost half of its population during the last famine, as I was informed. I asked my horse-cabby driver what the villagers thought of this slogan, but he didn't want to answer and just whirled his head. After I promised him it would be between us, he said in typically

146

short peasant's form: "It's spit in the peasant's face, but we've seen much worse. Now, once more we just wipe it off."

It was the end of a rich harvest, and people looked quite good, though there were no smiles or laughs.

The orphanage also was not in bad condition. There were even sheets and blankets on the straw-filled mattresses. The children looked quite healthy. Since the spring they had had enough simple healthy food like fresh vegetables, fruit, bread and milk, but they looked small for their ages. After visiting a number of orphanages in different districts, I noticed a similar phenomenon: all of them were smaller for their age. The younger children (approximately up to the age of five) behaved more or less like any children of that age group, but the older children behaved differently from children of their age group usually do. They remembered and understood what happened to their parents and other people in the village. They were withdrawn, watchful, and their eyes, sometimes with the painful expression of adults, showed disbelief in one's words. Some of the oldest didn't hide their bitter frustration, saying for example, "Go to school? What for? I am a peasant. Maybe next winter I will die."

I talked to them and then to Komsomol members, helping to plan the talks with children in the school and also in the orphanage. I also took other measures depending on local circumstances. Again in the Kharkov Oblast, I didn't notice the same interest in the Komsomol organizations as I had in the Voronezh Oblast, which had bad food shortages but not major starvation as in the Kharkov Oblast.

At the beginning of 1933, Stalin sent Pavel Petrovich Postyshev, the popular secretary of the Central Committee of the Communist Party of the USSR, a man of half Russian and half Tunguz descent, to the Ukraine as the secretary of the Ukrainian Central Committee of the Communist Party. He had to deal with famine and to stifle Ukrainian Nationalism. Soon a thorough purging of the Party was started and carried out for several years. Chubar, a Ukrainian, the Chairman of the Council of Ministers, and Lubchenko, a Ukrainian, the President of the Ukrainian Republic, were removed from their offices and later executed. There were many more. Mukola Scrypnik, the Minister of Education and Lenin's oldest friend, committed suicide. Many thousands of members were expelled from the Party. The Ukrainian intellectuals like Nekhvorostny, the Rector of Kharkov University, and the well-known historian Professor Hrushevsky, were persecuted. The struggle against "Ukrainian Nationalism" became the hot problem of the day and often Russians or Jews were appointed to important positions instead of Ukrainians. The fight was being carried out not only in the Ukraine but in all the national republics.

Ideological Changes

Profound ideological changes occurred in the years of the second Five-Year Plan, 1932–1937. These were manifested in cultural affairs and in the relationship between the State and the citizens. Stalin reintroduced the use of terminology and ideas condemned since the October Revolution, words and ideas like "Rossiya (Russia) our Rodina (Motherland)" and the duty of every citizen to love it and to know its history. Before this, the history of Russia was treated as the story of a dark experience and of people's sufferings. Now there was a gradual return to historical tradition with stress on the specifically Russian. There was an attempt to restore the links with the Russian past, synthesizing nationalist and Marxist ideas. Homage was paid to the Grand Dukes and Tsars, to the Saints and military leaders, and to those who had built or "collected" Russia. Films and theaters, literature and the arts, rediscovered and glorified the Russian past. Eisenstein created the famous films, *Ivan the Terrible* and *Alexander Nevsky*. Count Alexei Tolstoy, who had returned from abroad in 1923, wrote the grandiose, colorful novel *Peter the Great*, which was made into an outlandish movie. *The Hymn to the Tsar* was no longer suppressed in Glinka's opera *Ivan Susanin*. The hundredth anniversary of Alexander Pushkin's death in 1837 was observed as a great national holiday.

The schools were also involved in this trend of restoration. History was reintroduced instead of social studies. A number of laws were passed to protect the family, reinstating the family once again as the basis of the State. Divorce was made more difficult. Abortion was declared a criminal offense, except when medically authorized. This was necessary to replace the victims of collectivization and the famine of a general need for a larger population to fill the huge, sparsely populated Soviet Siberia.

In the armed forces, many laws were enacted to return to tradition and discipline. Universal military service was reinstated and was described as the honorable duty of every Soviet citizen. Most surprising was the change of attitude on church matters to stress the "progressive character" of Christianity, the important role played by the Greek-Orthodox Church in the education of the Kievan Rus, and the activities of the monasteries in the colonization of the Russian interior, specifically Siberia. However, the devastation of churches and of the Church's cultural wealth was not stopped. All these reforms were dictated by the necessity to improve the national consciousness and patriotism of the Soviet people; and to regard the Russian culture and history superior to the other Republics so as to makes the glue holding together all the National Republics in addition to socialist ideas. Finally, Stalin invoked the Russian autocratic tradition, specifically Peter the Great and Ivan the Terrible, to justify his own tyranny.

Policy Toward Children

Perhaps children were the primary winners of this policy: "Children, our flowers, are our future" was the motto. It was repeated often that Lenin had once said something like this, "If you give me five years to teach the children, the seed I have sown will never be uprooted."

From the very beginning of the Revolution, government and society had emphasized children's education, not only in school but also out of school. In the 1930s, 40s, and 50s, the government was in the process of creating the most formidable education system in the world. The Soviet child had to absorb in ten years a good deal more than an American child gets in twelve, as I found the American education authority maintained. The pedagogical method was to guide the development of the mind, of teaching how to think. Although the American perception of the Soviet educational system was just the opposite—that children didn't learn independent thinking—this perception was mistaken. It was right only about the teaching of the communist ideology. No high school graduate with an acceptable scholastic record was prevented from going to college for lack of money. Education was free.

The final aim was to create educated, obedient citizens of the Soviet state, but they had to be healthy, well-disciplined, and above all, intelligent and well-informed about the world, of course, ideologically according to the communist view. Hence, the firm accent on children's books, theaters, clubs, summer camps, sanatoriums and, above all, on schools and teachers.

Neglected children still were a major urban problem at the beginning of the 1930s. Lack of housing, collectivization, and famine in the villages often contributed to families breaking up. Orphans from villages ran away to the big cities or officials in small towns and villages forcibly put abandoned children on trains bound for cities. As after the Civil War, big gangs of children populated the cities. But by the end of the 1930s, the network of juvenile institutions absorbed them.

The Young Pioneers' Palace

Kharkov was the first among the big cities to start building a Young Pioneers' Palace. Though Leningrad (St. Petersburg) started work on its Palace much later, they outdid us and opened it before us, to our big disappointment.

In the center of the city is the beautiful Tevelev Square. A very long three story building of simple architecture built for the Nobility Club and their offices situated along its east side. Two main streets to the north—Pushkin and Sumskaja—started from the Square. This Nobility Club was given to the children as the Young Pioneers' Palace. It took about two years to reconstruct the inside and equip it for the children's needs. In jest the people called it the Fairy-tale Palace.

There were (if my memory still serves me) about fifty labs and rooms for various activities, for instance: the aviation rooms with a real miniature plane and everything that was needed to work on and construct it, all donated by the aviation plants; a few rooms for mechanical engineering with machinery given by the machine builders' plants; clothes-modeling rooms with many kinds of sewing machines given by the sewing machine factories, here kids created and sewed clothes; the music rooms with all kinds of instruments, starting with pianos. Eventually the Palace had its own symphonic and brass orchestras and even a few composers. The writers and poets lab was where they learned and even wrote some pieces for the theater and the chorus.

Thousands of children from all the schools were enrolled. Every two years or so, depending on the activity, membership changed and new members came. In addition, the mass children's festivities like New Year or the October Revolution celebration were held inside in the Hall and outside in the Square. A part of the Palace's activities was the Railroad "Pioneer" in the city's Forest Park. It was a small-size railtrack with a small real engine and cars. There were two fully equipped small railroad stations. All these things were donated by a number of plants. Children built up the tracks and stations with professional help. This railroad was very popular especially in the summer time. Each passenger had to buy a ticket for one kopek. It was real, great fun and learning, with children running it under close professional supervision.

Kharkov was the first city in the country to undertake this huge enterprise. The whole country helped; it would have been impossible to accomplish it without help from very high political echelons, specifically P. P. Postyshev and many other higher-ups.

The closest relations and interest I developed were with the Kharkov's Children's Theatre (TYUZ), which opened at the end of the 1920s. The first professional children's theatre was opened in Petrograd in 1921 (the name of St. Petersburg from 1914 to 1924 when it was changed to Leningrad). At the beginning of the 1930s there were over a dozen children's theaters in the country; all of them worked under the influence of the Leningrad Theatre. They were searching for a new form of theatre to reflect the specifics of children's perception. This new form was found in the unity of pedagogical psychology with theatrical art. First of all, it demanded the creation of a new dramaturgy, specially for children, differentiated according to children's ages, and the creation of a new physical appearance of the theatre employing the circus hall form and an open circular stage with a prestage in front of it. All these things allowed children to have active participation in the play. I observed children call out to warn personages on the stage of some danger or disapprove of some behavior. A director of Kharkov's Children's Theatre was Bella Rogosin—a beautiful, soft-spoken woman in her 50s, a genuine enthusiast. The whole collective was like her, enthusiastic, with first-rate actors, actresses, musicians, pedagogues, and a very important group of artisans who made specific things for fairytale productions, puppets, and

Petrushka theatre. I developed a friendship with the wonderful Bella and took part in the theatre's collective discussions about new or already staged productions.

The theatre had its own playwright, Makariev, and a composer. Makariev's play *Timoshkin Mine* was on the repertoire of all the children's theaters. Many well-known playwrights, composers, artists, and pedagogues collaborated with the children's theaters. For instance, there was Samuel Marshak, a writer; Shaporin and Strelnikov, composers; Makarenko, pedagogue, and many more. There were four main categories of productions: fairy tales, historical plays, contemporary mode of life plays, and puppet and Petrushka plays. Some of the productions were *The Humpbacked Steed, Cinderella, The Golden Cockerel* by Rimsky Korsakov; *Kat's House, The Adventures of Tom Sawyer* by Mark Twain; *Don Quixote* by Cervantes; *Fairy Tale about Yemelia, Little Red Riding Hood; Petrushka Leader*, and many more.

Olympiad

What about the village children of the Kharkov Oblast, who recently suffered famine and witnessed death from starvation? The Oblast Department of Education, on my initiative and idea, and the Young Pioneers Department of the Oblast Komsomol Committee, worked out a plan to organize the Oblast's Olympiad. In Russia, we differentiated between a *Spartakiad* (sports) and an *Olympiad* (music, singing, dancing, and acting). Our plan had to be accepted by: the Bureau of the Komsomol Committee; the Oblast Executive Committee (government); and last and decisive one the Oblast Communist Party Bureau. Naturally, the main problem was the budget, which was quite impressive. The Chairman of the Executive Committee gave a recommendation to the Oblast Party Committee as to where to get the money from or to disregard the whole Olympiad.

Novak took me with him to see the highest person of the Oblast, the Party Secretary Mikola Nesterovich Demchenko, to present our case for the Olympiad. Novak instructed me how to behave and to speak in Ukrainian since Demchenko was a Ukrainian. We stepped into Demchenko's big plush office which not long before had belonged to Kosior, the First Secretary of the Central Committee

Communist Party of the Ukraine before the Capitol was moved to Kiev. I looked at Demchenko and was almost intimidated. He had a big face with a strong expression. I couldn't take my eyes off him. Then he stretched out his hand to me and smiled, and in a second I saw a strong, pleasant human face. Funny talk developed. Demchenko asked Novak since when had he been employing European or American models (I was dressed well) and I had to tell him my short biography. I advised him to ask the older workers at the Kh. P. Z. (Kharkov Locomotive Plant) or other plants around about Dr. Bilyk-Pichka, my Grandpa. Much later Demchenko told me that he had asked the workers about my Grandpa.

"It's a pity that he passed away; we would take him as a good example for our young doctors."

He told me that his oldest grandson was my age, so he could call me a granddaughter.

"Superb!" Novak exclaimed. "You have to help your granddaughter." And he told him about my difficulties in getting an apartment in the city.

Demchenko said, "It is done!"

He was impressed with our plans for the Olympiad. But that was a lot of money. Where to get it? Although Novak instructed me not to talk about the famine, I felt now I had to. I told him what I saw in the orphanages and schools—that it was pshychologically extremely important to take children's memories away from their dark experiences and the pictures of death to the realm of children's normal behavior, playing, singing, and laughing; to fight their lack of belief in anything possibly good for them in their futures. We must help them grow up as good citizens of our country and not as cynics or even covert enemies, I said. I was very upset but kept my tears back.

Demchenko bent his head so we couldn't see his eyes and there was no sign of what we should expect. Then he got up, came to me and kissed me on the forehead, picked up a phone and talked at length with the Chairman of the Executive Committee (government). When he finished, he said, "Healthy ideas have to win. You have money. Together with the Komsomol, send your instructions to the Districts to start preparations and we will send ours to the Party's Committee."

In parting, he said to me, "Your exterior is of the capitalist world model, but you have a big Russian-Ukrainian heart."

Novak told me Demchenko was a good man from a peasant family and felt bad about the peasants' condition. His fate was tragic; he was arrested and executed.

I started an incredibly exciting time in my life—the organization and carrying out the Olympiad in the summer of 1935 and after that starting preparation for the *Spartakiad* in the summer of 1937. But in 1936, I resigned from my job and entered the University.

The schools of the whole Oblast were shaken as never before. An Olympiad? What is that? They started preparations enthusiastically: practicing singing, dancing, sketches, declamation, one-act plays, and more. It was the beginning of the 1934–35 school year. In July 1935, competitions and selections of the best started in the districts. Our working committee consisted of the Komsomol (Young Pioneers Department); Education (myself); representatives of the Trade Unions; the Department of Health; theaters; musicians; composers; writers; women's committees; and many more. We had the big "working active." All this time I was working in the Oblast Komsomol Committee Building, the seat of our committee. Once, Novak's secretary called me to come immediately. Rushing up, I thought something serious would happen. I saw Novak flashing a big smile and joggling keys in his hand.

"It's the keys to your apartment!" he said.

"I can't believe it! In just two weeks?"

"Do you know why Demchenko likes you?"

"No."

"Because you speak good Ukrainian, although you did not live in the Ukraine, and because you love the peasant kids, specifically the orphans, and you respect the peasants."

The head of the administrative section of the department told me he was giving me a truck to use until the end of the day, a chauffeur would take me to the apartment and then move in my parents and me. It had to be done that day, because he wouldn't receive another truck again soon.

Sadovaia Street was a one-block beauty. The huge four-story building of the Kh. P. Z. where my father worked stood on the corner of Sadovaia and Chernoglazovskaia streets and had six entrances. The Chernoglazovskaia part with three entrances was fully occupied by the middle echelons of the Secret Police, the NKVD. The Sadovaia part was occupied by the bureacrats and the intelligentsia. Although the building belonged to the Kh. P. Z. and was built for their employees, only my father was an employee of the plant. All of the forty-eight apartments were occupied by somebody "better" than the workers or engineers of the plant. The dictatorship of the workers started to change into a cynical slogan. My apartment was a dream at that time of housing shortages—two good sized rooms, a nice kitchen, a bathroom with a bathtub, and a large entrance hall. I never would have had it if not for Demchenko's direct help. We arrived at my parents' home. I told Mama to start packing.

"What can I take? Is the room big enough?" she said.

Papa became excited and ran to a neighbor to borrow a bottle of vodka to treat a chauffeur to dinner. We arrived at Sadovaia close to midnight, trying not to make noise and not to present ourselves as savages. Papa and Mama were simply speechless. They didn't believe the whole apartment belonged to us. I had to tell them the story of how it happened. Finally, after four years, we were set in the city.

Olympiad fever started to infect many organizations and plant-factories; they sent more money than we expected. We decided to dress all members of the Olympiad in uniform. It wasn't easy to execute this because of the goods shortage. The Chairman of the Oblast government asked the manufacturing mill to send textile fabric to the districts. They sewed them up and we paid. All together there were about 850 children.

The opening of the Olympiad took place on a Sunday in the middle of August with a parade of the participants on Dzerzhinsky Square, which, as we liked to brag, was the largest square in Europe. In fact, the square actually was huge. In the center was the big platform for dignitaries from the Oblast Party and government, from different organizations and plants, many District Party Secretaries who brought their district children, as well as the shock-workers from the plants and *kolkhozes*, the best "excellent" pupils from Kharkov's schools, and many more. The city's residents filled up the huge square, including, of course, my parents and Mama Rosa. I introduced them later to Demchenko. There were several children's brass orchestras. The participants were organized by district, in smart uniforms with red young-pioneer neckties, the standard with the name of their district on the front.

The marshal of the parade and the Olympiad Committee, wearing the uniforms, opened the parade and then we took our places on

155

the platform. The atmosphere was not only festive, but highly emotional; many people were crying as they saw hundreds of happy children's faces. After years of famine and abuse, something really wonderful on a big scale involving the villages' children was happening. Hope was alive once again!

After passing the platform, the district groups were lined up next to it. After the parade, Demchenko, Novak, and the Chairman of the Olympiad Committee walked along the columns, talking to and thanking the children. Then the orchestras played and the children and public sang the anthem "International." It was the most powerful performance I had ever heard. A joyful celebration erupted—singing, dancing, mixing public and children.

The Olympiad competitions were going on for four days in two theaters: the Children's Theatre and the "Beresil" which were fully filled up by children and adults. The juries in both theaters as well as the general public were highly impressed with all kinds performances. The press broadly reported the event, speaking about the gold mine of the people's talents. For that time, this event and its organizations were completely new accomplishments.

After five days of incredible activities and triumphs, we bid farewell to these exceptional children. During those days, we tried to talk with many of them, to encourage and to praise them. I talked to many orphans, including that "cynical" boy. But he was now a different child, a little shy with smart, lively eyes who happened to be talented in many ways. He received an award and when I kissed him on the forehead (as I usually did) he looked at me with eyes full of tears. During the time I worked, I met hundreds of children. Some of them left a trace in my memory. Later, I wondered what could possibly have happened to them, thinking that probably WWII had gulped most of them down as their parents had been by famine.

All the newspapers of the oblast published Demchenko's long letter to the Olympiad Committee and to all who actively participated, praising them as educators of the socialist morals and ideals. He mentioned me as the originator of the idea. He provided an analysis of why the Olympiad was very important and what had to be done to preserve and further develop the Olympiad experience. Thinking now about what was done to children at the time of those abnormal hardships in the country still makes me both amazed, indignant and proud. What was done for children in the Kharkov city and Oblast was the accomplishment of local leadership and the people. Human progress among other indexes is judged by how the society brings up and treats its children. Now, I am afraid that humanity at large is falling much behind in this important task.

All the children were gone. I had a deep feeling of satisfaction with the work we had done. I was in my office writing a report about the Olympiad, rushing to finish it before Misha's arrival. It was the last summer he spent on some Industrial Project building in the Urals. There was a knock at the door and a tall, elegant, handsome man with a broad smile and lively, happy eyes stepped in, shining like a sun. It was Misha.

I introduced Misha to Novak. After some teasing, Novak told me that my vacation would start the next day and the report would be just as good in two weeks. At home, a company was gathering already. Misha's parents arrived. It was a happy time; everything was falling into place as we could only have dreamed and our expectations were only for the better. We didn't see any dark clouds over our sky. Incredibly, Misha stayed for two weeks, the first time in our two years of marriage. It looked as if we were a normal couple!

Misha was already accepted to *Asperantura* (the Graduate School), which meant after university graduation the following year, he planned to be in Moscow only two more years. After that, in 1938, it looked as if good luck was waiting for him.

"Do you know what kind of construction is starting just about ten blocks from here on Pushkin Street? It's the Scientific Institute of Experimental Physics, which will be under Academician Kapitsa's general direction. And, I will apply for a position as a junior scholar after graduating from *Asperantura*."

I planned to enroll the next year at Kharkov State University and at the night school at the Theatre Institute.

In spite of our general satisfaction, we were troubled by the new domestic upheavals. These were set off by the murder of a prominent Party member, the Leningrad Party Secretary, Sergei M. Kirov, on December 1, 1934. It immediately started a chain reaction of arrests and executions which had its climax in the great purge, the *Chistka* of 1937–38. The trial of the Kirov assassin, Nikolayev, was held in the jail "camera" with any legal assistance denied to him. In his famous secret speech of February 25, 1956, Khrushchev made known that Stalin himself was involved, and knew about or even ordered this assassination. Kirov had been in disagreement with some of Stalin's policies and wanted a more moderate political course.

On the wings of the Olympiad's success, considerable achievements were made in organizing children's clubs, sports places, and in improving schools. I visited a number of districts and more than once I was touched by the thanks of ordinary people for helping children. But I was starting to concentrate on preparing for the university entrance exams.

On April 1, 1936, I was relieved from my work and completely absorbed myself in studies. I successfully passed the exams and was accepted to the Faculty of History and Philosophy. Misha graduated from University in 1936 and took a few short courses on the graduate level because he didn't want to come home, fearful of disrupting my studies. Therefore, after my exams I left for Moscow for a whole month.

Kharkov, ultra-modern building on the Dzerzhinsky Square, built in 1931, by the Russian architect, to both disapproval and pride of Kharkov's people.

7

University Years

Visiting Misha at Moscow University

It was my first visit to Moscow—a city I had never seen before, but I loved it like something very close to me. It was a natural feeling—in a sense, Moscow was like a parent, guiding our everyday life. We disagree with parents sometimes, but usually we trust and love them. As Alexander Pushkin once wrote: *Moscow: those syllables can start/ A tumult in the Russian heart.*

The poet Shchipachev wrote, *"Moscow has a right to be proud of the glorious greatness of its fate."* Really, it is true! How many times since its birth in 1147 was the city destroyed, burnt out by invaders? Yet each time it rose from death and rejuvenated itself.

Misha and I explored the city and its history—its historical and architectural monuments, churches, museums, and art galleries, theaters, the Metro, and the Moskva River and parks. In 1935, the government accepted a general grandiose plan for Moscow's reconstruction. Thirty years later, for the 800th birthday of Moscow, the facts and numbers concerning that reconstruction were really hard to imagine. For instance, in the sixties, four-fifths of Moscow territory was occupied by the newly-built regions with a population of four million. Moscow has seventeen city regions, only four are the old city, inside the wide Boulevard ring which once completely encircled the old Moscow. It's a green strip of trees and flowers, very popular with people and children. Also, in the middle of this ring is a wide track for fast moving cars and buses.

Moscow is not only an administrative and political center, but a huge industrial, cultural, and scientific center as well. A few of them are the Academy of Science of the USSR (with many branches); the University; over 80 institutes (colleges); 66 museums; 26 theaters;

and more. Walking the streets of the old city, I was stunned and even more bewildered by the nation's history revealed all around by thousands of memorial plaques on the houses. Old Moscow is the huge historical and emotional museum of my nation.

Moscow is full of literary monuments. My favorite is the one for Alexander Pushkin on Pushkin's Square. The lines that he wrote are engraved on the monument:

> *I shall be loved and long the people will remember*
> *The kindly thoughts I stirred—my muse's brightest crown*
> *How, in this cruel age, I celebrated freedom*
> *And begged for truth for those cast down.*

These words are from the biographical poem *Monument,* which I loved and recited often. Although it was written about one hundred-seventy years ago during the time of Nikolay I, it reflected on our time in all respects.

What impressed me, as well as any non-Muscovite, was the city's vitality and something contrasting to that—the drabness of the people's appearance, the prevalence of the dreary black and brown colors of their clothes. Some faded and rusted signs over the stores presented an appearance of negligence.

Moscow State University (MGU) was established in 1755 by the first great Russian scholar, Mikhael Lomonosov, son of a peasant-fisherman from the north. After it burned in 1812 during the Napoleonic War, it was reconstructed and new buildings were added. It's situated on the Manezh Square facing the Kremlin. The new MGU was built after WWII on Lenin's Hills.

The early years of the university were very slow. The nobleman Novikov was exiled by Catherine from St. Petersburg to Moscow made Moscow University the center of intellectual life. Moscow returned to being a center of the revival of the pure Great Russian culture and past, developing a distaste for the French obsessions of St. Petersburg's upper crust. Here were born new ideas, radical ones included. A pleiad of celebrated personalities developed—scholars, political leaders, and literary figures. Belinsky, Herzen, Lermontov, Turgenev, Chekhov, S. Vavilov, V. Kliuchevsky, and many more, all educated at MU.

The appearance of the city was changing so fast that even a Muscovite could get lost. Architecture as an integrated art rooted in the classics adorned Russia in the late eighteenth and early nineteenth centuries. Later, the Russian National style was born by incorporating some additions from the old Russian style. Stalin's architectural style was characterized by the heavy outlines of civic buildings, sometimes with spires and other frills. One of the best monuments of this style is the Moscow Subway: vast, lots of light, beautifully ornamented by chandeliers, sculptures, mosaics, and stained glass. The luxury of the subway had a purpose. Citizens were told that this kind of accomplishment and beauty would be achieved in every field, including their personal lives. The Metro carried more than two million passengers a day to any destination for about a nickel. It was built primarily by the Moscow Komsomol as a monument to their selfless enthusiasm.

The appearance of the new Moscow with its wide green prospects, boulevards, parks, and monumental buildings made us feel good and proud. All around were the locomotive cranes used for building or moving buildings, or destroying the old wooden houses, often with their beautiful and priceless artistic wood carvings on the doors, around the windows and roofs. Churches were the first target for destruction.

At the beginning of the Revolution, Lenin gave a directive and a law was passed that all architectural historical monuments, including churches, had to be preserved. But after his death a *bacchanalia* of destruction was started, even over four hundred centuries-old architectural monuments were destroyed. From that great and unrepeated architectural human genius, only pitiful remnants are left. It was a crime!

Student Life

As a graduate student, Misha shared a dormitory room with another graduate student who moved out to the big general dormitory room for a month to give us privacy. "Room for two, but it's small for one," as the students ironically and rightly noticed. It held one narrow bed, one dilapidated couch, two small tables, and one chair. But we were unspeakably happy to have our privacy for a whole month.

161

Misha told me, "Now you understand why I didn't want you to enroll at Moscow University, and believe me, I tried hard to get a larger room at the dorms or out in the city, but no luck."

Every day hundreds of workers were coming from the villages to work in the city's reconstruction, to build the Metro and the industrial complexes around Moscow. Although it was summer recess, the dorms were far from empty. Some students were taking summer courses; others were working on building the Metro or something else. Understandably, these students were from the periphery, not Muscovites. I was amazed at their poorly-dressed appearance but, in contrast, their basic behavioral culture was acceptable. As students called themselves, "civilized beggars." In addition to the shortages in everything and the poverty in the villages, the outlook of the first decades of the Revolution was yet preserved, specifically that important was not one's appearance, but one's belief in a socialistic society and honest work for its realization. More than once I felt out of place, but Misha was wise and said that I belonged to the next step in the development of our society of well-to-do people. Stalin had already said he wanted to make all *kolkhoznics* rich.

At the university, Misha was well-known. He held various positions of leadership in Komsomol or general students' organizations.

Girls, the Komsomol members, building the
Moscow subway, 1934.

Now his friends were really interested in meeting his "secret." Misha told them his wife was very simple and her exceptionality probably consisted in her natural ability to feel and understand a human being, and her outstanding talent as a dramatic actress.

In the students' refectory, several students were waiting for us for dinner. I met them like good old friends. As usual, really exciting discussions developed. I felt intimidated because my knowledge and intellectual strength, compared to the best graduate students and intellectuals of the best university, were inadequate.

What did Soviet students talk about? Cars were not yet a reality. Neither were apartments, specifically well-furnished ones. Money? The more important was to get a position in a prestigious institution on a good track for advancement. Girls or boys? Naturally, that's an immortal theme for youth, but open talk about sex in mixed company was still unheard of; modesty prevailed. Understandably, talk about teachers, classmates, and one another was ever popular. Our main interest was concentrated on politics, both at home and abroad. This was followed by talk about books, movies, and theaters. But we considered ourselves the children of the Russian radical intelligentsia of the 19th century. Consequently, intellectual themes about the purpose of a human being's life, and belief in the goodness of the simple people all were in our blood. We were great idealists.

But now somehow conversation came around to the young people's subject. Misha's closest friend, Dimitry (Mitia), told us the secret of his heart, although Misha already knew it. He was planning to be married. His future wife had just graduated from the Institute and was a smart and intelligent girl from a well-educated working class family living in their own house in the Moscow suburbs. But somehow, he was afraid to go ahead and that's why he wanted to open his heart to Misha and me, and another married couple, both graduate students. We asked Mitia if his girlfriend excited him for her appearance, her behavior and thinking, and if he prepared himself to look and sound his best when meeting her.

"Is there an emotional joy when you look into her eyes," we asked.

"Not necessarily. It's normal."

"Then it sounds as if your love is not a holiday, not a celebration of a unity which lifts your soul, but a trivial routine of life."

"Have you read Stendhal's writing about love?" That wise man traveled into ever new regions of the human heart?

"Did Stendhal eulogize physical love?"

"Stendhal? Just the opposite. He thought if physical love was the basis of a relationship then it would be unsteady and probably love would be short-lived."

"What about Nikolay Chernishevsky's outlook on love in his book *What is to be Done?* It's interesting, but sometimes like a sermon, instructive. Chernishevsky had gone far beyond the idea of equality between the sexes. He thought what was needed was to grant women superior privileges, to compensate them for centuries of male domination."

"I followed some of Chernishevsky's advice," I confessed. "Do you remember how Chernishevsky wondered why a woman who is going out, where there is no one in particular whom she cares about, makes herself more attractive, although at home for her husband whom she loves, she doesn't care to make herself attractive but maintains a rather sloppy appearance with her hair in disorder. I try to avoid this feeling of triviality."

"Love as a mainly psychological feeling needs continuous attention and strengthening."

"When is love born?"

"Most often it is born in seeing a beauty or something attractive in the appearance, or behavior. That's why it's important to preserve what was seen that stimulated admiration."

The relation between the sexes and the problems of love were the hot topics of discussion among students. Some young women still conducted themselves as they did in the 1920s, aping men's behavior, signifying equality between the sexes by adopting a gruff voice, a cigarette on the lips, a leader jacket, and loutish manners, although among students this wasn't popular anymore. Once in our dinner discussion, the girls angrily protested some poets and writers still described women's beauty as being comprised of sumptuous breasts and tight hips, and it was a humiliation for women to be represented as a sex interest for men. The boy's comments were:

"Our time demands both that we adore women's natural beauty and that we respect women as equal members of our society."

"On the other hand, women themselves must not be allowed to cheapen love. Women's freedom in love doesn't mean they may have promiscuous relations with men. We are not in favor of Kollontay's ideas of the 'free love.' It means first of all that women are free to select their partners in life. Otherwise, it would certainly happen that love as the most deep and beautiful feeling of the human being would lose its value and lust take the place of love."

"That could be very dangerous and might bring the degeneration of our society if families were to fall apart."

Another time we were joined for dinner by a group of girls who wanted to know how and why a Ukrainian girl is better than a Muscovite.

The boys answered them, "You don't know yet, that Ukrainian girls are the most beautiful? They are tall with slim figures, not round barrels like some Russian girls are. Besides, Ukrainian girls are more conservative. Their demure bearing makes the boys easily lose their heads."

"Misha, is it true?"

"One hundred percent truth!"

The other time discussion turned to politics. Someone had read a new foreign book about a future political and social system for the world. There were several pretenders for the leadership role. It's hard for us to intelligently judge them—we don't know their scales of judgment, and their values we know superficially from our press and books. We judge each other from far distances, although close-ups always present a different picture than what is seen from a distance. Could we exist and survive together like that?

The claimed biological superiority of a nationality by Hitler's party as well as rule by a wealthy social class in Europe—both are antihuman. For us, our idea was the only righteous one, despite the fact that already we had seen the rude violations of that idea. We justified these "mistakes" as unavoidable, because what we were building was not yet known in human history. We were paving the way, making mistakes, correcting them and putting signs up for those who were going to follow us how to avoid them. We were the newest, the youngest country in the world, but what we created in eighteen years was not matched by any world miracle in history. We were already spoiled. Nothing astonished us anymore, even Alexei Stakhanov, who in one shift mined 102 tons of coal, exceeding the normal quota by 1,300 percent. We noticed more shortcomings than achievements.

This was dangerous for our political thoughts and behavior.

Misha's behavior toward me was still not much in practice among students—like kissing me on the cheeks in company, embracing me over the shoulders while walking. Once, a group of students whistled at us (a sign of disapproval). Misha stepped up to them and asked, "Tell me why innocent feelings of love for a wife have to be hidden?"

They agreed with Misha and said they just envied him. Then they asked me, "If we go to Kharkov, will you find us girls like yourself?" I promised I would if they would be as nice as Misha.

The old "cursed questions" were still part of our conversation. They were about human nature and the purpose of humans on earth, as well as about the role of the arts. These ideas had occupied the minds of the liberal and radical intelligentsia of the 19th century. Now someone asked if Prince Myshkin (from Dostoyevsky's *The Idiot*) was right in his statement that the single most important basic law for the whole human race was compassion toward a human being. A hot debate developed.

"This negates our Marxist idea of the 'class struggle.' Now, the human race consists of wolves and sheep. When humanity does away with the wolves, the greedy exploiters, then we will follow Prince Myshkin's ideas strictly. Certainly, no one would dare disagree with this Marxist dogma in public. Then, what is the "proletarian humanism," our ethical view? Those two basic views of ours—the "proletarian humanism" and the "class struggle" are contradictory. They cancel each other out. "Class struggle" is annihilation, even physical, of certain classes and their ideology. Humanism is freedom and tolerance of beliefs and thoughts. Any party ideology is not humanistic."

Misha's young professor and friend invited us to dinner while his family was vacationing. We brought some food and wine. Dinner preparation was a joint effort and a lot of fun. Hearty, witty conversation, but I couldn't stop watching him. His face was very expressive and handsome, but of different bone structure; as he explained, he was a mixture of Scythian and Polovets ancestry. Scythians were an Asiatic tribe who came to the south, now Ukrainian territory, in the eighth century B. C. and subjugated the Slavic tribes living there, but with time were assimilated by the Slavs. As Alexander Blok wrote in his famous poem, *To the Slanderers of Russia*, "Yes, we are the

Scythians/ Yes, we are the Asians . . . "

The professor gave a broad picture of higher education, specifically of humanities at the universities.

"It's not the best time to study humanities. Why? The majority of universities, especially in the Ukraine, have serious shortages of professors. To say this is not to present a full picture. There's practically an absence of scholarly-prepared professors to teach on the University level. We haven't yet replaced those who left the country in the 1920s. Now, some of those who stayed home, as well as many new professors considered as Nationalists, have been arrested.

"Also, Universities don't have textbooks in Russian history, general philosophy, literary criticism, and in other subjects. Two excellent multi-volume histories of Russia by Professors Sergey Soloviev and Kliuchevsky are both now withdrawn for usage, as well as Pokrovsky's sociological approach to history. A book created for the guidance of the science of history could be ready in a few years. Unfortunately, our intellectuals still have not resolved to what extent our culture has to absorb the heritage of the past, including spiritual life because of its political meaning. But over sixty-five percent of our students are in the science faculties—physics, mathematics, chemistry, biology, geology. These are our country's urgent needs.

"Our National policy is overhandled now," he said and asked for a secret between us. "Look, in 1918 Lenin's government reconstituted the country as a multi-ethnic empire, USSR. Even the name Russia was struck down. It's constituted of the ethnically-named territorial administrative units, like the Ukrainian Soviet Socialist Republic, the Bashkir Authonomous Soviet Socialist Republic, and others. The government did a great deal to encourage development of non-Russian education, history, ethnography, and folklore. It was an aim to create a United State, consisting of the cultured and economically developed societies from the Siberian eskimos to the Soviet European Republics. *The dogma was that the Soviet culture has to be National by form and Socialist by content, ideology.* The Party fight against nationalism has to be not against a form, like language, but against the forces for the National exclusiveness, separation. In theory the Party aspires to provide the psychological basis for the creation of a Soviet nation of the multi-ethnic cultures cemented and based on the well-developed Russian European culture. It was developing, but recently it is overhandled, exaggerated to a level against the country's interests."

Once, at dinner in a cafeteria, we had an exciting conversation about books. Russians have a passion for books, probably like no other nation. A book for any occasion, especially when it is an unusual one, is a welcome present. Even for a newborn baby, a subscription for one volume per year of the Soviet Encyclopedia was proudly presented. Now Misha's friend wanted to find a book for his girlfriend's birthday. But it wasn't easy because she was from an Old Bolshevik family who worshipped books. They had a philosophy about them: the book never dies, like a sequoia tree, which lives for thousands of years, though if it is deprived of water and sun it will die. The source of the book is the human soul, human ideals, which never die. Therefore, the book is the immortal reality of the human world. Great personalities of the world were also great readers.

"So, what kind of book would be the most appropriate?"

"How to furnish an apartment when you get married," someone sneered. We laughed.

"For sure, they would show me to the door."

"How about existentialist philosophy?"

"I couldn't find anything about it." We discussed this philosophy a little and summarized it as "A human being in a situation."

"Who knows where to find anything of N. Berdiaev? His analysis of the Russian character, Russian soul, and Russian Revolution is eventful."

Another time, we were having a good laugh when a group of students joined us. They were irritated and laughing, talking about English tourists, women from some women's organizations who had come to their class for a talk. Ivan Turgenev, a writer, was right that Russians have some dislike for English tourists because of their haughty behavior, and disdain of everything foreign to them. He wrote their appearance was not pleasing: cold eyes and long, rabbit-like teeth. The other students disagreed, saying the English girls were attractive with their healthy white teeth.

"The women didn't even try to conceal their suspicion of us. But when they told us that communism is an immoral system, we stopped smiling and methodically compared two systems: communism with captialism. They had no choice but agreed with us that communism is a moral system by design (the Stalin terror still was in the future) and capitalism is less moral because it does not practice social justice. Their ignorance about Russia's past and present was simply comic.

They understood it and tried to cover with self-assurance and a superior tone of voice."

Many-sided problems of *culturnost* were of great significance for us. We understood it as the civilizing process of self-control and self-transformation; personal acquisition of knowledge in all fields from geography to music, and certainly ideology and politics. Above all, active participation in collective life, egalitarianism.

In the library, we took a few books on culture and discussion erupted. Books published in the beginning of the 1920s emphasized personal hygiene, proper behavior, and etiquette. Books published at the end of the 1920s and later propagate creation of a Soviet specific behavior, in the sense that Soviet men and women must be a unique creature, cultured, and not greedy for material possessions. A book just published looks like it was addressing the new class of rulers: the Party, and the intelligentsia elite, who may accept general values of a good life, refinement at home, in behavior, and in speech, but still some Soviet exclusiveness expressed in egalitarianism. Later, in the post-Stalin era, consumerism became a normal feature of *culturnost*. It was a clear evolution from the Soviet exclusiveness to the general values, especially for *nomenklature*.

The Two White Doves

Mitia was from a family of Russian radical intelligentsia and lived with his grandparents in a suburb of Moscow. Misha had been a guest in Mitia's grandparents' home, but now Mitia wanted to introduce me. We bought several bottles of wine and some food and took a suburban train, which atypically started to run on time. It was an exciting treat. I met true representatives of the famous radical intelligentsia of the second part of the nineteenth century. We had studied and read a lot about the extolled heroism of that unusual movement. Husband and wife, were in their middle eighties, slender with white hair, white faces with young eyes, clean white clothes. Something pure, like holiness, emanated from them.

Their appearance made me very emotional. I stepped up to the grandmother and made a deep bow, took her hands and kissed them. Her husband didn't want to let me kiss his hands.

"Please, let me express my deep respect for you as the living truth of that heroic and selfless historical movement."

We spent two happy days of talk and fun. In fact, we mostly listened and asked questions. I walked around their home, looking at old pictures, letters, news clippings, attestates, presents from the bygone days. With my love of history, it was hard to even imagine a more perfect place. The excitement overcame me. From these "two doves," as we called them, emanated a serene calm and we were drawn into it.

The elder man was talking with pleasure. He gave us a look into the heroic Populist movement:

"In the middle of the 1870s, when I was a Moscow University student, the Populist movement seized our hearts and minds. We were captivated by the German philosophy of Hegel. The Germans accepted the Hegelian idea that the state was an expression of the world spirit. But for us, our state was immoral because it treated over eighty percent of its population not as Christian humans but as cattle. Consequently, this state had to be annihilated. The leader of the Westernizers was an outstanding personality, one of the 'conscious-stricken gentry,' Count Alexander Herzen. He and others developed the socio-political program of Russian 'Populism.' It's a mistake to think Herzen wanted Russia to follow the West in all of its economic development. He thought, in accordance with Russia's specific character and national history, the ideal for Russia would be to have free peasants' communes. Herzen's call to the intelligentsia, 'Go to the people! Educate them!' was answered by a whole generation of idealistic young people. Populism was deeply rooted in Russian mystical views about *muzhiks*, peasants. Vissarion Belinsky, Chernishevsky, and Nekrasov idolized them, and many publicists, critics, writers, and poets were inspired by this movement and saw their work as their 'moral obligation' to the people. The whole of Russian culture, especially literature, was under the remarkable influence of Belinsky's ideas which played a formative role in changing society, in disseminating new ideas. In the 1890s, when Marxist ideas from Europe flooded Russia, the public mind was ready to accept them."

The "two white doves" were great lovers of poetry, especially Pushkin and Nekrasov. When Misha told them about my talent for reciting poetry, I had to recite (without exaggeration) for hours. They were happy as children, kissing me. I had given them deep emotional and aesthetic pleasure, they said.

The elder said, "In the summer of 1874, thousands of idealists went to the villages. I, too, with a friend rushed to a village. We dressed in peasant clothes and walked, then talked to peasants in their *izbas*, explaining our ideas and plans for their future. They agreed with our general ideas and liked to listen, but sometimes merely considered us not wholly sane, laughing at our lack of knowledge of peasant life. But they told us more than once, 'You are good Christians. You have a heart for poor people.' We were lucky. The peasants snatched us out of the village before the police arrived to arrest us. Many of our people were not as lucky and spent many years in jails and in Siberia. The Populists' generation of 1874–75 and the years after were more than heroes; they were saints who, without hesitation, gave their young lives for the lofty purpose of improving peasants' conditions and changing the whole of Russia's political and social structure."

He recited the lines from Lermontov's poem *Borodino* for fun:

Yes, there were heroes in our time
Not like the contemporary generation
They were the knights, heroes, not you.

His wife was also an active revolutionary. They met in the revolutionary circles. "Our idols Herzen and Dobroliubov were dead, Chernishevsky was in Siberia, and Nekrasov was dying." He was the publisher of a radical magazine, *Contemporary* (Pushkin had originated it).

The elder continued: "On December 27, 1877, Nekrasov died in St. Petersburg. A group of us rushed to his funeral. There were huge crowds and all political groups were present. A group of socialists organized the singing of revolutionary songs which were censored, but the police did not stop the singing and this was clearly a political manifestation. Among the speakers at the funeral were Dostoevsky and Plekhanov. Dostoevsky spoke softly and looked tired. He put Nekrasov's poetry equal in importance to Pushkin's—the highest in Russian literature. The Socialists cried out, 'No! No! Nekrasov was higher!' Dostoevsky was a little confused, but repeated his position. Plekhanov, who introduced Marxism to Russia, was a good orator. He spoke about Nekrasov's deep love for the Russian peasants and how, in his poetry, he gave a broad picture of their hard life and their overall good character."

The grandpa had met and talked to many well-known revolutionaries, including Lenin whom he worshipped. It was extraordinary information.

Mitia was still disturbed. He felt obligated to his fiancee, but his physical attraction to her was waning. "Look," he said, "it's funny, odd thinking, but it has a serious meaning. When we walk on the streets or in the art galleries, people look at Nina with an expression of approval for her classic appearance. You, Misha, proudly hold her hand. No one looks at Lena, though she is not bad-looking. But her whole appearance and conduct are not appealing. I like that she is a smart, intelligent and a good human. I don't know what to do."

Misha got mad at him for confusing appearance, really *shmatas* (clothing), with the essence of a human being. In Misha's opinion, Mitia's point was superficial and shallow.

Mitia was still holding his ground. "I remember some lines of the poet Vasiliy Fedorov: *She is not a girl/ She is not pretty/ If no one looks at her.*"

The New Theatrical Art

In the 1930s, Moscow had twenty-six theaters. The most famous ones were the Bolshoi, the Art Theater, Maly Theater, and Tchaikovsky Conservatory. We visited the Maly, situated across the square next to the Bolshoi. They were built simultaneously; the Maly opened in October 1824, and the Bolshoi in January 1825. Close collaboration existed between the Maly and the dramatist N. Ostrovsky, who wrote forty-eight plays for the theater depicting the life of the merchant class, the peasantry, and the morals of Russian society. It was the theater of realism with the most famous actors ever, like Shchepkin, Mochalov, and Yermolova. I wanted to see *The Thunderstorm*, in which I had acted the leading role of Katerina, but it wasn't in the repertory at the time. My passionate wish to see *The Seagull* in the Art Theater came true. I dreamed of acting the role of Nina in that play.

Finally, we were at Pushkin Street in front of a three-story building with the Seagull emblem on the front, the theater which changed theatrical art in Russia and profoundly influenced it in Europe and

America. It started on June 21, 1898 when Vladimir Nemerovich-Danchenko, a nobleman, met Konstantin Stanislavsky (Alexeyev) in a private room of the restaurant *Slaviansky Bazaar* for a "chat" at two in the afternoon until six the next morning. These two theatrical visionaries came to the same conclusions and conceived the same hopes. Later, Stanislavsky defined it. Their program was revolutionary; they rebelled against the old way of acting, false pathos, declamation and exaggeration, those routine expressions of grief, joy, or love, with the accepted hardened body movements. These were usually played with bad production and sets. It was against the star system which ruined the ensemble, its whole presentation of the play's meaning, and the spirit of the performance. To make it worse, they had insignificant repertoires.

A new era had begun for the Russian theater; on December 29, 1898, the Theater presented Chekhov's *The Seagull*. The whole company was in a state of incredible tension. Two years before, the play was crushed at the Alexandrinsky in St. Petersburg. But here, after the third act, there was frenzied applause and excitement in the Hall and then celebration and triumph of the whole company. It was a theatrical miracle: the Moscow Art Theater had found its style. It produced modern plays using realistic (naturalistic) detail for the purpose of creating a psychological mood and character. Chekhov's style of psychological plays was marvelously fitted to the aspirations and experiments of the theater. It was an "ideal marriage," as it was later called, this fateful alliance between the playwright and the theater. When the theater moved into its permanent building, the flying seagull ornamented the curtain, programs, posters, tickets, and the building itself.

Later, the "Stanislavsky method" known to the world could be expressed in general as a system in which the poet (the playwright), the actor, the painter, the stage designers, the dressmakers, and the make-up men all worked toward one goal: to express the meaning, the essence of the author's idea. The actor had to find genuine and fresh ways to express the physical and emotional characteristics of the character, to find the right voice intonations and gestures. After seeing *The Seagull*, I better understood what was involved in being an actress and I wanted to be one with all my might.

Across the street from the Maly was the Children's Theater which opened in 1921 when the Civil War was still going on.

Forty years later in 1976, I witnessed in Moscow something that was hard to believe was true. At the Taganka Theatre was staged *The Master and Margarita*, a play based on the novel by Mikhail Bulgakov. The modernist director Yuri Lyubimov produced this mystical fantasy about a Devil who came to Moscow and played his Satanic tricks on various people. It was a biting, sardonic critique of Party policy and Soviet life. For instance, people go to the street where Satan lives, but all of them mysteriously disappear. The obvious analogy was to Stalin's NKVD. The audience simply went crazy. The play was done cleverly in high artistic creativity, subtle, but on the edge of danger to be in Satan's corner of no return. It happened to be a period of "softness" in the Party's cultural policy.

Maxim Gorky's Death

Once, in the morning we heard funeral music on the radio and then an announcement of Maxim Gorky's death by the Communist Party's Central Committee and the government's Executive Council. He was a very popular writer as well as a good human being. He was of a simple background, from the lower Volga region, Nihzniy Novgorod, now Gorky. He had genuine Socialist convictions and before the Revolution, lived in exile on the island of Capri while Lenin lived in Switzerland. They were close friends.

His early works were in the romantic style, presenting the strong positive characters of simple people (*Chelkash, Makar Chudra*). Later he wrote epic novels in the realistic style about Russian society. The popularity of his literary works was great and brought him a good income, which he spent in helping the revolutionary cause, specifically in publishing the newspaper *Pravda* abroad before the Revolution. In 1934 at the First Congress of the Union of Writers, Andrei Zhdanov, Stalin's aid for cultural affairs, pronounced the doctrine of "socialist realism." To give it a measure of respectability, Gorky was make president of the Congress and then of the Union of Writers. He was a human with a "big" heart. He wrote about a dreadful old custom among the peasants in his short story *Conclusion*. But he omitted the fact that he was a witness and a victim of this custom.

The story: A young *muzhik*, a peasant, standing in his cart whipped his horse and his young wife, herself almost still a child, completely naked, badly flogged and running next to the horse to

174

which she was attached. The *muzhik* thought that she was unfaithful to him. The crowd along the street was noisily laughing, supporting the husband. By chance, a young man saw this frightful scene and came running to stop it. But the crowd would not allow this and the strong man, was left to fight against the crowd alone. They beat him badly and threw him in a ditch. He survived and the broken ribs healed, but the pain remained forever. The young hero was Gorky himself. That was his character, to react immediately to any injustice.

During the Civil War famine, Gorky received some government support and helped writers, actors, and intellectuals to survive.

In Moscow for some time rumors had been circulating that Gorky was a prisoner in his own *dacha*, his death was not natural, but he was poisoned. At this time, Andre Gide, the prominent French writer, was in Moscow at the Soviet government's invitation because he had openly proclaimed himself a sympathizer of the Soviet Union and of Stalin personally. There was a rumor Gide would speak at Gorky's funeral on the Red Square. A group of students from the dorms organized themselves in a column, took a red flag and the university standard, and we marched to the Red Square. But the big organized columns, as usual, would not accept smaller sized ("wild") columns and the police cordons told us, "Get out, we don't know who you are."

Gide was standing on the reviewing platform on the Lenin mausoleum beside Stalin and other leaders. He was not allowed to speak or talk to Bukharin and other opposition members, nor to tour the country freely. Later in his book he expressed much praise for the country, especially for the people, their humanism and enthusiasm. But he also revealed some criticisms, specifically about freedom—that on any subject there could be only one opinion, which Stalin pronounced. Gide, a product of the French skeptical tradition, understood that the unanimity of thoughts because of state control over the arts could cause the death of the culture, the original and rich Russian culture. After this book, Andre Gide was out of favor in the official Moscow.

The Show Trials Begin

An event of immense historical proportion occurred during the time I was in Moscow. On August 19, 1936, the first show trial of the opposition leaders began, the group of sixteen defendants, the so-called "Trotskyite-Zinovievite Terrorist Center." It was an unforgettable shock for the whole country.

Zinoviev and Kamenev were close friends of Lenin. After the Revolution of 1917 they were the very top leaders of the country. Now in calm voices, presumably willingly, they told about their roles in the assassination of Kirov and their plans to kill Stalin and other members of the Politburo to take power and establish a government headed by Trotsky. All of them, except one, gave uniform testimony about their treasonable plans and deeds. They mentioned that Bukharin, Rykov, Tomsky, and many other heads of various government branches and organizations and members of the Central Party Committee were involved in a conspiracy. Throughout the country in the factories, government institutions, Universities, Colleges and villages, public meetings demanded the execution of the "mad dogs" and an investigation of the others. The majority of people believed in Stalin. Doubts easily vanished after reading newspapers or, more decisively, listening to the radio the defendants' personal confessions. It was a blood-chilling experience, when one after another they calmly told about their vicious crimes.

The behavior of students also changed noticeably. Each one had a newspaper in hand and sat in small groups in the cafeteria, reading and discussing it. Usually, their discussions were rather loud, but not now. In our group discussions were open and sincere; trust existed among these few friends. What distressed us incredibly was the question of whom to believe. Those "sixteen" were the Old Bolsheviks, Lenin's cohorts. We had no choice but to believe in Stalin. We thought we knew what had gone wrong in our government planning and its realization. But we didn't know all, didn't understand, and consequently were not able to make judgments. We were positive that the defendants were telling the truth about their dreadful plans and deeds. Therefore, we thought, there had to be a very significant reason for them to take these actions by treason and terror. They knew in advance they would lose their heads, but did it anyway. Why?

All of us were obsessed with this trial and talked about it endlessly. I don't think it frightened us. We made the logical historical comparison: the French Revolution of 1789 after a while split and the Jacobins sent the Zherondists, Danton, and the "mads" to the guillotine.

"We destroyed first the Social-Revolutionaries, then the Mensheviks, then Zinoviev's faction together with Stalin destroyed the Trotskyites. Each revolution passes through different phases and accordingly, different classes and parties take part. Consequently, the actions of the Revolution come into clashes with the interests of certain parties and classes. It is an inevitable development of any revolution."

"But if it's a normal process, then when does the Revolution start to evolve peacefully?"

"Who knows? If never, then our country and people are in danger."

Silence. Everyone lowered their eyes, except for Misha. "You are not right. All of us know that our society will consist of working people—peasants in the field, workers in the factories, and intelligentsia. The division of wealth will be among those who toil. It's not too long from now when we will have a classless society, meaning that there will be no reason for class conflicts."

Even though hundreds of "why" questions overwhelmed us, we looked for explanations and most often thought we found them. Our spirit was still courageous. We didn't know the extent of the terror.

After four days of the trial, all "sixteen" were sentenced to death and execution was carried out the following day. Stalin waited late into the night until the executioner reported to him personally that all of them were dead and how it happened. After hearing this news with sadistic satisfaction, he went to bed. He did the same every time there was an execution of famous people, his friends, with some of whom he had spent years in Siberian exile or jails.

There were two more trials like this one. They involved the well-known Old Bolsheviks who prepared and carried out the Revolution. They were the first group destroyed by Stalin with the help of his morally and politically corrupt lieutenants, while stupefied members of the Politburo and Central Party Committee were silent.

In 1989, an excellent 900-page documentary book titled *Let History Judge* by historian Roy Medvedev was published. I am using some factual material from this book. I lived and suffered through this time of terror, but while reading Medvedev's work, I was not only in emotional pain, I was profoundly ashamed of the top leaders around Stalin whom we practically worshipped and imagined as human-giants, though in retrospect, they looked rather like pygmies. They were afraid to stand up for the truth and inform people about it.

Medvedev made clear all show trials of the 1930s were completely fraudulent. Devilish and skillful forms were employed to break each prisoner physically and psychologically, including physical methodical beating, artful tortures, like keeping a victim on a "conveyor" sometimes for days, practically without food or sleep, and using certain will-depriving medications and hypnosis. It's worth noting that a well-known hypnotist, Arnoldo, "disappeared" after the trials. Some were given promises. Bukharin was told that his young wife (his recent first marriage), baby son, and father would not be touched. They continued living in their Kremlin apartment and his wife was allowed to deliver him books, letters, and photographs of their son till Bukharin was broken and began to "testify" and signed the confession composed by the NKVD. Then at once everything was changed: his family was evicted from the Kremlin apartment, and his wife and father were arrested and sent to Gulags.

In his famous testament, Lenin considered Bukharin as "the rightful favorite of the Party," meaning he was a leader of the Party. But Stalin could not stand anyone, not Bukharin or Kirov, whose popularity and intelligence were greater than his. On many occasions, Stalin played shameful games of cat and mouse with Bukharin, trying to break him psychologically before his arrest. In one, a group of Chekists (NKVD) came to Bukharin's Kremlin apartment and served him a notice of eviction. Bukharin panicked. What to do with his huge library and archives, besides his young pregnant wife, the big love of his life?

Suddenly, the internal Kremlin phone rang. It was Stalin. "How are you, Nikolay?"

Bukharin told him what was going on and Stalin roared, "Chase them the hell out of there!" They left immediately. It was planned: possibly Stalin had ordered them to be sent.

In February of 1936, the Plenum meeting of the Party Central Committee expelled Bukharin and Rykov (head of the government after Lenin's death) from the Party, slandering them as most ignoble criminals. Waiting for his arrest and death, Bukharin wrote a letter, "To a Future Generation of Party Leaders," and asked his wife Anna Larina to memorize it. After testing her several times, he burned it.

Anna Larina spent many years in prisons and exile, but survived.

178

After the Twentieth Party Congress, where Khrushchev exposed Stalin's crimes, she submitted the text of the letter to the Party's Central Committee. In her memoirs, she said she often recited the letter to herself in order not to forget it. Their baby son was taken from her. When a teenager, he was sent to prison and spent years in different prison camps. His mother met him when he was in his twenties.

Before he was arrested, Bukharin kissed his nine-month-old son, then fell on his knees before his wife, asking tearfully for forgiveness and telling her he was not guilty of anything. Just before his execution on the night of March 15, 1938, a calm Bukharin asked for a pencil and a sheet of paper. His brief letter to Stalin began with the words, "Koba, why did you need my death?"

Tretiakov's Gallery

We were in the Tretiakov Gallery of Russian Art. In the 1850s, the wealthy Moscow merchants and outstanding personalities Pawel Mikhailovich Tretiakov and his brother Sergei began collecting pictures of Russian artists and icons with the patriotic idea of establishing a national museum. It was a time of almost stormy growth of national consciousness. Russia had outgrown her feudal serfdom and turned to the capitalist way of developing. The new social and democratic forces came to life.

In 1863 at the Academy of Arts in St. Petersburg, which had the tradition of being a neo-classical academy, a group of fourteen graduating artists declared their secession. This heroic gesture could have been economic suicide for them. Their ideal was of "bringing art to the people." They called themselves the "Wanderers" and planned to organize the traveling exhibitions all over the country. The "Mighty Five," the nationalist composers Balakirev, Moussorgsky, Borodin, Rimsky-Korsakov, Kui, and their followers such as Tchaikovsky, and others accepted the ideas of Russian nationalism in music. The writers and poets Tolstoy, Turgenev, Dostoyevsky, Nekrasov and many more as artists and composers who were in the avant-garde of this movement thought their cultural activities must be useful to society to educate people. In 1892, the Tretiakov brothers gave their Gallery as a gift to the people of Moscow.

I wanted to see first the icons in the collection and here we were standing in front of the *Trinity* of the monk Andrei Rublev (1370–1430). His icons are the artistic summit of Russian iconography. Rublev's masterpiece is unsurpassed in aesthetic and theological refinement. The visitors to the Biblical figures Abraham and his wife Sara, the three angels representing the Holy Trinity, are depicted in an unobtrusive circle, a symbol of eternity, dressed in transparent garments. The general characteristices of the icon are the light brilliant colors, the purity of lines, and simplicity of composition.

The first public "Wanderers" exhibition in 1872 was bought by two influential collectors—the future emperor Alexander III and the Tretiakov brothers. The Slavophile Tsar Alexander III did much to collect Russian medieval and contemporary art. Several museums were opened including the best *Russian Museum of Emperor Alexander III* in St. Petersburg, now the State Russian Museum. The superb Neo-classical Mikhailovsky Palace was given by the Tsar for this purpose. If in the 18th century art was collected by the aristocracy, now in the 19th century that practice was replaced by the new concept that the arts were a means of education and cultural advancement of the general population. The aristocracy and wealthy individuals were giving their collections and money to the museums and galleries.

Ilia Repin (1844–1930) was the greatest and the most influential artist in this new movement. He made the genre painting specifically important not only by its contents, which generalized and depicted the realism of life, but by its lofty aesthetic standards and psychological treatment of characters. He created several images of the populist-revolutionaries. One of these was *They Did Not Expect Him*. It depicts the episode of a political exile returning home and realistically shows the psychological reaction of the members of his family. I felt the emotions of those people. The clearness of the composition and the light strengthened the dramatization of the picture.

Repin, as well as Surikov and others, created several big paintings on historical subjects. *Ivan Grozvy and His Son Ivan* melodramatically conveyed the horror of a father who unintentionally killed his son. We saw only a father, not a Tsar, crazy with grief, with his fingers trying to stop the blood flowing from his son's temple. He embraced him, but death had already touched him visibly. The only lighted figures are the two tightly embracing on the floor, father and son against the red carpet with puddles of blood and the dark chamber. People who had soft nerves were advised not to see this picture as it exerted a powerful psychological effect.

The other picture which made a sensation at home and abroad in France was *The Volga Boatmen*. It reflected the social problems of the hard life of bargehaulers. Repin's mastery of portraiture depicted many famous people like Tolstoy, Dostoyevsky, Tretiakov, Mussourgsky, as well as many of the Tsar's ministers and a gallery of peasant characters. A spectator has the sensation of seeing people each with his own different life and nature.

Vasily Surikov, *Sibiriak* (man from Siberia), created many large canvasses depicting the Russian past. The most famous of these are *Boyarinia Morosova* and *Morning of the Streltsi Execution*.

The Golden Age of landscape painting is connected with the name of Isaak Levitan (1860–1900), who continued the work of the talented landscape artists Polenov, Kuingzhi, Savrasov, and many others. Levitan felt the character of the Russian people was the incarnation of the Russian landscape, with its expansiveness, broadness, feeling of endlessness and the eternity of life, longing for God and for His truth. I had in my home copies of two of his famous paintings, *Golden Autumn* and *Vladimirka*, the endless road on which arrestants walked to Siberia.

The most remarkable collectors, the industrialist Savva Morozov and Sergei Shchukin, were pioneer purchasers of Post-Impressionist French paintings, like those of Cezanne, Gauguin, and Matisse, and some of the Impressionist paintings including Renoir. These paintings are now in the Pushkin Museum of Visual Arts in Moscow. The collection served to reveal to the young Russian artists the latest developments of the French school. Also purchased were works by Van Gogh and fifty paintings and drawings by Picasso.

At the same time, Savva Mamantov, an intensely patriotic railway magnate who played an important part in the cultural developments of the country, organized an artists' colony at his country estate of Abramtsevo near Moscow. Great artists, some with their families, settled there and worked together and a new cultural movement developed.

Particularly interesting were two young artists, Valentin Serov and Mikhail Vrubel. Serov implemented the technical innovations of Western painting. Later he became the Court painter. His outstanding portrait of Nicholas II is among his best psychological studies. It's unusual to make a portrait of a sovereign in the form of a character study. Vrubel' fell under the influence of Byzantine art techniques. Later, he infatuated himself with the depiction of a Demon as a lonesome, unhappy figure searching for love. They and others were pioneers in the "World of Art" group which reacted against the aesthetic values of realism of the "Wanderers." They were subsequently headed by Sergei Diaghilev, an aristocrat and impresario who introduced to the West the new revolutionary Russian art, the Russian opera with Fedor Shaliapin, and Russian ballet with Anna Pavlova, Kazimir Nijinsky, and composer Stravinsky.

In the beginning of the 20th century, the avant-garde movements emerged, different groups each engaged in revolutionary techniques. The artists Larionov, Malevich, Tatlin, Chagall, Kandinsky, Goncharova, and many more presented Russian Suprematism, Abstract Expressionism, Primitivism, Cubism, Constructivism, and more. All of these artistic movements were using different techniques, yet almost all of them followed a similar philosophy. Instead of realistic records of life, they presented interpretations of their emotional feelings toward reality. Moscow became a meeting place for the most revolutionary movements in European art. I simply fell in love with Larianov's and Goncharova's primitive style of painting and with Goncharova's icon paintings, characteristic of her brilliant range of color and strong linear rhythm. European and American art was profoundly affected by these Russian revolutionary movements in art.

Many of these paintings are exhibited in Tretiakov's Gallery. Self-declared prophets tried to judge, "What is art and what is not art." It didn't sound convincing. History again provided an insight: archaeology, in digging deep into human beings' pasts, discovered no stage in human existence without art, and yet all of them were different.

Frankly, this sketch of the Russian art presented in Tretiakov's collection does not do justice to the subject. I have been in the Tretiakov Gallery many times and each time I had an extraordinary feeling I saw Russia, I had passed through the centuries of her life, and saw her people and her landscape. I felt her happiness, her grief, her pain. It is an absolutely unique National Institution.

"Boyarinia Morozova" by V. Surikov, 1887. The old believer taken to her imprisonment and death is driven through Moscow Streets.

**Andrei Rublev's "Trinity," painted in 1411. Rublev influenced
a style of Russian religious painting.**

Our Parting

After a month of being together, our parting was painful as never before. The inner, quiet, emotional and physical happiness intensely united us. We believed that happiness was inside a human being, and wouldn't come from the outside if the inside were not serene.

In parting, Misha gave me an exquisite and exceptional present, a small book of Alexander Blok poetry of intimate lyrics about women and to women. We read some of the poems together aloud and felt he was writing about our feelings, making us understand each other's souls and love more deeply. Blok's poetry was poles apart from the modern Soviet poetry published in newspapers and magazines, which sounded like a drum beat calling for action, but left no feeling of warmth in the heart for another human being. To find a book of Blok's poetry was an almost impossible task. It was not yet republished.

At Home

My mood was like a roller coaster—up and down. My personal life was happy: a loving husband and family. All around there was progress, changes. Yet it was clear something was going very wrong. No one, myself as well, dared to express thoughts freely if they were even a trifle different from what was in *Pravda*. Although this phenomenon was not new, what was new was the fear, the knowledge the "justice" of the NKVD was dangerous. A saying that was spoken in a whisper between friends:

"Who yet wasn't there, will be in time. Who was already there and is still alive, will never forget it."

Afterwards, when I visited my *Krestnaia* and family, I would also visit my friend, Lida, who lived on the same street just a few houses away. Lida worked at the Department of the Young Pioneers of the Oblast Komsomol Committee. We had worked together on the Olympiad Committee. She was a wonderful human, a model for me. When she talked, everyone listened, although she spoke in a soft, gentle voice. She was always kind and ready to help anyone in need. Always neat in appearance, she had big gray eyes, a pleasant smile, not tall but rather plump. She liked to repeat whoever is sloppy in appearance is often sloppy in behavior and thinking as well.

We usually went to lunch togerher. Then, Abrahm, a worker of the City's Communist Party Committee began to join us. After a while, I told Lida that he was in love with her.

She smiled. "Yes, he told me."

"And what is your feeling about it?" I said.

"Guess!"

"Are you in love with him?"

"Yes, we are going to marry. My parents like him very much."

It's hard to imagine a pair who were created to match each other—two really good human beings. A few weeks later they were married. Abrahm's friend and I were witnesses at the registration office and then we had dinner in Lida's parents' home where the newlyweds were living. Her parents were known all over Kharkov. Both were Old Bolsheviks together in jail and then in Siberia. They were the very opposite of Lida—both very loud and straightforward. Probably they were the only people who still spoke their thoughts openly, but were always saying "our Stalin," giving him full support. Her father liked to have fun and told amusing stories about his revolutionary activities. People liked them and came for advice and help. Later, Lida left her work and had a baby daughter.

After a visit with my *Krestnaia*, I stopped to see Lida and her family. Both Lida and Abrahm were home, happy to see me, but they had changed. It looked like they had lost half their weight. I adored their baby and brought her a present. Then Lida, in her gentle voice, told a horrible story—her parents had been arrested and she was not sure if they were still alive. She was expelled from the Communist Party as a daughter of the "folk's enemies." Abrahm was expelled from work and a decision about his Party membership not yet made. Lida advised me that I'd better not come to see them. I answered I would and did several times, brought some food, and gave them some money.

More Painful Questions

Since 1936 the whole country had been in a high fever of struggle against the "enemies of the people," who were supposedly all over and planning to destroy the Socialist state. The newspapers were publishing stories about "spies" and "wreckers" caught sometimes just by the young pioneers. Stories like this:

A group of young pioneers noticed a foreign man, not from their village and dressed differently, walking through the fields of wheat. They were positive he was a spy, so they took big heavy sticks and ran after him, telling him they were arresting him. They didn't believe what he said he was and they brought him to the village council.

"O, Tovarishch X, where were you?" the chairman of the council said. "We were looking for you to show you our fields."

He was a representative of the Oblast Party Committee. Anyway, the young pioneers were highly praised for their class vigilance.

The tragical truth was that the "enemies of the people" and their crimes were created in the terror chambers of the NKVD where defenseless, powerless, more often good people were barbarically terrorized and made to sign any political criminal deposition against themselves composed by NKVD investigators. Stalin created a situation in which many (not only people in NKVD uniform) faced the choice of killing and terrorizing or being killed. Would it have been possible in any European country for the wife of the President of the USSR, Michael Kalinin, to be arrested on Stalin's order and sent into exile on Altay? Zhemchuzhina, the wife of the minister of foreign affairs, Vecheslav Molotov, a beautiful, educated, outstanding woman—a minister of culture of the USSR—was arrested on Stalin's order and sent to the GULAG. Both men begged Stalin to bring their wives back, but it was no use.

After this fat appetizer, Stalin plunged into even more frightfully bestial campaigns of mass terror against Russia's own population, my family included, a campaign unequaled to anything in world history. Even the Nazi's Holocaust, which for them served a Satanic purpose, was not equal in sheer numbers to Stalin's destruction of up to thirty million people.

It's an irony of history: by the middle of the thirties, the whole socio-political process had already culminated in the cult of Stalin. He presented himself as the only heir to Lenin's legacy and his authority grew beyond measure. He became known as the "Beloved Father of the People!" when we knew he was a killer of millions. But that was only the tip of the iceberg.

University

On September 1, 1936 my dream of being a student became reality. The University had expanded—the original site on the University Hill now housed only the Science faculties, the Administration building, the Central Scientific Libraries, and the students' club. The others were scattered throughout the city. My faculty of History and Philosophy was just two blocks away from my house on the corner of Pushkin and Sovnarkom streets. The latter was two short blocks between the city's two main avenues, Sumskaia and Pushkinskaia. Sovnarkom Street was famous. A popular riddle at that time was:

What street is the longest in the country?
Answer: A Sovnarkom street in Kharkov.
Wrong. It is only two blocks long.
But there stands the NKVD building. People who get on
that street can be back in ten years if they are lucky, because
it goes through Siberia. Otherwise, they never come back.

Our class was huge—about 120 students—the first of this size. The upper classes all together probably amounted to about forty students. This change in enrollment reflected the political changes in the country. In 1936, Stalin's new Constitution of the Soviet Union reintroduced the old concept of *Rodina*, Motherland. It was the duty of every Soviet citizen to love his *Rodina* and know its history. Soviet patriotism had been connected with Russian history and traditions. They reintroduced teaching history and reestablished the Departments of History-Philosophy at the universities. The importance of Russian history and patriotism was underlined by the fact the Seventeenth Party Congress in 1934 was debating the reform of teaching history; a textbook was published but had not been accepted by the Congress. Stalin, Molotov, and Zhdanov had to work on the outlines. I believe we all received it in 1939, including all the National Republics of the Soviet Union, not only Russia. Although the focus was on Russian, Russian national tradition and patriotism was a cementing force.

On the very first day of class I remembered what Misha's friend, the professor, had said and it was right. The dean of the faculty, Kassiy Markovich Vich, came in, welcomed us and informed us of our schedule.

"1. Ancient History. We dont' have a professor yet, but it looks as if Professor Semenov-Zuser from Leningrad University has agreed to a one year term. I am waiting for his arrival.

"2. Marxism, study of 'Capital.' In the next hour the professor will be here.

"3. History of World Literature: 1st semester—mythology; 2nd semester—Classic Greek and Roman. We are still waiting to

188

get a professor.

"4. Languages: Latin and German/English. We have excellent professors.

"5. History of Philosophy. The prospects for having a professor for this year are not good. But for the next year a professor has been appointed from Moscow Institute of Philosophy and Literature.

"6. The Russian language. We have a good linguist."

The First Class. Marxism, "Das Capital"

A pair entered the classroom, a lady leading a tall blind robust man by the hand. *"Zdraste"*—"Good day," he thundered out, pronouncing it in the "street" fashion. The woman, his wife, settled him down into a chair on a cathedra. He introduced himself and was noticeably nervous. It was his first try as a university professor. After explaining the aim and the format of the course, he started the introduction which was closer to the leading article in *Pravda* than to a university academic lecture.

The second day we had only the languages in small classes. For German, we had a pleasant, good-looking, and wonderful lady—an excellent teacher. She reminded me of L. L. from the tekhnikum. Her fate was tragic: during the German occupation they ordered her to serve as an interpreter against her will. When the Soviets came back in 1943 for a short stay, they shot her as a German collaborator.

Latin was taught by Ippolit Nikolaevich, a diminutive man in his fifties, but childish looking and, an enthusiast, in his behavior, the true type of Russian idealist intelligentsia. His two-year class gave us high academic benefits, pleasure, and fun.

On the third day we started to mix, introducing ourselves. A jubilant Kassiy Markovich entered carrying some kind of record player followed by a man who gave the impression of being two round parts: his head and his body. He was not big, not really fat, but somehow he had a round appearance. Kassiy Markovich happily introduced Professor Semenov-Zuser, a renowned scholar of ancient history. Zuser stood on a cathedra and looked at us seriously. He started playing music, said nothing, just looked at us.

Only one student, Riva, in her early thirties, exclaimed, "But this is from the *Gold Ring* by Wagner!"

She was the only one among us who recognized that famous piece. We were quite ignorant about classical music, especially foreign music. She was the daughter of a professional musician. The music stopped and he gave a few outlines of the opera's contents.

"What is the idea of this great prophetic music of Wagner? The human race is headed on a road toward self-destruction. Greed, greed for gold, means wealth and power, competition, hate and envy, because of the struggle between humans for more material possessions and power. Is this an inconstant unfriendly struggle or an inherently human characteristic? No! It's a developed system of values of wealth and power which have now become an incarnation of the world's capitalist society. The human race can be saved only through the abolishment of the system and the values of this society. Now we are starting a journey from the very beginning of modern human civilization which provides us with an understanding of our past and consequently what our future has to be and how to achieve it."

Our Zuser , as we called him, was not only a knowledgeable professor but an actor on the cathedra. We liked and respected him. He stayed in Kharkov preferring the sunny south to misty Leningrad. In addition to Ancient History, he taught archeology, supervising our university's archeological digging in Olvia (lower Dnieper), and a course in mythology. All his courses gave us good knowledge and a lot of fun.

Kassiy Markovich Vich was a small, skinny man in his late fifties with a smiling face and perfectly organized wrinkles that resembled the folds of an accordian. An Old Bolshevik before the Revolution, he had to flee abroad and lived there for some time, mainly in Switzerland getting some assignments from Lenin. During the Civil War he was Commissar of the *Divisia* (which consisted of four regiments). In his last years he was a professor in the Institute of the Red Professors in Moscow. He was lucky—the Central Party Committee (or Stalin) sent him to take a small position in Kharkov before the mass arrests happened in the Institute. He was a good man. In my life, I knew a number of the Old Bolsheviks, and almost all of them were exceptionally good human beings. They did not hesitate to sacrifice their own young lives for the sake of improving the human race.

The Rector of the university, Nekhvorostny, was arrested as a Ukrainian Nationalist as were many professors and administrators.

This policy of ideological screening affected not only the university, but the whole educational system of the Ukraine. That's why we did not have teachers. The evident, sometime comical ignorance of the "new" professors was not surprising in such a state.

In Mythology class, gloomy Kassiy Markovich introduced a renowned Ukrainian writer, Comrade X, as teacher of mythology. For a whole hour he talked about himself and his writings. That was okay. The second class he read the general outlines. The third time, his lecture was a funny mixture of Ukrainian folklore and mythological terminology. Riva and I had some knowledge of mythology and wanted to straighten out at least his terminology. When we questioned him, we found out he didn't have the slightest idea about the subject and, trying to save face, made simply laughable "academic" explanations. The City's Party Committee had sent some teachers to the university. Vich and Sazonov, the Rector, were in a very difficult position because no one would dare to reject such a candidate at once.

The fourth day, a joyful K. M. introduced "our Zuser" as the mythology professor and we gave him a standing ovation. Zuser was quite biting and couldn't tolerate our ignorance, but he fascinated us with his brilliant knowledge and wit.

In spite of many difficulties, the first year at university was probably more "pure" academically, when academic conclusions were still drawn from facts. With each higher step in our studies, the methodology became more perverse, even actual facts being adjusted to the accepted theses of the communist ideology. Our faculty was ideological, the first line of the ideological forgeries that was presented as historical facts. This mainly concerned the history of Russia, particularly the Communist Party. Although in Ancient, Middle and New Age World History, the facts were soundly presented, perhaps the conclusions had some ideological coloring.

The Philosophy of History adopted a new concept, specifically the class struggle had been the motivating power of society's development throughout the ages. Although the teacher of Marxism was less than inspiring, for me and surely for all of us, the idea of studying the basic work of Marx, a work responsible for the changes going on in the world, was extremely exciting. Jesus with the Bible as his teaching had changed the world; Marx and his *Das Kapital* we believed was in the process of changing the world. I studied a lot and with true pleasure.

As is normal among youth, groups of close friendship developed. Mine consisted of four girls and Isaac, a blind man with an excellent mind. Our friendships survived through grave political hardships, but the most emotional friendship was with Ina Khristenko. Unfortunately, our class hadn't yet become a place where friendship, joking, laughter, and academic questions were normal activities. Five to ten minutes after the last lecture, the classrooms were empty. Usually, each one went home alone. We didn't even know the names of all of our students. It was far different from my experience in the tekhnicum.

Who were we? Yes, we were different from five or six years ago. Although belief in our ideal has not changed, but disillusion with the present policy and conditions in the country were creeping in. Students from the villages were quite different from those I knew in my tekhnicum years. They stayed together, and didn't want to mix or express their opinions.

I found out two girls who stuck together were orphans. They were serious students, but shy and very small. I invited them to my home. They tried to be cheerful but when Mama served some food, they cracked and tears filled up their eyes. One girl asked for a piece of black bread. She put some salt on the bread and cut in four pieces. Tears ran down her cheeks and she breathed out her story.

"I was fourteen years old, and my younger two brothers were crying. They were hungry and had bad pain in their stomachs. Father left for a city to get some bread or any food. He didn't have a passport, so police arrested him with many others and sent him to Siberia for work. Every day Mother brought from *Kolkhoz* one piece of bread. She cut it in four small pieces, put a little salt on them, and gave it to us with warm water. My brothers died. *Kolkhoz* didn't have any more bread.

"The last piece of bread Mother brought she cut in the four pieces and told me to have it for four days, and she didn't need it anymore. She died that night. Her last words to me were to go outside and dig the grass roots under the snow, which started to melt. Then in a few days the buds and small leaves will appear on the trees. Get them and eat them."

This is a picture of Stalin's Russia during the years 1931, 1932, and 1933.

A change in our relations came at the beginning of 1939 when we "sang songs together" and knew that each one was "ours." "Mr. Fear" was not as busy as before—it made people breathe much easier.

Exams were over and I was satisfied. My grades were good. But I was very sad. Misha wouldn't be coming home; he had received some assignment from the Komsomol Central Committee. For the New Year's Eve of 1937, our group went to the Students' Club celebration. After a dull concert, I went home; my parents were waiting for me. The streets were almost empty: people were already in their places of celebration. I was walking alone and a drunk was following me, telling me how much he would pay me for a night. I was upset and almost crying, thinking about Misha.

At home, a table was covered with many "goodies." Mama and Papa were excited for the happy New Year celebration. About a week later in the morning, I was alone. As usual, Mama was out hunting for food. I got up and was changing out of my nightgown when I thought I heard Mama come in. Instead, I heard: "I like how a good wife is meeting her husband! Don't dress—I'll be with you in a minute!"

At dinner, Misha laughingly tried to tell this story, but I was so mad at him and closed his mouth. In many families, it was not proper, even shameful, to talk openly about sex in company, especially in the parents' presence. However, it was perfectly normal to ask a mother's advice on the subject. The next day, Misha's parents arrived and happy times were with us again.

Everyday Life

In everyday life, the Soviet Union was a unique case. The State was both the only producer and only distributor. From the late 1920s and onward the big cities were a complete mess, overwhelmed by a sudden huge population growth due to industrialization, tight budgets, and collectivization. The shortages became endemic, the worst were housing, transportation, and cities' amenities. It was not unusual for people to sleep and live in hallways or basements filled with coal. Basic food stuffs were short, and even worse was the supply of clothing, shoes, and all kinds of consumer goods.

The leaders, besides using normal, logical explanations for the abnormal difficulties, had to find the "scapegoats." The *kulaks* were first, then the "wreckers," specifically in the distribution chain, and finally the "enemies" in the middle and top eschalon of the Party.

The average citizen's survival depended on *blat* and the black market. The speculation was a thriving second economy. *Blat*, that phenomenal Soviet "creature," in English renders as "pull." In Soviet jargon, it means something like bribery, protection. In reality, it was acquaintances and connections. As the Russian proverb says, "One hand washes the other."

My mother had a "friend" salesman in many different stores who saved product for her they would receive that day. Usually only part of the people who stood in line were lucky to get the product. For that kind of favor, my mother gave some money or more often a piece of clothing, which she got through another "friend" salesman in the clothes store in exchange for some food she got in the food store. The favors were done in a discreet but normal way. The salesmen who do this *blat* were careful in dealing only with those they trust.

Blat penetrated the whole system, in everything from the small means of survival for the average people to the highest Party bureaucrats, who helped in promotions or receiving apartments. The whole press constantly wrote about this shameful condition and many people were punished.

A *Krokodile's* cartoonist once wrote:

Two clerks talking:
"Our store manager is a courteous man."
"Yes, he calls all the customers by name and patronimic."
"Does he really know all the customers?"
"Of course. If he doesn't know someone, he doesn't sell to them."

The new semester continued with the same programs. In Moscow there was a new trial of the famous Old Bolsheviks—the "Trial of 17." Our Komsomol meeting condemned those "mad dogs" and praised to the sky the "beloved Stalin." Our most well-known chatterboxes, David Bernstian and Vasia Pavlov, were busy writing resolutions and sending them to the "beloved Father." In whispers, friends were saying to each other that many "black ravens," the small, black vans in which the NKVD carried arrested people, were working hard through the nights. Many people still thought if someone was arrested it meant that he or she had done something wrong.

Later in the semester we read a long article in the newspaper against Andre Gide, the famous Frenchman. After he returned from the Soviet Union, Gide published a book called *Return from the USSR* in which he told a lot of the truth, but with love. He said that the Soviet people were happy, and he was happy as well. Only in the USSR did he feel himself a part of humanity, he was a comrade, a brother. But the happiness of the Soviet people was a result of their hope, their belief, and their ignorance. He was right. Even in Moscow, people didn't know what was really happening in the country and why. It was a kind of intoxication with gigantic achievements, especially technological and cultural. In spite of the fearful present, the country's hugeness, the unlimited natural resources and the moral strength of people—all these still kept our belief in the messianic role of Soviet Russia in the world and in our good future.

Crimea, Yalta

It was the middle of June 1937. Our train from Kharkov to Simferopol, Crimea changed speed and started going very slowly. Misha and I were on the Arabat *strelka* (spit) the very narrow stretch of land in shallow waters connecting Crimea with the mainland as well as the Perekop Isthmus to the west. The *strelka* railroad always made me excited. In some places one can see only a very narrow stretch of land alongside the train—just shallow water around as far as the eyes could see.

A historical fact came to me and I told Misha. In November 1920, the Red Army stormed Crimea, where the remnants of the White Army had concentrated. It was accomplished by walking, and in some places swimming, across these half-frozen shallow waters while carrying ammunition, machine guns, and more. It was one of the dramatic heroisms of the Civil War.

Misha and I were going to Yalta for an unprecedented six weeks vacation together, after four years of marriage, a luxury for the first time. In Yalta lived my Godfather Fedor Yaropolov. He had a high position in the city government and a nice villa in the mountains. He

195

and his wife, Anna Ivanovna, were very happy to have us. About a year and one half later we received a letter from her. She wrote that my Godfather was arrested. Over forty years later, I was in Yalta and tried to find out what had happened to him and his wife. I even went to the NKVD, but there were no traces and nobody knew anything. I didn't expect anything different.

Our train was now hurrying through the northern Crimea, which is open to the mainland and is quite similar to it in climate and vegetation. Farther to the south, the mountain ridges protect it from the cold winds of the mainland and the south coastal lowlands are Mediterranean in climate and vegetation. Through the centuries, the Crimea was overrun by dozens of nomadic people. Then the Greeks and Romans colonized it and founded those beautiful cities like Eupatoria, Sudak, Theodesia, Sevastopol, Simfiropol, and a number of other "pols" (Greek for city, courts). Italian Genoa ruled Crimea for two hundred years. In the 13th century, the Tartars occupied Crimea and in 1475 came the Ottoman Turks. Many wars were fought for Crimea between Russia and Turkey. In 1783, Catherine II annexed Crimea to the Russian Empire, calling it the "Tavrida Province." In October 1941, the Germans occupied Crimea and the Soviet armies reconquered it in April 1944. Almost the whole Tartar population was deported to northern Russia and Central Asia for their alleged collaboration with the Germans. Simfiropol, the Capitol, is inland.

We wanted to see Bakhchisaray (*saray* in Tartar means city, court), the old Capitol, specifically the Sultan's palace and Bakhchisaray's famous fountain of tears. Composer Asafiev wrote a beautiful ballet, *Bakhchisary Fountain*, on the basis of a legend later written by Pushkin. It's a masterpiece of Soviet ballet-drama choreography, the same genre as *Romeo and Juliet*. In the end of the first act, in the war raid on Poland shown in energetic, pointed classic dance, Sultan's army took among the prisoners Maria, a beautiful daughter of the Prince, just days before her wedding. In the next act, the bearers carried Maria on a stretcher. Sultan Girey showed he was impressed. The contrast in emotions was expressed between the blonde in white innocence of Maria and the passionate Oriental beauties. Girey was in love and wanted to bend Maria to his will. He was not interested in his harem or even in Zarema. In the third act there was a strong emotional classic dance like dialogue between Zarema and Maria.

196

Zarema is telling Maria about her love for Girey but he doesn't want her anymore. Passionate and crazy from love, she is begging, "Give me back my Girey!" Maria doesn't understand and expresses surprise and even fear. Later, in a rage of jealousy, Zarema kills Maria with a dagger. Girey was greatly shaken by Maria's death. He meditated on how to execute Zarema.

The development of character is masterful: In the first act, Girey is a despot; in the last he is a human. He orders a fountain of his tears to be built. It was still there: a big white marble block with winding grooves and through them the drops of water slowly run down and drop as tears. We listened as this legend was wonderfully narrated by the guide.

We explored all of Crimea—its famous places from Livadia, the Tsar's summer residence—the meeting place of "three:" Franklin Delano Roosevelt, Winston Churchill, and Stalin in 1945—down to the "Pigeon Nest Palace" on the cliff's top over the sea; the Chekhov House museums; and certainly the "Artek," the Soviet Union's Young Pioneers permanent camp, a wonder not repeated any place on the planet. Then we saw the famous Botanical Garden, Massandra's winery, and many other sights.

The Palaces and big houses previously belonging to the aristocracy and rich people were now given to different organizations, such as Trade unions; the Ministry of Health; the peasantry; the Komsomol; the Young Pioneers; writers-composers; the Theater workers; the Party's Central Committee; and others. Some palaces in Livadia were given to the peasants. Thousands of ordinary people had a good vacation and cure for free in these sanatoriums. People were sent there by their respective organizations, mainly the trade unions.

On the beaches we met ordinary people from all over the Soviet Union, from Kamchatka to Leningrad, Arkhangelsk to Astrakhan. We were satisfied and proud—it is a country of the working people and for the working people.

On the wide, crowded boulevards of Yalta, many of the walkers wore the same clothes, as in a prison. They wore pajamas because many of those people never in their lives had them and in the sanatorium each received them. "They were too good to sleep in, but just right for walking around"—garments in black, green, and white stripes.

Once, after dinner still in daylight, we were promenading on

197

the boulevard. Walking toward Livadia, we passed a group of women loudly swearing the most dirty Russian curses. Unbelievable, all of them were dressed in very fancy nightgowns. The picture was comical.

The young and middle-aged *kolkhoz* women, *udarniki*, produced the most, working at a shocking pace driving tractors, ploughing or harvesting, milking and taking care of cows, and doing other tasks in the *kolkhozes*. Their reward was a rest in Livadia. It was unusual a store had such expensive merchandise. They saw these nightgowns and bought all of them to use as fancy gowns. Why not? The "Beloved Father" said that all the *kolkhozniks* would be wealthy. They dressed up and were proudly walking on the boulevard. Two *rotten* intelligents stopped them and told they were "*ne kulturniye* (lacking in culture)," are shame of our great country, foreigners laughed at us. The women would not take such insults and let them feel the strength of their fists. It was especially the word "shame" that offended them. Their pictures were in the newspapers as the pride of the country.

I found all this out when I approached them. "*Babochki* (an endearing diminutive form of *baba*), what happened?" I calmed them down. "You are the pride of the country, so behave accordingly. No dirty swearing." I told them their gowns were really nightgowns. "But put a nice shawl or another fancy top on your shoulders and it turns into a gown. Besides, who dictates whose fashions we have to follow?" They invited us to visit and instruct them. The next day we did and it was a lot of fun.

Evenings were equally fascinating. After dinner, we sat on the veranda, looking down on the sea lit fantastically by the moon, and on Yalta lit by the variety of colored electric bulbs. But the greatest pleasure was listening to Anna Ivanovna narrate the Crimean legends. The peninsula was full of them. Different peoples who had lived there had left some cultural traces. Anna belonged to an old Crimean family, so it was normal for her to know the multitude of legends, the old and the new about Pushkin, Aivazovsky (the famous painter of water), Tolstoy, Chekhov, Gorky, and many others. I wrote down many of those legends, planning to work on them, maybe to compare them with Russian and Ukrainian legends.

We drove to the Tartar village to listen to the legend teller. She was a skillful artist, an old Tartar lady, really a lady: a small dignified woman who spoke Russian with a strong accent. First, she put on the simple wooden tables the *chebureki* (baked dough stuffed with vegetables and meat), grapes and cold water, asking us to try some of it. One of the oldest legends, probably known to every Crimean resident, is called *Ayu-Dagh* in Tartar, *Medved' Gora* in Russian, *The Bear Mountain*.

The legend goes: It was a small round land in the sea and only huge grey bears lived there. Then a beautiful girl in white appeared. All the bears fell in love with her, most of all the master bear—the biggest one. One day the young human-hero came on a boat, snatched the girl and went out to sea. Bears can't swim, so they decided to drink up the entire sea and that way they could catch them. They drank, getting larger and larger, and their land was getting bigger and the sea was getting smaller. Then they started to die. They burst, changing into mountains, hence the Crimean mountain ridge. The largest bear, still with his head in the sea, died last and turned into a mountain that looked like a huge bear drinking the sea water, *Ayu-Dagh*. That's how it happened that a small land became a big peninsula with wide coastal lines and mountain ridges which produced a warm climate for human enjoyment. And all these things happened because of love.

Misha and I proudly sported deep suntans and every day repeated the words of Goethe's Doctor Faust: "The moment, you are wonderful, stand still." We liked to dance at our favorite restaurant, *Poplavok*, a cork float about one hundred meters out in the sea. Anna Ivanovna was a good dancer and she trained us so that we became passably good.

Next to our villa was a smaller one of interesting architecture. Once when we were walking by, the owner called to us. We sat down next to him on the bench and he asked about us. We felt the man was in distress. He said he envied us—we were young and in love, but his wife had left him. And suddenly he burst open and told us things which can be said only by a human faced with death. He was a local NKVD interrogator.

"Many people's fate have I decided...I don't know if I was right." He paused. "But I didn't want to decide the fate of probably innocent people anymore, to send them to the gulag or to death. I have something like a quota of people to unmask, not less than two or three 'enemies' per week. I decided to try to do it the honest way, without torture and other inhumane means. So I did not unmask 'enemies' anymore for several weeks. My chief told me to stay home. Today or tomorrow my colleagues will come to arrest me, but they will find my body. Now in my profession you have to send innocent people to death or otherwise you become one of them. My wife left me because of what I am—a killer. I was an honest young man, a graduate of a law institute, until the NKVD hired me. Then, my life lost its meaning."

He talked more. We were shaken and tried to soothe his pain. A few days later, the NKVD took his body from the house. The Yeropolovs didn't want to tell us about their neighbor. Possibly the arrest of my Godfather was connected to this episode. The NKVD couldn't let anyone know the truth about them.

We were at home. As it had to be, we brought some presents for all our parents, but the best present was several kilos of grapes. We visited the Institute where Misha would be employed in a year, which was in the process of being built. We met the head man and were elated that Misha's name was already on the list of future employees. The wonderful, happy summer of 1937 came to a close.

University, the Second Year

The first day back to the University was exciting: over one hundred friends meeting after summer vacation greeting each other made our big classroom sound like a thunderstorm going on inside.

My friend, Sofa, beautiful and excited, ran to me. "I am a married woman, too, but my parents don't like my husband, Seva."

Our group and the other students congratulated her, and she openly told the story of her marriage. Seva was a young Professor of Marxism-Leninism at the Pedagogical Institute. He was from a small village at Donbass, near coal mines. People from that region were known by their proud, stubborn character and their indifference even to basic cultural norms. Seva was a genuine representation of that group; he sneered at cultural behavior. He was very handsome, tall, smart, and well-trained in his academic subject. He considered Marxism the only right way for life. We called those kinds of people

200

yanichar (a Turkish word that denotes the special boys prepared in the military schools to be patriots—warriers without deviation).

Sofa met Seva in June; they were bicycling together. Once, during their trips Seva asked Sofa, "Why don't we get married?"

"Okay, let's get married."

"Why not right away?"

As they were in dirty clothes they went to the Office of Registrations to register their marriage. Sofa brought him home to her parents.

"I want to introduce my husband, Seva, to you," she said.

When finally her mother understood what happened, she fainted and became seriously ill. Dr. Rosenfeld, Sofa's father, was a Director of the important Scientific Research Institute. A member of the Party's intellectual elite, he was trained in Germany and was a perfect European gentleman. Her mother was a beautiful woman in her late forties, a medical doctor. Their apartment displayed their importance. It was spacious with four big rooms filled with the finest furniture I ever saw. Cultural disharmony between Seva and Sofa's parents was normally inescapable.

Later, we wanted to give Sofa and Seva a wedding party, but we needed a place with a lot of room. Sofa invited us to have it in her home. Although her mother gave us a lot of good food from the *nomenklatura* store to which Sofa's father belonged, she excused herself from the party. We girls didn't know much about organizing a big party, even though the Rosenfelds had a permanent, live-in service woman, so I asked my *Krestnaia* to organize it. She became a friend of Sofa's mother who asked her to represent them at the party. It was a great party with a lot of good food, dancing and singing.

We had a new course: history of the Middle Ages, taught by Professor Pakul, a good scholar and an excellent professor, a man in his early sixties, tall and erect with a handsome face, which looked older than his age. He was formal, skeptical, and somewhat arrogant. He liked to repeat that true history does not require hyperbole; it naturally provides fascinating insight into human activities throughout the ages. Sometimes Pakul liked to laugh over our cultural ignorance, specifically at students from the villages. I felt ashamed for that good professor. Why humiliate those poor students who only four or five years earlier had been close to starvation and death?

An event happened which exposed the Communist Party

National Policy. For the first few days, Pakul was lecturing in Ukrainian. Then, he switched to Russian. A student from a village, who preferred Ukrainian as did the majority of "villagers," asked Pakul to lecture in Ukrainian. The Komsomol "active" protested, demanding he lecture in the "language of our Socialist Motherland." Pakul was angry and left. A hot discussion developed, the "villagers" against the "active." The "villagers" pointed out that Kharkov University was the oldest Ukrainian university and that the official language of the Ukrainian Socialist Republic was Ukrainian. The majority of students were silent, myself included.

The next day, an avalanche of meetings began—the Communist Party, the Komsomol, and the Trade union. All of them discussed "the case of violation of the working discipline when a professor had to leave the class." The "villagers" who broke this discipline, as it was said, were reprimanded. No one in all of those meetings uttered a word of truth—that it was a case that illustrated the denationalization of the Ukraine and that the Ukrainian youth spoke up against it by asking for lectures in their language.

In our Faculty, only one subject, the history of the Ukraine, was lectured in Ukrainian and the professor, Professor Boyko, was the only faculty member who was Ukrainian out of about seventeen professors. I think only ten lived permanently in Kharkov. The others were mainly from Moscow. Some of them were teaching half a semester in Kharkov, and half in their permanent place. All of them were Russians or Jews. The Ukrainian professors not arrested were not allowed to teach anyway.

We were not allowed to use *The History of the Ukraine* by the well-known historian Grushevsky, nor the histories by the historians Kostomarov and Doroshenko. It seemed that the policy was not to let the Ukrainian people know and love their history.

I met Professor Dmitro Doroshenko and his wife, Natalia, in Germany and we became good friends. She was a well-known dramatic actress in Kiev until their emigration. She was from peasant stock, pretty and vivacious, and he was a very handsome man from the Ukrainian aristocracy, which showed in his bearing. His great-grandfather, Petro Doroshenko, was the Hetman of the Ukraine, a strong personality.

One of the many stories she told me happened just a few months before we met. They had arrived at Augsburg, by invitation of their friend, a scholar historian.

"So we have a place to live, but we need food, too."

She went to see the American head of the Displaced Persons Services. He rejected Mrs. Doroshenko's petition and refused to see her. She was persistent and waited. Meanwhile, among the books on the shelf in his secretary's office she found *The History of the Ukraine* by her husband. Finally, the head of D. P. Services stepped out of his office and the secretary introduced Mrs. Doroshenko.

"I don't have time to talk. I am receiving too many petitions like yours."

"This book, *The History of the Ukraine*, is by my husband. It looks like it belongs to you."

In a moment, he changed his demeanor and sat down next to her. "Yes, this is my book. I studied the history of the Ukraine."

Naturally, he assigned the best ration of food for them, visited often, and in general was taking the best possible care of them.

We finally had a course in the History of Philosophy. The teacher was a recent graduate of *Aspirantura* (the Graduate school) of the Moscow Institute of Philosophy and Literature. He was friendly and knowledgeable. It was a good and a bit of an unusual course! After taking up the philosophies of classical Greece, and eighteenth and nineteenth centuries of Europe, he concentrated on the classical German philosophers, specifically on Hegel, the creator of the dialectical method formulated as: thesis (point of view), antithesis (counterargument), and then synthesis (new view). Then he took up Feuerbach, who developed a materialistic view which traces all reality to matter. Karl Marx's "dialectical materialism" is built on these two philosophies: the dialectic and materialism. It was a surprise to know that Russia has the fully-developed Russian idealistic philosophy.

· Since the Napoleonic Wars, the educated Russian nobility had avidly consumed the ideas of French, English, and German romanticism and the idealistic philosophy, and they developed their own prolific philosophical-religious ideas. Vladimir Soloviev was the first among them to develop a full formal system of philosophy. Then, a big group of young thinkers, former Marxists—Struve, Berdiaev, Frank, and many others—published two anthologies. The sensational one was *Vekhi* (Landmarks). They criticized the views and philosophy of the Russian radical intelligentsia, Marxist materialism and its rejection of spiritual values. They called for a renaissance of religious and social ideals. This was the beginning of the well-known philosophical school called *Russkoye zarubezhie* (Russians Abroad) that was still active in the 1930s. Our Professor presented their critique of the Marxist philosophy first and in depth, rather than the Marxist critique of their philosophy. This was an unusual and unaccepted practice in our time. We were surprised.

The class in political economy was a really strange course. The teacher was somehow an incomplete looking man who usually entered the classroom looking down at the floor, sat down at the table and started reading his lecture in a monotonous voice with a strong northern Russian accent. Our "activists" found out that the faculty office typist typed his lectures and made them into a book. Apparently with Kassiy Markovich's permission, she made several books for the class. We made a schedule so that in small groups we would have a book for a few days at a time so that we could read it together. Another schedule was made for class attendance, so there were at least twenty students each time. Otherwise, no one would come and we and our K. M. would have big trouble from the University Bureau of the Communist Party and the Rector. But in reading those lectures we found out to our surprise that they were very good, well-written and informative. We didn't have any other textbooks for the course. As we learned, there was a good textbook on the subject, but recently the author, a professor, had been arrested and his book withdrawn from the library and from class use.

There was still no professor for the Classic Literatures and Arts class. K. M. divided the course between the professor of art from the art department and our "bag of knowledge" enthusiast of the Classics, Ippolit Nikolaevich. It turned out to be a good course.

New Year's Eve, 1938

I had an idea to organize a New Year's Eve celebration in our Faculty Hall and K. M. and everybody enthusiastically accepted it. I planned the whole event, selected the organizers for the different activities, and asked the Bureau of our Komsomol oganization to discuss it with us and confirm it for action. The idea caught on like fire: an orchestra, chorus, dancers, individual performers, decorators all began preparing. Students from the other faculties brought their own talents. K. M. and I were the most excited and busy. "Our Zuser" asked me to recite a legend with him. We did it with great success.

The Hall was festively decorated. Many parents, including mine, Misha, his parents, *Krestnaia*, students and professors from different departments and institutes came. Even some university Party and administration functionaries attended, as they said, to see this new undertaking that they would rather promote instead of drinking parties. Accompanied by K. M., I opened the festivities. K. M. welcomed the guests. I wore a long black skirt and a white formal tuxedo shirt— a novelty in Soviet fashion. The public enjoyed it and made loud remarks, "*Krasivo!*" which means, "It's beautiful!" *Krestnaia* was beaming with pride; it was her creation.

Our chorus and orchestra performed with zest. The orchestra— violins, guitars, down to spoons and gypsy bells—was trained by Riva's father, a professional musician, and the chorus was prepared by a student from the Theater Institute. The pianists were Ina and Riva, both quite accomplished amateurs. I had a long list of the individual performers, starting with the opera's arias down to the short comic scenes, and of course, dancing: *Gopak*, Ukrainian, and *Komarenskaja*, Russian. Dancing on the floor and singing by all was the most enjoyable. I was ready to start floor dancing, waltzing with Misha when Professor Pakul came up and in a beautiful, gallant, old-fashioned way, asked me for the opening round and Misha for permission. Everybody stepped aside from the floor to watch the incomparable Pakul give a "lesson" in how to behave and to dance.

At midnight, K. M. and Vania, the secretary of our Komsomol organization, greeted all with the New Year and the powerful "International" shook the walls. The real Russian festivity began when the big crowd became as close as a family, singing, dancing, and laughing. Meanwhile, I introduced my whole family to K. M. and to the professors. All the girls, especially of my group, fell in love with Misha and asked him to dance. He was happy to oblige. At about 3:00 A.M., with regrets K. M. had to close the evening. The festivity, as ususal, revealed the Russians' and Ukrainians' immeasurable initiative and gaiety. Later in my life, I read in the foreign press that Russians don't have initiative. That's entirely wrong. The problem with Russian character is having too much free initiative, making it difficult to develop an organized democracy.

A few days before leaving, Misha didn't conceal his sadness. He thanked me emotionally for the happiness I gave him.

He told me that several leaders of Moscow Student Council, of which he was a member, were arrested. He knew them well. Tears welled up in his eyes. The pattern of the NKVD's "honest" defense of the country against its enemies had become fairly well-known to the public. If they arrested one man from the organization, certainly more would follow. The first victim "cracked" under terror, indicating other innocent people, and it went like that on and on. The NKVD supplied the list of those innocent "enemies" to the victim and terrorized him until he signed it.

At the railroad station, saying good-bye, Misha held me tight, and wiped his tears. I cried and my parents did the same. Something like this had never happened before.

"It's better if I don't go," he said. At that moment the train conductor practically snatched him up because the train started to move.

Momentarily, I realized what he had said and ran alongside the train, screaming, "Get off the train! Get off! Get off! Get off!" I didn't see Misha.

I immediately wrote him a letter asking him to come home at once. He answered everything was okay. I had no peace of mind. Some kind of dialogue was going on in my mind constantly:

"Misha is innocent. They don't take the innocent."

"Really? Then what about that person and that person . . . "

At the faculty, relations between students and teachers changed considerably, becoming more informal, and relations between students became very close. Dancing and singing together as a collective at the New Year's Eve celebration definitely helped. The university newspaper published a glowing article about it. Students now called me Ninok, as they had heard Misha called me. Studies and good friendships were somewhat helpful in setting my mind to rest. My closer friends in our group besides Sofa were Ina (Khristenko), the most intelligent and gifted student in our faculty whose father was a known Ukrainian linguist, an author of several books; Lena (Maslenikova) whose father was an old Communist, a worker, and she was an exceptionally honest and pleasant human being; and Isaak. Two among us were Jews and, believe me, I didn't even know Isaak was one. It was entirely of no importance to any of us. Unfortunately, a notion of "what is his/her ethnicity or race" developed in me later here.

For about a week, Ina hadn't shown up for classes and I asked K. M. about it. He took me to his office, closed the door and said, "Her father was arrested, but don't say anything about it until her expulsion from the University is officially announced by the Rector."

I comprehended what K. M. said. I tried to say something, but could not. He sat me down, gave me a glass of water and calmed me down.

Several days later I visited Ina at home with her mother. The picture was very depressing. They were in fear of the possible arrest of her mother, also a linguist scholar. A couple of years before, she had been in an accident resulting in a crippled leg which still wasn't healed. Later, she was arrested, but incredibly they let her go home after holding her for several weeks.

At the meeting of our Komsomol organization, one of the questions on our agenda was the expulsion of Ina Khristenko and another, "X," as children of the "enemies" of the Soviet people. X was not a favorite of ours. He was overbearing, but quite smart. In his long speech, though it was not new, he said that he was firmly and steadfastly renouncing his father and changing his last name because he didn't want to bear the name of a traitor of the Soviet people. He received applause and "not expulsion." In spite of the fact I was in agreement with all the kids, my feeling was different. To renounce your father? I could never do it!

Ina, in a short speech and soft voice, said her father was not an enemy of the Soviet people and system. She was positive he would be vindicated. Now, she would stand by him until they would make a decision about his case. There were the voices of indignation at her words:

"How dare you doubt the Chekists (the NKVD) who are saving our country from enemies like your father?"

"Our glorious Chekists don't make mistakes."

We applauded. There was a long sermon by David, a member of the Komsomol Bureau, followed by other speakers in the same pattern.

"You (Ina) showed us how your father educated you. People like you don't belong in the Komsomol and the University."

"You had to know that your father was a Ukrainian nationalist. His book on the Ukrainian language is already suppressed."

207

Not one of us said a good word for Ina. The majority voted to expel her. A small group, including me, voted not to expel. As she left, no one, not even me, looked at her. Later, I asked myself why I behaved in such a dishonest way. Fear? Or did I still have some trust in our "beloved Father," who was calling for cleansing our country of unreliable people. Like so many Soviet people, I was not yet ready. We still held as a revolutionary axiom left over from the Civil War that when historical necessity of preservation of the new Soviet State came into conflict with ethics, even carrying on terror, certainly historical necessity had to prevail. We didn't bother to look more deeply, to see that in the Civil War we had truly been fighting the enemies. But now the historical necessity argument was not acceptable. It doesn't reflect the real situation in the country and its needs.

Terror: Misha Disappeared

I took my semester exams in the main subjects before the scheduled time. I asked the professors for this favor. Misha had to be home no later than May 15. It was May 17 and he was not yet here.

My papa called Misha's father, Peter Nikolaevich, who was also concerned and said in a few hours he would leave for Moscow to find out. Late in the evening on May 22, there was a knock on the door. Peter Nikolaevich came in and collapsed. For five days he had had to control himself, and now he relaxed and broke down. After we put him on the bed and helped him regain his strength and sense, he started to wail loudly. Mama and Papa wept bitterly with him. I went to my room, but I didn't cry. I believe I was psychologically frozen, in shock, and probably I never have unfrozen completely.

Mama prepared food and vodka. P. N. didn't remember having eaten in three days. Now he was eating and telling what he found out in Moscow. Tears were rolling down his cheeks, as they were on Mama's and Papa's. I didn't want to see this picture; I closed my eyes and listened.

Misha was arrested at night on the thirteenth or fourteenth of May. Nobody knows exactly—he was living alone in a room. All his possessions were thrown on the floor and bed. The university's rectorate answered that they don't give out any information about such matters. With the help of friends in the Ministry of the Railroads, he finally found a lawyer who had permission to take political cases, though there were not many of them in Moscow. This morning, the lawyer told him that Misha's name was among those arrested. When? Where was he now? It was a secret. And probably, the lawyer said, he would not find out soon.

The elders talked almost throughout the whole night. I didn't know what to say. Then I noticed that they looked at me. Papa Peter changed, stopped wiping his eyes, and told me Misha would be vindicated. Mama gave me some medication and I fell asleep. When I got up, Papa Peter was gone to soothe Mama Rosa. He didn't want Mama to go with him to help. It was better if he didn't tell her the truth now.

I don't remember anything that happened for four or five days after that night, only my physical discomfort—throwing up and diarrhea. Then suddenly the words from a popular song hit my mind— "Siberia is also Russian land"—*"Sibir' ved' tozhe Russkaya zemlia."* How many thousands of Russian women starting with the two beautiful Princesses Trubetskaia and Volkonskaia and, over thirty years ago, Nadezhda Krupskaia (Lenin's wife) had followed their husbands into Siberia? With her mother, Nadezhda traveled to Lenin's exile in the Village of Shushenskoye in Siberia as his fiancee. They were married in the village church and she stayed in exile with her husband. Why couldn't I? I felt energy and a happiness filled me. Singing the song, I ran to Mama's room. She looked at me and hid her face in her hands.

"No, I'm not losing my mind. I'm happy because I've decided to follow Misha into exile."

Mama became enthusiastic, too, and we started planning. When Papa came home a plan was ready: P. N. had to find the concentration camp where Misha was. I would get permission from the Ministry of Education to be a school teacher in the closest possible region. After I established myself in some place and school, I would work on the problems: how to send a letter to Misha or how to get into the camp's perimeter. My aim would be to let Misha know I was there with him. After some connections were established, then I would know how to help him with food and money and resolutely support his psychological state.

A couple of days later, Mama and I went to see my in-laws. From the train we went straight to their apartment and found Mama Rosa sitting alone in the kitchen. What had happened to her beautiful face? It was swollen with two red slots instead of eyes. Seeing both of us smiling, she thought that Misha had to be there. No? Clearly, she didn't comprehend. We took her to the living room, sat her down on the sofa, and I told her my plan. She felt better, kissed and caressed me. Then she went down on her knees and prayed in her own words, as Russian women usually do, asking God that if her perfect flower, her son, had to go through this torment, then to let this selfless daughter help him to carry his cross.

Now she was more relaxed and showed her fatigue. We made her comfortable on the sofa and she fell into oblivion. Mama looked through the kitchen and found no food, but some bread and sugar. My practical Mama knew what to expect here, therefore, we had brought some food with us. A big pot of *borshch* turned out to be a lifesaver for Mama Rosa.

I went to the station office looking for P. N. but he wasn't there. I found him in the station's food store. Seeing me he was overcome with joy, but a few minutes later he told me that his wife wanted to die, wouldn't eat anything, and had thrown out a lot of good food.

Mama prepared dinner. We woke Mama Rosa and she ate well. I expressed my wish that a year from now, Mama Rosa and I would be having dinner in some place in Siberia and would have established connections with Misha. She seemed to be looking through us into the future, not noticing us. She slowly and painfully unburdened herself.

"It happened thirty years ago. I was leaving my father's home. Father allowed Peter to come inside. He said to me, 'You are leaving us, rejecting our God for another God. My heart is broken. I understand that your pure human love overpowered your sense of duty to and love for your father and mother, family, and the Jewish people. You are not my daughter anymore. You are not a Jew. But I am not cursing you, although by our law I have to, and I am not asking my God to punish you.' Since then, I've had a happy life and my son, my perfect flower, was a reward for the pain of my heart. But all this time, I knew the Jewish God would punish me and I prayed to my Christian God to defend my son and just punish me. The Christian God is a God who forgives. The Jewish God is a strict God. He punishes the apostates and their relatives."

210

She had a bad feeling that Misha was doomed, he would be a sacrificial lamb. My Mama, a believer, disagreed, saying there was only one God, though we humans created many more of them.

At the time of our leaving, Mama Rosa felt much better. "Maybe fortune will smile on Misha and us."

Back home, I was preparing a *kozhukh*—a sheepskin coat. After two weeks of my absence from the Department, friends inquired what had happened and why I had lost so much weight. I lied and said I was sick. I saw K. M. and told him the truth.

He closed his eyes and said, "No. It's getting to be too much."

The second year of University was finished. Petr Nikolaevich didn't have any news from Moscow. I went to see Novak, told him the truth, and he promised to give me good papers for getting a position in Siberia. Several days later he was arrested.

In the late evening of June 21 there was a knock at the door. Petr Nikolaevich looking bewildered with wide open eyes stepped in and asked Papa for a glass of vodka. Mama prepared food for him. He drank at once a whole glass of vodka, and ate a lot, all silently. We were sitting around the table waiting for his words. He finished eating and took his *partbillet*, the communist party membership card, from his breast pocket and put it on the table.

"This card is burning my heart. I don't want it anymore. The revolution and socialism are betrayed. I revered it for twenty years. I carried it with pride. I see how the ideals and aims of my life are gone, treacherously betrayed. My life was dedicated to my wife, my son, and my communist ideals. Now my son is dead, the ideals are betrayed, and my wife is dying. They said my son never existed. His name is wiped out of any place or paper where it was before. Not only my son, but the leaders, the cream of the Moscow student organization, were executed and the case is under the NKVD's highest secrecy. Why? What would people think if they found out that Moscow students were against Stalin and the government? The truth is that they believed in Stalin, were ready to defend communism with their lives, but the Dictator knew and was afraid they would become the avant-garde in a struggle against him to save the revolution and communism."

He spoke very loudly, looking straight ahead. It was obvious he was not well. "Tomorrow, I will give back my communist membership card. But before they get me, I will tell people what is going on in our country."

Everything around me detached itself and disappeared. I heard Papa Peter's voice. When I think about that faraway time, I can still feel that dark emptiness.

The next morning, Mama helped him to the railroad station. About a week later, Papa went to Belgorad and found out that P. N. had done what he said he would do on that dreadful night and was arrested and, of course, executed. Mama Rosa died and friends buried her. Going to Belgorad, Papa concealed himself, avoided the station where people knew him and went to the town. For me, that family is an image of Russia itself. Three really beautiful human beings—honest and bright, dedicated to the ideals of making human life better. They helped in small, everyday tasks, and the needs of the country. Their love was strong and faithful. Life for them was a joyful wonder to appreciate, but suffering was also an inseparable part of life. How many millions of beautiful people like them were destroyed, making the country weaker?

Sixty years ago when it happened, I wanted to bury my grief inside me and close it up. I didn't want to talk about it. I didn't wish to see my friends, afraid of being asked questions and of having to reveal myself.

Father's Arrest

Papa called his cousin, Yakov, in the city of Sumi, asking if he would accept two undemanding guests—Mama and me. He was glad to have us, and we were invited many times.

Uncle Yakov was a huge, gregarious man, director of probably the biggest commercial alcohol plant in the country. In their youth, my father had saved my uncle's life and they were really close friends, although they seldom saw each other. Papa warned us not to tell them what happened, and secretly informed only uncle. I liked to be there. It reminded me of Krasnaia-Yaruga, my childhood, the same arrangement: a plant circled by workers' houses, apartments, and the plant's offices and organizations.

On July 22, uncle brought a telegram. I opened it, read and understood, but my mind somehow closed itself up. "I don't understand it," I said.

212

Mama took it, read it, and collapsed in a chair. Uncle read it aloud. The telegram said: "They took uncle. Come home. Signed, Shura."

Shura was my youngest cousin from Krasnaia-Yaruga. She came to keep Papa company and to do some shopping. We decided that I would go alone and uncle drove me at once to the railroad station. I caught a train at the last minute.

When I arrived home, I saw Shura with red swollen eyes. She burst into tears when she saw me. Everything—books, papers, clothes, dishes, small things—was thrown on the floor in both rooms and the kitchen. It showed that the search couldn't be called thorough—it was rather unprofessional and barbaric.

The next day Mama arrived. The *dvornic*, the janitor, from our building came and told us some of what happened that night. Father was completely at a loss. He couldn't imagine that something like that could happen to him. He was a good, honest man who loved his country and was a loyal supporter of socialism. Shura made a small bundle of underwear, a shirt and socks, and put a coat on him. He was mumbling something rather senseless. As usual, the *dvornic* had to be present during the arrest procedures. He was a friend of Papa's, sometimes they had a drink together. Papa was a member of the House Management Committee.

He advised us not to be home nights because the NKVD might come back to arrest us. We knew it often happened. Where would we sleep? A question impossible to answer. There were so many places.

First we were at Grandpa's apartment. In spite of the fact that we were careful and came in late, the neighbors in the hallway (lately another two rooms were taken from my aunts and each given to a couple) noticed and asked. We didn't want to put my aunts and Grandma under suspicion or even worse. Certainly, friends were out of consideration.

We became the "night ladies," wanderers, sleeping during the day at home. In reality, it was an animal living, just preservation of life. We didn't care about life, though; I wanted to commit suicide, but I couldn't do it on account of Mama. And she couldn't do it on account of me. Someone told us about a "hotel" and we joined it. It also became our "university."

Our Agony

From our building, three or four blocks down on the cobblestone Chernoglazov street to the River Lopan', across the narrow bridge, we walked into a small park of trees, lush bushes, and flowers. The place was bustling with secret life, mainly women sitting on benches or already lying on their "beds" made of newpapers and sacks under the bushes. We got acquainted with some of them. Some were like us, afraid to sleep in their homes. But the majority of women and men were here to see the Prosecutor, to ask just one question: "Where is my husband/daughter/son/father?"

Around this park were three offices of Prosecutors: military, for the Military Industry, like my father's plant of the railroad engine which was now making mainly tanks; the second was this region's Prosecutor; and the third was for some other purpose. In order to see the man in the office, people came before midnight, signed the list someone was keeping because the Prosecutor's assistant would usually see only a certain number of people. Sometimes, people had to spend two or even three nights before being lucky enough to see him, who routinely answered, "We don't have this name on our list."

His list consisted of one or two pages, when in reality in just this small park every night up to one hundred people came to ask that question. At the sight of a policeman, everybody crawled under the bushes and were silent. Very seldom a policeman stopped pretending that nobody was there and gave a command to scatter at once. Men and women ran away like hares.

The next night, Mama signed the list and saw the man. She received the routine answer: "This name is not on our list." It was an excellent "school" for us, learning how many different Prosecutors' offices there were in the city and how many jails, and that all of them gave the same answer: "This name is not on our list."

Some of them didn't even bother to pretend to have a list. Every day there were hundreds of people in each of those offices asking the same question and we were among them. It looked as if the sense of human normality was gone and some invisible cruel power was devouring innocent, unprotected people. I felt we were defenseless. Mama had gone with other women several times to the freight station outside the city where "they" packed "convicts" on the way to Siberia. Women were running on and back alongside the train's box

214

cars, each calling out her relative's name. Policemen were trying to keep the women away, sometimes beating them with riflebutts. The park became for us not only a "hotel" and "university," but a healing place as well. These people were suffering the same as we were; it became a way of life. I was asking myself. What could be done?

There was no doubt in my mind that the Revolution was betrayed. The majority of people didn't know the dimensions of this pogrom. Many still believed the whole country was penetrated with enemies of the Revolution who were damaging and slowing down the building of socialism in our country as "Beloved Father" was proclaiming. Our huge country resembled a psychiatric ward. Stalin cleverly and craftily used people's revolutionary passion and hatred for enemies of the Revolution. He used oversimplified slogans about the "intensification of the class struggle" to draw in the masses by the millions. Essentially many honorable folks guided by the best motives were poisoned by suspicion, looking everywhere for spies and "wreckers." Even children, the young pioneers, became psychotic.

Once when we were coming home in the morning, several weeks after father's arrest, our *dvornik* met us in the entrance and in a whisper told us that "last night some guests were looking for you. It might be better for you to go to the movies earlier, before it's dark."

We understood his message and that our "night walking" had to continue indefinitely. We were lucky again that we were not home when "guests"—NKVD—came to arrest us.

I was standing in a long line of mainly older women along a wall of a jail on Kholodnaia Gora. When it was built many years before the Revolution, it was on the outskirts of the city, but now it was in a huge workers' region, a town. People were walking by our queue. A group of three men stopped by me and familiarly lectured:

"Why are you standing here? You married a man and didn't know he was a *svoloch* (villain) an enemy? You lost your proletarian vigilance. Spit on him and join us, the workers' brigades, to clean our country from the villains. Our fathers and grandfathers saved our country during the Civil War and we will save it now. We are the workers. It is our dictatorship."

The line got silent, but one old, old woman stepped up to them. "Don't bother us. Otherwise, I will make a cross on your forehead with this, my *klyuka* (a cane with a few nails on the end)."

They were astonished at such heroic behavior in an old woman.

The policeman quickly stepped in. "Order, order! Boys, go your way."

Mama and I, worn out physically and emotionally, stopped running at night. We did not care what would happen to us. But the worst case we hadn't foreseen befell me—my digestive system was badly affected by the condition of my nerves. Any food I consumed was thrown up. This weak digestive system has seriously bothered me all my life and is Stalin's personal "present" to me. Yes, I do remember that humanoid devil. Some doctors, as we heard, didn't want to help the relatives of "enemies," so Mama went to see Dr. Volovnic, a younger friend of my Grandpa. He came and helped well enough so that I was able to go back to my Faculty.

I had to report to K. M. about my father's arrest. It was September, and classes started. K. M. looked at me and bent his head low. He was silent for awhile.

"Who?"

"Father."

"When?"

"July 22nd."

"Husband, too?"

"Yes, in May."

"Are you going to renounce them?"

"No!"

"I have to report your case to the Rector. But it looks like good news, if it is true, that children of arrested parents will be reinstated in their schools if nothing politically compromising is found against them. Don't tell anyone about your husband or this conversation."

I was getting weaker, just lying in bed preoccupied with thoughts: what Misha was thinking and doing just before the execution. My psychic feeling and vision became so sensitive that I saw the scenes of execution and I talked to Misha aloud and heard his answers, which I repeated again and again. I saw Papa in a big room where many other men were sitting or lying on the beds and floor. My kind father looked like a skeleton and was crying. I was talking to him aloud: "Papa, we are in normal condition. Don't think about us. Do what is better for you."

We were really lucky; the House Committee didn't throw us out of the apartment onto the street, but only took the smaller room and gave it to a middle-aged couple. They were very happy because they could use our furniture. They hadn't any of their own.

Our lawyer found out (with difficulty) that Father was accused of counter-revolution: propaganda against the revolution and "wrecking." On the propaganda point: at Sevastopol in 1918, Father had spoken a few times at the Ushakov Ravine meetings, just expressing doubts about the Bolsheviks. On the "wrecking" point: in Father's big department, there was a cooling unit which produced ice for the plant. In the accusation, it was said that the cooling unit produced "empty ice." We never found out what that meant. For these "crimes" he was executed.

This special lawyer himself only had the right to find out information if "they" allowed it to be given to him and to write a petition for us. He wrote one in which we asked for a review of the case. We sent this petition to twenty-one places. They went to the city and Oblast Prosecutors; the Ministry of Jurisdiction of the Ukrainian Republic; the Military Industry Prosecutor; to M. Kalinin, President of the country; to N. K. Krupskaia, Lenin's widow; and many more. We received two answers. One was from the Central Military Prosecutor of the USSR addressed to my mother on 9.1.1939. The second was from the Prosecutor of the Kharkov Oblast addressed to me on 7.10.1940. Both answers were the same. They did not find any grounds for revision of the case.

Much later, during the war, we found out that the formula of the sentence "ten years of strict isolation without the right of correspondence" meant execution. That sentence by *Troyka*, the special three-man commission, was given to my father. My letters about Misha, asking for a revision of his case, were never answered.

At that time, we did not know that Kalinin's wife was exiled again to Siberia for the second time by Stalin because she tried to tell the truth. Along with his adult children, Kalinin begged Stalin to bring his wife home. But it was in vain. N. K. Krupskaia was offended by Stalin and he tried hard to exclude her from the Kremlin's inner circles. When she persistently asked Stalin to free some arrested Old Bosheviks who had worked with her and Lenin, Stalin once told her: "Do you want me to make Comrad N. as the Lenin's widow instead of you?" Stalin spread a rumor that she (Comrad N.) was Lenin's lover. It was a lie.

My Visit to the Information Bureau of the NKVD

We never found out what happened to my father. In the summer of 1939, I went to Moscow to the NKVD's Information Bureau. I lived with the wife of one of Mama's distant relatives who had recently passed away. For several days early in the morning, I stood in a line outside a big hall, signed the list, and received a number when I entered. It was like a barn with benches along the walls and several long tables. About half a dozen assistants to the Commissar of Internal Affairs, Lawrenty Beria, were receiving people. There, I saw representatives of every nationality or ethnic group, from all parts of our huge country. All of them came to ask the same question as I, about the fate of a close, beloved person.

Finally, at the end of the third day, my number was called. The assistant was a young man, not in uniform. I gave him our new petition and asked for answers to the questions: Is my father still alive? If so, then where is he? Can we have his address and write to him?

"We will read your petition," he said and threw it in a big box. "What are you doing?"

"I am a student."

"Where? What are you studying? Ah! History and Philosophy—the most political subjects. The Party has high trust in you, and you defend your father who is an enemy of our country. You have to know that the responsible workers of the NKVD don't make mistakes."

Now I saw a fanatic with a sinister look in his wicked eyes. And in those seconds, I realized that my time could come to an end.

"You are a potential enemy," he said. "I have seen many like you. I will kill you now and won't be responsible. Go to that corner and face the wall."

"You can kill me," I said. "But I prefer to sit and look into your eyes. My father was not an enemy."

"Okay. You can go now, but we'll remember you."

I walked "home" fast. I was not shocked. Instead, I had a deep feeling of satisfaction with my stand against that ugly fanatic. Thinking later about this event, I realized that the experience and suffering of the last year made me invulnerable to any fear or threat. Certainly, we never received any answers from this Information Center. For three more days I went there. Now in a short letter, I was asking,

"Where is my husband?" It was a vain hope to expect an answer.

I wanted to talk to a someone who had been present at Misha's arrest, so I went to see the Commandant of the University's dormitories. According to NKVD's rules, during the search and arrest, someone from the outside, usually the Commandant of the building, had to be present and sign a paper attesting that everything had been done properly. "Democracy" had to be preserved.

A secretary let me in to the Commandant's office. He asked me what I wanted and I told him, practically by signs, that it was confidential. He asked me to sit down. People kept coming in with various papers for him to sign, or to receive some instructions.

Two workers received their orders and asked, "What *marka* goes there?" (What number bus goes there?) It was known that only in Kharkov did people use that word.

When I heard them saying this, I said, "Kharkov."

It was then that the Commandant asked the secretary not to allow people in. He sat down next to me.

"You are Nina. I have a couple of pictures of you with Misha. I will give them to you. I was present at Misha's arrest. The NKVD people called me and told me to be in my office after midnight. It had happened often. Misha was packed; in the morning he was going to leave, going home to Kharkov. He got dressed in a good, prepared suit to wear going home. They told him to stand in the corner and I sat in another corner in that tiny room. We watched those two officers doing the search. Everything from the suitcases was thrown on the floor. When they emptied a sack of books and notebooks on the floor, and made an awful mess, Misha asked me aloud to take those books of the latest research to his faculty for the graduate students; they were priceless.

"During this search, which lasted over two hours, Misha was standing straight in that corner. He was oblivious as to what was going on around him. His thoughts were in some other places. I was watching him with deep pain. I saw a beautiful human being in that corner. I knew that honest, smart young man quite well. I tried to talk to him. Misha's last words were: 'I'm glad *it* happened here and not at home in Kharkov. I spared my wife from this ordeal, although I would like to kiss my wife good-bye forever.' He knew pretty well what was waiting for him. Almost all members of the Moscow student leadership had already been arrested and probably executed.

Rumors were circulating that they were organizers of the Moscow students' counter-revolutionary organization and wanted to kill Stalin and commit many other crimes against the Revolution. All of those accusations were vicious fakes, lies."

The Commandant told me to take Misha's two suitcases with his belongings which were stored with many others like his. I asked him to do me the favor and send them to Kharkov, and I gave him money for that.

Mama took care of the things, sold them on the market, and what was left I bartered for food in the villages during the war. All these transactions were very painful for us. But they helped us to survive. It's a horrible irony that the most complete repudiation of a human's rights happened when the seemingly democratic Constitution in 1936 was adopted, when Stalin and all the organs of oppression and bureaucracy spoke in the name of the free Soviet people and real Soviet Democracy.

Now Back in Time

Classes started on September 1, 1938. I was too weak to walk the three blocks to the Faculty, but mainly I didn't want to show myself to the class in such deplorable condition. No one came to visit me but that was normal and understandable, because they could have been accused of helping the enemies. About a week later, I received a letter from K. M. and the Rector of the University, Sazonov, with an order of expelling me from University. Interestingly, it did not say as it had before, "as the daughter of an enemy of the Soviet people," but "according to the law." This meant some political changes.

I expected this, but it still hit me badly. Days of sometimes hallucinating and sometimes a clear mind, followed. I thought my life was over. There was nothing left to live for. My love, my friend, my husband was gone. My father, whom I loved and respected, was gone. My ideals and ideas, which made my life meaningful and worth living, were gone. What was left? I didn't see anything in the present or in the future that made it worth living, except that I couldn't leave my Mama.

I talked to Misha aloud sometimes. Knowing that he liked singing, sometimes I sang, imagining him sitting next to me. It was truly a tragic picture, when love songs full of emotions were addressed to the empty chair. At night, when I couldn't sleep, I recited poetry. It was probably a good exercise for my mind.

The hallucinations were getting worse and repetitive, occurring with the rapidity of films. One was very persistent and made me realize that I was not well. I saw an endless and deep abyss filled up with running ants. Suddenly, all that mass started to grow upward, like leavened dough, and I heard a terrible noise coming from it. It was not ants, but people, and I saw Papa and Misha. They shouted something to me, but I couldn't hear them. Then I saw that the people around me were throwing ropes down into the abyss. I did the same, trying to fetch up Papa and Misha. The ropes were stopped in the descent on an invisible roof and weren't sliding down to reach the people. I realized I had to find a heavy, iron object to crash through. Now all of us were running, looking for that kind of an object. But there was none.

Dr. Volovnic helped me, talked to me, and gave me some medication. But I wanted to die; life had lost meaning. Ninok was dead. The new Nina was different—her character and appearance had changed and her aim in life was lost.

It was late autumn. I had lost track of time—day, night, season. Once, in a moment of mental clarity, Pushkin's line came to my mind, *Ne day mne Boh soyty s uma* (Don't let me, God, lose my mind). I clearly understood that it was happening to me. It hit me terribly. I got up, dressed myself, sat down at the table and tried to write verses. It was not the first time I had tried, and as before it came to nothing. What to do? Mama and I discussed what to do with our lives. One choice was to die by suicide. Another was to shut off our past as if it never happened and live a normal life. The last was to live with our past, remember it and be unhappy. We selected the second way which called for strong character and we acted that way.

I remembered that the years before I had prepared some books and notes for research on the theme of "Komsomol in the Civil War." Much information on the subject was scattered in many publications. I wanted to summarize it and in addition to show how those heroic Komsomol deeds were reflected in poetry. This unintentional and unorganized work helped me, preoccupied my mind and saved it.

Our economic situation bothered Mama. Savings wouldn't last

for too long, although the last time Misha was here he transferred money from his savings into mine. It helped for a while. Mama decided to look for a job, which she had never held. She wanted to work in the kitchen of a restaurant or a "closed" dining room. She lied and said her husband had left her, but they didn't believe her because the others said the same. One "boss" said to her, "Get away. You are a liar. You can poison our good people." Finally, she got work as a cleaning woman in a furniture store.

Krestnaia came often to keep me company and to prepare food. She was not afraid to be with us. She hadn't overcome her personal tragedy. Her fiance, a scholar in the Ukrainian Academy, was a defendant at the trial of the Ukrainian Nationalists Center in 1928 or 1929. He was sent to Siberia, but *Krestnaia* and his parents never found out where. It was a secret. They were very much in love and wanted to marry but she had to stay with the family for a while until he received an apartment. However, Grandma with her old-fashioned customs would not permit it.

Reinstated at the University

It's the end of December. A knock at the door, and smiling, happy Ina appeared.

"Why are you lying down? Get up! I've come straight from the department. You and I are reinstated at the University with all our rights. You see, Comrade Stalin said that a son does not answer for the crime of his father. K. M. was very happy to see me and asked me to come see you and give you this order from Rector Sazonov. Get up! Get dressed! No more lazy life! I am going to make lunch for both of us."

I told her where to find food, not to take our neighbor's. Two soft boiled eggs for each, bread with sunflower oil, finely sliced onions with salt and oil and tea.

"I can't eat this. I will throw it up."

"Try it. Eat little by little."

We were talking excitedly and did not notice how I consumed my food and did not throw it up. Mama came home. For the first time in almost a year, tears of happiness mixed with laughter were heard in our home.

"Now listen to my mother's wisdom." And Ina laid it out with her customary clearness. "Number one—we have only one Motherland with a certain system and government. It will not be changed to another system. It's our National system. Number two—our political system is on a mistaken road now. Why? We don't know. But it is clear that we can't change it from the bottom up. It will have to be adjusted from the top down. Number three— it logically follows that if we can't fight the system, the only way for us to proceed is to continue to be a part of it. Maybe not sincerely and enthusiastically as before, but honestly. Lastly, number four—Ninok, your past was beautiful, but it is the past. It's not wise to continue to dream about it. You will be a loser. It's wise to dream about the future. Put some flesh on your bones and start fighting in your nice way for an honorable place in life. That's what I'm doing. Life is a gift; preserve it and use it!"

This day was the other important break in my life. Unfortunately, even though I tried hard to overcome my tragedy, I could not. I was too emotional. I was not happy with myself. I kept my feelings inside and was often too apathetic to stand up for my interests. "It does not matter," I thought. With time, I understood that it was intuitive self-preservation. Negative, painful occurrences were usually followed by a reaction of my digestive system and nerve disturbances. Better to avoid them.

At the Faculty, friends and the majority of students treated me as if nothing happened. Everybody had become used to having sons and daughters of the "enemies" around, although the Komsomol active ignored me.

The lecturer of the History of the Soviet Union class, Professor Rubach, was impressive, knowledgeable with his lively, friendly delivery. The rumor was that he also was arrested but was freed. Before his arrest, he was the head of the Communist Party Committee Publishing House. Soon, *The Concise History of the Communist Party* became the new Bible, not only for us but for the whole population of the country. In it, Stalin was the hero of the Revolution and afterwards. We admired the orderly and clear system of the book, simple in language with what looked like a good analysis of Marxism and Leninism. Later, we found out that the book was a falsification of the history of the country, Party, and revolutionary philosophy. The work falsely asserted that Stalin was Lenin's only true disciple and close friend. The other Bolsheviks happened to be traitors and deserters. The purpose of the book was to justify Stalin's dictatorship on historical grounds.

Expulsion from the Komsomol

At a meeting of our Komsomol organization, a couple of us sons and daughters of the "enemies," myself among them, were on the agenda. A boy renounced and disowned his father. He was reprimanded, but not expelled. A girl who did not disown her father was expelled.

It was my turn. "I know you will expel me." A voice from the hall: "Yes, we will. You are the daughter of our enemy."

Even I knew my new political standing was that of "daughter of the Soviet folks' enemy," but this was the first time it was said in public. I felt I was losing self-control; there was no way out of this frightful injustice. I started screaming, but was stopped right away by David, the secretary. I was ashamed of myself and became self-possessed. "For ten years, the Komsomol was for me not only a political school in action, but a second family. I can't renounce my father. He was not an enemy of the people. He would defend our system of socialism with his life."

"Are you saying that our NKVD is wrong?"

"No. I'm saying that a mistake is possible."

"Our enemies around the world and here try to slander our defenders of the Revolution, the NKVD, and Nina is helping them." My friend said this and was followed by others expressing indignation at my defense of my father. I knew what to expect, but it was hard to take more beating. Particularly painful was facing the changes by my friends. Just a few hours ago, they encouraged and calmed me down. They acted like friends, but at the meeting they said I was their enemy. They didn't act like fair-thinking humans, but like puppets on strings, being pulled by some evil power. I was expelled.

The next day, a few of them showed some sort of embarrassment. The others, "activists," didn't notice me at all. Days later, they seemed to be normal humans and talked to me, but at the meeting they enacted a ritual prescribed to them. Stalin's aphorism, "A human being—that sounds proud," was a delusion, a deceit. Independently thinking humans had disappeared or become silent.

The words became useless. That was the true tragedy of my time. People learned the art of talking, but saying nothing. Smooth revolutionary words were a necessity for the defense of one's own life. I preferred to be silent, instead of uttering useless words. I tried to occupy my mind completely, not to have any free time. Otherwise, Misha's image dominated my mind and feelings.

Trying to Relax

My third year of university was finished and it was summer vacation of 1939. Anna Ivanovna, my Godfather's wife from Yalta, visited us. Mama took a vacation. Four of us—Mama, Anna, *Krestnaia*, and I—all wives of executed "enemies" of the Soviet people, tried hard to have a good time, relax, and not speak about our husbands. But their images, their souls were with us, making us feel guilty even for our innocent pleasure.

Every day we picnicked in the park; in the evenings after a good dinner, we went to the movies, or theater, or to the City Park to listen to the orchestra, and dance. *Krestnaia* was forty-one; I was twenty-five. She was a really beautiful woman, slim, not tall, with very fine facial features, chestnut colored hair, greenish shiny eyes, and a reddish complexion like an American Indian. In general, this was unusual for the Russian appearance. I jokingly protested that not many men gave me a second look, but practically every man gave several looks to *Krestnaia*. It was not unusual that she was asked to dance by two men at once. Anna also was quite popular and an excellent dancer. I didn't want to dance.

The Fourth Year of University

On September 1, 1939, the fourth year of university started. Professor Rubach continued teaching the history of the Soviet Union. Once, speaking about the revolution of 1905, he said that on the ninth of January thousands of working people went to the Tsar's Winter Palace to beg him to help and intercede for them against His

225

Majesty's bureaucracy to change the unfair laws against them. People still believed in the Tsar as their last hope and help. They were greeted with bullets, cossacks' sabres, and whips. Hundreds of dead bodies covered the Palace Square.

The outcome was three-fold. First, the hope and belief in the Tsar as the people's only defender was lost. There was no hope left at all. Secondly, they realized that they could only help themselves. Lastly, no more begging; only through their organized power and mass uprising could a new political regime be established to change their grim lot for the better.

Momentarily, I was lost in my saddened, frightful thoughts. This historical lesson was one of many and now we were in the situation of the ninth of January, 1905. Our government with its system of fake, so-called socialism had to be abolished. That was the first time I had the clear thought that our anti-socialist and inhumane government was not viable and had to be eliminated. Afterwards, this shocking idea lived with me in secret. The more I thought about it, the more assured and calm I became. I was for the real socialism, understanding it as a truthful democracy in which all human rights are safeguarded. I talked to Ina and she agreed with me. But the entire history of the world is full of uprising, civil wars, and revolutions. Although those actions were justified, they more often brought just another oppressor, another brutality. How could this vicious circle be changed?

In spite of the terrors, horrors, and endemic lying to the people, we thought that the Soviet Union was stable. The rulers were deceiving the public, but not themselves. Their grip on reality was yet unshakable. However, the more they relied on the forces of coercion, the more dependent they became on them. People were opening their eyes and minds to this. Instability and revolution can follow, resulting in a political system and political parties which could be no better.

We still expected that our system would evolve into a good society after Stalin died. The new, very secret joke became an enjoyable political propaganda:

What does the SSSR (USSR) mean?
Smert Stalina Spaset Rossiiu—Death of Stalin will Save Russia.
That kind of thinking was spreading.

The most original course was the History of the Colonial and Dependent Countries. Professor Nina Semenovna was borrowed, from Moscow as was the majority of our professors. She was about forty years old, good-looking, vivacious, and a "big flirt." All of us were fascinated with her, especially the boys. She was fluent in Chinese, having spent more than three years with the Mao-Zedong army teaching Marxism. She joined them during the "Long March" from the south to the northwest of China.

In the 1920s, the Chinese Soviet Republic was created in south China which could not survive under China's Nationalist forces attacks. Mao-Zedong, the communist leader, made a desperate gamble. He led 100,000 communists on an almost impossible 6,000 mile trek, with constant fighting. In 1935, only 3,000 of them reached their goal. They reestablished the Soviet Republic, now bordering the Soviet Union. The last sustained them and helped organize a strong communist movement.

Nina Semenovna, sent by the Central Committee of the Soviet Union Communist Party, lived there in the caves as the majority did, teaching and helping Mao and all his comrades. She gave us unbelievable insight into that movement, and the character of the Chinese people.

It would be unrealistic to expect myself to be as comfortable at the Faculty as before. After all, I was the daughter of the "enemy" of the Soviet folks, and expelled from the Komsomol. The Komsomol active still tried not to notice me.

Once, my blind friend, Isaak, asked the class for a minute of their attention. This was normal practice, just before a professor would enter.

"Let us nominate Nina to organize *Kult Pokhods*," he said. The class answered *da*, [yes].

Kult Pokhods is the collective attendance of theaters, philharmonic, and other cultural institutions. Usually about forty or fifty of us would go, a few students of the Theatre Institute would bring whole scores of the opera. Normally we were seated on *Gallerka*, or "Student's Heaven" on the second or third floor. These *pokhods* were very enjoyable and generated a lot of playfulness.

Sometime later, we would discuss the performance. Once again, I was close to all the students. It was a tremendous help for my psychological condition.

A course in Russian literature, which started the previous semester, was good and a little unusual. The professor, an outsider, from Kiev was excellent. Later, when we studied the views of the "Russians Abroad" group on Russian culture, we realized that our professor had expressed many elements of their outlook and philosophy.

The great Russian culture of the 19th century—classical literature, music, theater, and art—was not an end in itself, but a means to inspire spiritual and cultural changes in human beings. All 19th century literature had philosophical, religious, and sociological direction: the Christian themes of searching for salvation, deliverance from evil, and from the sufferings and deep anguish with the condition of man. The age of Realism dominated Russian literature in the second half of the 19th century and it is Russian's principal contribution to world literature, including the literary giants Tolstoy and Dostoevsky. The main characteristic of this literature was a sympathetic attitude toward all human beings, "good" or "bad," depicting their intrinsic moral significance.

In most of the Russian culture existed some kind of unity subordinated to the certain quest, philosophy. In its importance, our literature was like another government, but more trustworthy as it professed the truth. Pushkin and Nekrasov were like contemporaries to us because they exposed tyrannical regimes. The professor's treatment of Dostoevsky was hardly acceptable in the 1930s. From the 1930s until 1956 (Krushchev's denunciation of Stalin), Dostoevsky's works were banned, except for a few like *Poor Folk*, which was presented superficially as an expression of social injustice.

The professor unfolded the story of the novel *The Possessed*. Dostoevsky had wanted to open the eyes of the public about revolutionaries and the catastrophe that they would bring Russia. A young man, Petr Verkhovensky, arrived in the city, aiming to organize a revolutionary movement. He established an underground group, which accomplished many devilish acts, including the execution of one of them, a revolutionary, with the purpose of binding all of them together by the blood of that crime. The type represented in the character of Petr was the most ugly that Dostoevsky had ever depicted. His moral code was the "catechism of the Revolutionary," in reality written by Bakunin, a revolutionary, and it expressed the idea that anything was permitted and justified for the aims of the Revolution. He had lost the criteria of "good" and "evil," of "right" and "wrong." In discussing this novel, the professor wanted us to know the real reactionary Dostoevsky. But it made us doubt our professor's intentions. His interpretation of Dostoevsky's *Legend of the Grand Inquisitor* confirmed our doubts. This *Legend* is Dostoevsky's philosophy and prophecy about the human race. Jesus came to the Earth to give people truth and freedom. The *Grand Inquisitor* promised the weak humans to burn up Jesus and make them happy. Instead of freedom, which means to make a choice, take a step into the unknown, which can be dangerous, *Inquisitor* gives them bread, leading to an irresponsible and peaceful life. The *Inquisitor* makes choices for them. They don't care about their slavery.

Although the main statement that he liked to repeat in this course was the great concept of Karl Marx: "If human nature is conditioned by its environment, then we must make this environment more humane."

Stalin's era in culture stretched the Realism of the 19th century to "Socialist realism," which often appeared as a distortion of realism (Stalin himself favored a melodramatic art). The wonderful, far-reaching innovations in all forms of culture which flourished at the beginning of the 20th century were suppressed, forced to die, or to develop with considerable changes. But the ontological and spiritual nature of this culture was preserved, though God was replaced by another "divinity," the communist society.

It's a mistake to think that Soviet literature was of an inferior quality, and the Soviet hero was an unattainable fantasy. This is only partially right. The list of great or outstanding writers and poets is long: Maxim Gorky and Mikhail Sholokov; Anna Akhmatova, a poet and creator of a true art, but not favored officially; Vladimir Mayakovsky, poet of the Revolution and his opposite, the writer Yevgeny Zamiatin, who could be called a dissident and whose *We* is recognized as a precurser to George Orwell's *1984*; Konstantin Fedin and Alexey Tolstoy, excellent novelists in the classic tradition; and Leonid Leonov, a "psychological" novelist. These are just a few before the later appearance of Boris Pasternak and Alexander Solzhenitsyn.

Pasternak themes were on how man should live his personal life.

Basically the Soviet literature follows traditional Russian conception, preoccupied with a search for the meaning of life and the destiny of mankind.

Solzhenitsyn was the first to give a truthful, unvarnished account of Stalin's concentration camp life. He is the most prolific author, presenting a panoramic view of the communist Russia. He was critical of the West, similar to the later Tolstoy, and specifically close to the position of Alexander Herzen. His character and his traits are traditionally Russian.

Socialistic Competition

Our department had a socialist competition with Kiev State University's department of history. Usually, every year a delegation of students and professors visited alternately—one year we would go to Kiev and another year they would come to us. In the summer of 1940, I was a member of our delegation. It was my first visit to Kiev and I was very impressed.

We knew the story behind the red color of the University building that made the Kievans so proud. About 150 years ago, students of the University staged a strike against the authorities. Later, when the Tsar, probably Nicholas I, was visiting Kiev, he told them to paint the University building red saying something like this: "If the students do not blush with shame, at least the building will show their shameful behavior."

Kiev is a beautiful green city with a much more relaxed atmosphere than Moscow or even Kharkov. It's neither too businesslike, like Moscow is, nor cold like St. Petersburg , and known instead for its friendliness and warmth. It's a sophisticated, ancient city. The supreme sights were the St. Sophia Cathedral, built in 1037 and considered to be a replica of the St. Sophia of Constantinople. Now it is an imposing white beautiful structure. Another, St. Andrew's Cathedral with five blue and white spike domes, was built by Rasterelli, who also built many famous buildings in St. Petersburg, including the Winter Palace. According to legend, St. Andrew's stands on the site overlooking the Dnieper River where the Apostle St. Andrew stood and erected a cross called St. Andrew's Cross and proclaimed from that place that God's faith would spread all around.

The most interesting sight is the Pechersk monastery, Lavra. The oldest church in the Pechersk (Ukrainian for cave) compound dates from 1051 and the bell tower was the tallest structure in the city at a few hundred meters. The Nazis, when they were evacuating Kiev, demonstrated as usual their "high culture" and with great difficulty blew up most parts of the Pechersk monastery and the famous bell tower, although it hadn't any military significance. The whole monastery lived in caves underground, including the graves for their saints. Probably because of the earth's consistency there, the bodies turned into well-preserved mummies. The Church claimed this as proof of sainthood. Lavra is regarded as the holiest institution in Russia, together with Zagorsk monastery near Moscow, called *Sergiev Posad*.

In a socialist competition the two sides—Kiev's history department and ours—had an agreement by which each side took a pledge to strive for and fulfill certain obligations. Specifically, the three main fields of activity were:

First, academic work consisted of different measures to raise the general quality of knowledge and to help students with some academic difficulties.

Secondly, the social work which was mainly the university lectory. Members of the lectory were not only professors, but also students. It provided speakers, lecturers, and just simple talk to hundreds of different organizations such as factories, plants, schools, young pioneer clubs, cultural and official government establishments, the farms around the city, and many others, with little or no pay for us.

Thirdly, our own cultural activities like going in groups or as a whole class to the theaters and opera and then discussing it afterwards. Our favorite activity was skiing in the park.

Both sides presented the record of fulfillment and the new pledges and agreement. After this, at a meeting of the whole department (professors and students), each side made a report of accomplishments and discussions of a new agreement, which was accepted.

Lectory

I was now a member of the Lectory. The theme of my lecture was

231

"The Komsomol in the Civil War." According to the rules, each student member had to write a lecture and present it to the Professors' committee, which made a decision on whether the work was "academically sound" and "ideologically sound." My case was very touchy. I was expelled from the Komsomol but I was talking about Komsomol heroism. K. M. told me straight about the extremely difficult position of the lectory, his and my own.

"Look what can happen. You present an excellent lecture. Then in the question period someone who is very vigilante asks you why you are not a member of the Komsomol. And you have to tell them what happened. In a minute, your lecture will be forgotten and harsh criticism will start with the demand to find out how it happened, whose fault it was, whether you are a *dwurushnik*, a two-faced person who stole into the Lectory. The next day, there will be a big article in the newspaper. You would be made a secret enemy and the Lectory and I would lose our class vigilance. The City Communist Party Committee will start an investigation. You will be arrested. You see, we have to think carefully. The Lectory has already had a few requests for your lecture. I want you to deliver your lecture to your class instead of me giving my normal lecture. Then I will see what will be appropriate to do."

I delivered the lecture. I was very nervous; the poetry in it was very emotional and I finished with the poetry of Eduard Bagritsky:

We were led by our youth into sabre battle
We were flung by our youth on the Kronstadt ice
The battle-horses whirled us away
On the broad square they killed us
But youth is not destroyed
Youth is forever alive.

Isaak was the first one on his feet and clapping. The class followed him. Isaak's body was trembling from his cry. He lost his sight during the Civil War when he joined a Komsomol detachment. His left eyebrow had a gash across it that continued in a narrow shiny line across his forehead. He was receiving a special pension from the government. The class gave me an excellent grade.

Several days later, K. M. showed me the Lectory listing where under my name was all the information about my membership in the

Komsomol and my expulsions. "Now it's up to them to decide," he said.

My lecture became quite popular in the Lectory. Perhaps the "war is in the air" situation in 1940–41 intensified interest.

Fear of War

In the autumn of 1940, people realized that a tragic future was approaching us—a new war. We were going to be attacked. One of the military *punkt*, conscription offices, was on the next street, Pushkin, just across from our building. From my room's window, I saw the big back yard which every day filled with people who had come with a young conscripted man to see him off. According to an old custom, the relatives and friends would party the whole night and in the morning they would accompany him. They were singing, playing the *garmon* (accordian) or the guitar and the "old" people—mother, father, close relatives—would be in the back of the group, usually crying.

In our region of the intelligentsia and bureaucrats, it still wasn't a permanent picture, but in the workers' regions on the left bank of the river, these groups became the normal ornaments on the streets, especially toward the spring of 1941.

Who was going to attack us? This question excited us perhaps more than the general population. We were the first line for the military duties; almost all boys were petty officers and all girls medical nurses.

"Germans? No. We have a peace agreement with them."

"Hitler is not trustworthy. Almost a year ago, he declared that Germany shall defeat the Soviet Union and German rule will have to encompass the world."

"The Old Entente—England, France, and now America—they didn't want to sign the peace agreement with us."

Fifth University Year
Opening Our Minds

The last, fifth year of university started in September, 1940. It was the most exciting year of studies; we didn't have any more classes or lectures. In the fall semester we received the right to study at the "special fund" of the University Central Library. Speaking plainly, we were allowed to read forbidden books not in circulation. The rules of behavior in the reading room were very strict. Each of us had a specific identification card and if we left the room for even five to ten minutes, the book had to be put on the librarian's desk. This one semester provided me with a profound understanding of Russia, specifically in comparison with Western Europe. The factual knowledge that we had previously received made possible the critical understanding of the analytical material.

We organized our group's work very productively, spending every day in the reading room from morning to evening. Each of us made a short summary of the readings, and once a week we discussed what we learned and copied those summaries. The last (spring) semester was preparation for the State exams and taking them, only three subjects.

It was in the winter of 1940 that I was called to see the University Communist Party Secretary. I was very nervous, expecting something really bad. In his office, I met three students of foreign languages— German, English, and French—although I never exhibited an aptitude for languages. The Secretary told us that we would help to host a group of foreign journalists who wanted to see the collective farms. He gave me an additional assignment: to tell them about my father and that I was not expelled from the University and even now I was a member at the University Lectory.

The night before our trip with the correspondents there was a heavy snowfall, up to five feet of snow on the ground. I thought that our bus with the eight journalists and a number of the service people like interpreters and political watchdogs, would be stuck. But to my surprise, the road was unusually clear for the twenty kilometers to the *kolkhoz*, as were all the roads in that huge village—even passages to the peasants' homes were cleared.

At the *kolkhoz*, the journalists looked through the stables for horses, cows, pigs, and other animals. All the shades were clean, the walls freshly painted. The animals were clean and well-fed. The *kolkhoznics* who took care of the animals looked clean and happy as well. Then the Chairman of the *kolkhoz* led all of us to a few peasants' homes. They were well-furnished, clean, had running water and a sanitation room (bathroom).

Finally, there was a reception for us in the *kolkhoz* club. Naturally, there was a lot of good peasant food and vodka. The "bosses" of the *kolkhoz* and the village provided information about the good life there. It was quite true, because this *kolkhoz* was one of the best in the region. In spite of this good reality, there was also a *pokazukha*, a phony show put on for people of high standing to impress them.

Another epithet for this is "Potemkin village." In 1787, Prince Potemkin, the Governor of the Southern Province, had erected stage scenery to look like villages along the road that Catherine the Great was traveling, though at quite a far distance from it. All over the world, officials and people want to show their better side to visitors, especially to journalists. But truthfully, the Soviet *pokazukha* and *vranyo*, lies, were perfected in their great dramatic skills.

Our Perception of Russia Was Broadened

Our perceptions of Russia's past and present were immensely broadened, bringing some important changes in our assumptions. We were not looking for new historical facts, but for new views and interpretations that differed from the Marxist-Leninist philosophy, which was the only one acceptable to us. Our interest and fascination were concentrated on the famous authors who left Russia after the October Revolution, the "Russians Abroad," *Russkoye Zarubezhie*. We were already acquainted with this group from our philosophy class. The most famous among them were N. Berdiaev, G. Fedotov, G. Florovskiy, B. Zenkovskiy, L. Shestov, S. Frank, and many more. Their scholarly concentrations were in philosophy, philosophy of history, theosophy, Russian orthodoxy, in problems of the East and West, and in classic Marxism and Russian communism. Their contributions to European philosophy, history, and religion were considerable; many of their works were published in the European languages. But their great merit was in broaching the all-embracing problems of past and present Russia. The image of Russia became more diverse for us, but quite often made us confused. We wondered who was right.

Berdiaev's books, *The Russian Idea, The Roots and Meaning of Russian Communism, The Fate of Russia,* and others made our heads whirl and intensified our search for answers. We were astonished by Berdiaev's portrayal of the Russian character, which gave us a profound understanding of ourselves. Comparing the German, or European character in general with the Russian character helped me later to understand European politics better. After WWII, while living in Germany, I was convinced that Berdiaev was quite close to the truth in his depiction of the characters. For instance, he thought the Germans perceived the world as lacking in order. It had to be stopped by Germans, who claimed to be the bearers of order and organization, as they understood it. Hence, aggressiveness and egotism—no acceptance of anything outside of their own will and spirit. "It is right because I did it"—Hegel's well-known words. There are, certainly, many great traits in the German character.

The Russian people's specific attitude toward life and their specific mentality comprised of intense spirituality can be explained not only by Russian Christianity and history, but by Russian geography as well. Russia's endless space and broad flat land conditioned such attributes in the Russian character as unlimitedness, maximalism, extensiveness, and freedom. The cold climate and wooded plains shaped people's lives. Men led a rather sedentary life during winter. They could extract everything they needed from the forest: logs for the hut, fur for clothing, bark for shoes, wax for candles, meat, berries, down to sweet honey.

The tradition of extending warm hospitality to anyone, to meet them with drinks and bread and warm *shchi*, or *borshch* (vegetable soup) was a necessity in a cold climate and such a vast territory. It remains some to the present day. During long winters, there was really not much to do except to have a drinking party, to make shoes from bark, to tan animal hides for *kozhukhs* (sheepcoats), or to decorate utensils, home objects, stoves, and windows with carving and artistic painting. Sometimes a small *izba* looks like a little museum of ethnic art. In the *Old Chronicle* it is said the Rus took Byzantine Orthodoxy because of its *krasota*—beauty. Hence, the idea that Russian Christianity is aesthetic and Russians have a specific feeling for beauty. During the short summers, people worked hard and long hours. There was not enough time to do their work precisely and tidily.

Berdiaev expressed the thought that in the West, land and everything is partitioned, enclosed, deprived of broadness and wholeness. The same is true of the soul of the Western people; it is lacking in breadth, too differentiated, restricted. Russian people have a different geography and a different mentality, and soul. In their soul is endless breadth. They are freer in life and in their religious attitudes. They don't like to be bound by form, organizations, laws or rules.

Actually, two contrasting sources played prominently in the formation of the Russian character. In particular, the first was the natural spontaneous forces and the second was the asceticism of Orthodoxy and the autocracy of the State. Hence, the contradiction, the polarization in the Russian character. In *The Russian Idea*, Berdiaev formulated these contradictory virtues: despotism and anarchism-freedom; inclination to violence and kindness, and humility; ritualism in religion and freedom to search for the truth and God; individualism and collectivism; extreme passion and inertia; nationalism and universalism; endurance and riot. Russians were aware that keeping order in their huge country was a hard task and their traits of character were ill-fitted for that task. That's why they preferred to have strict authorities, though they had to be Russians.

Interestingly, the recent facts of *Romir* polling agency says that 85.7 percent of Russians said they believe only strong government is capable of bringing order into Russia.

Are Russians self-confident people? We debated this ardently and were surprised that a few non-Russian scholars expressed the opinion that Russians are not self-confident enough. We agreed that Russians are not as aggressive as other nationalities, are more modest and lacking in the superficial appearance of confidence. But we are very much a self-confident people. Although contrasting values can be found in each nation and in each human, only in Russian and Jewish people did they reach a tragic limit.

Also in the Russian character are two streams of World history—the East and the West came to interact and left their influences. The spirituality of the Russian people was expressed through the Orthodox religion. The Russian idea, the Russian calling in the world was connected to Orthodoxy, which taught a Russian to renounce the worldly life: materialism, greediness, attachment to private possessions, in other words, an attachment to the earthly kingdom.

Western Christianity created a great universal culture, but Russian Orthodoxy believed in the inner connection of a human with God. It's absolutely ontological. Until Peter the Great, Russian culture was religious and as a type, Russians are religious; they have to have spiritual aim. Their souls are not inclined to skepticism or partiality; they accept, rather, totality and orthodoxy. But they can switch from one wholly orthodox belief to another. That's what happened in 1917. Russians are apocalyptic people by nature. They strive to create the Kingdom of God on Earth or a Kingdom of Brotherhood and social justice without God. Someone compared the European character, which was like a formal English park that has been trimmed for several hundred years, to the Russian character which was like a natural park still growing fast and full of energy.

We agreed with many foreign observers who confirmed that Russians are more free from malice and vengefulness. Regarding Stalin, it was said that he was a Georgian reared in the tradition of the blood feud. Some foreigners admit that Russians can be very violent when their patriotic feelings are aroused. The others credited Russians to be tolerant of people of different nationalities. As well, their tolerance is traditionally extended to the religious sphere. This degree of flexibility was probably derived from centuries of living in a multinational empire.

These studies created discussions and disagreements among us. We rejected a number of Berdieav's characteristics, especially cruelty.

Russia always had differentiated between citizenship and nationality. Over one hundred nationalities and ethnic groups live in Russia. A citizenship was one for all—Russian, or the USSR from 1918 to 1991; a nationality was up to one personal declaration: Russian, Ukrainian, Eskimo, Armenian, German, Kirgiz, Buriat, and many more.

In 1940-41, when we studied these works of Berdiaev and others, we felt their ideas about Russia and Russians were sound. Sixty years later, after the Russian people have gone through several apocalyptic events and face yet another uncertainty, the character of the people is also going through profound changes.

The understanding of the nature of our State was a dramatic experience for us. In some connection we read about the peace of Westphalia, after the Catholic-Protestant strife in Europe. It pointed out that the Sovereign has the authority over the State and people have individual rights. It made us wonder about our State. Our Sovereign is the lawless Dictator, contrary to the constitution. As well the individual rights are only in propaganda not in the practical life.

The problem was too complicated and dangerous for discussion in public. Also, if the Sovereign policy is not in the interest of the public, how would people remove him? Finally, we understood reality, that our Communist State was an extension of the Communist Party itself. In reality, people's rights depended on the political situation imposed by the Party. Constitutional division of the State powers was not practiced. All and any decisions were made by Politbureau (Stalin) down to the Party cells (secretary), the same in the whole country.

In spite of Berdiayev's anticommunist philosophy, he affirmed that any form of social organization is justified if it serves the free human beings.

Roots of Communism

Another question we analyzed with great interest was where to look for the roots of communism in Russia. The roots of the 19th century's preparation for the Revolution can be found in Western Europe. Changes in thought—philosophical, political, cultural—were the outcome of the contacts with the West. Both Christianity and communism were children of the West and in changed forms they became the most penetrating ideas in the Russian mind because both of them are for human equality and justice. But the paradox was that Russia accepted those Western ideas and changed them in their application. They turned out to be in contrast to the norms and ideas of bourgeois society. Hence, the unique character of the 1917 Revolution basically conveyed the Western ideas taken by the radical intelligentsia and changed them specifically into ideas of social equality and justice and the rejection of capitalism.

To follow the outlook of some historians, it would be right to say that one of the important differences between the Revolution carried on by the Bolsheviks on one side and the ideas of the liberal and even radical intelligentsia was in Lenin himself, a leader of the Revolution. In spite of the fact that Lenin was a product of the Russian idealistic intelligentsia, he was a theoretician of the Revolution and its main point, how to take and hold State power. He combined in himself traits of the revolutionary-maximalist and the Statesman; in essence, traits of Chernishevsky and Nechaev united with Peter the Great.

239

There was no doubt in our outlook that the Revolution and the history of the Soviet Union could not be explained soley by Marxist ideology nor solely by the Russian heritage.

They Watched Me

I was called to the University Rector's office. The secretary brought me to a tiny room, the last one in the rear of the building with a small notch instead of a window. I noticed right away a big door heavily secured to prevent hearing from the outside what was going on inside. I realized they had not invited me for academic talk and I froze. A man came in and introduced himself. Our talk went more or less like this:

"Please, relax," he said. "I want to ask you several questions and it's better to tell the truth. We don't like those who are lying to us."

That's the statement of the century, I thought.

"We know who you are and we want to know who is paying for your good life and your very expensive clothing. Is it a man or a country?"

From then on, I understood I was in great danger. But I explained to him that my husband had bought materials in Siberia where Moscow University students worked on industrial projects. My fear disappeared. I was as mad as I was in Moscow at the NKVD Center; I didn't care anymore. The man continued to ask me many questions, repeating them and screaming at me, and I was screaming back at him. Then abruptly, late in the evening, he told me to get out. I told only my Mama about this interrogation. They did not bother me anymore. The political situation in the country became softer and besides, the war was approaching.

Moscow and the West

We realized that the history of the relationship between Russia and the West was complicated and torturous. In 1480, the Tartar-Mongols' yoke finally came to an end. Now backward Russia needed the European knowledge of how to move forward. Ivan III

240

(1463–1505) and his Greek wife Sophia Paleologh, a niece of the last Byzantine emperor, invited to Russia not only foreign merchants, but master professionals. In Moscow, a foreign colony was originated.

The Academician S. Platonov, in his book *Moscow and the West*, provided excellent information on relations between Russia and the West. For instance, Ivan IV (the Terrible, 1533–1586) sent a big delegation to Europe to recruit "knowledgeable people" in all the professions. Then the German Hans Schlitte assembled 123 people —scholars, architects, doctors, mining masters, gold and metal masters and others. But Ghanza Commercial Union and the Polish government and some of the German states sent a special delegation to the Pope and the Emperor of the Holy Roman Empire to explain to them what a dreadful harm would happen if Moscow learned the military and technological arts of the West. The idea of the "Moscow danger" was born. The recruits were no longer allowed through the borders. Since then, not much has changed in the geo-political conjuncture.

We found out that the notion about Russian cultural strata in the past and present as being against the West was false. The great Russian thinkers, philosophers, and writers exposed not the Western culture in general, but its condition of ungodliness in practical life and bourgeois injustice and excessive materialism. We dreamed of seeing European culture and at the same time rejected its economic and social systems. We were sincerely afraid of the West's anti-Soviet position and believed they were preparing war against us.

The Role of the Intelligentsia

The Russian intelligentsia was a unique creation in world history. The titan Peter the Great raised Russia on his own shoulders and created the intelligentsia from the nobility who were educated primarily in Germany. It was an absolute necessity for the state to have an educated elite. But it split Russia into two societies: the educated aristocrats and noblemen and the rest, including the illiterate peasants. The new intelligentsia spoke not Russian, but German or French, and scorned Russian traditions and culture. These two parts of society didn't understand each other anymore. Western culture and technology were brought to Russia at the price of alienation of the upper class from the lower classes. But Peter created a powerful and more contemporary Empire.

The liberal intelligentsia from the nobility were the first breeze of the expression of liberal ideas on Russian soil. Petersburg, which had started to become alienated from the rest of Russian culture, slowly was coming back to its roots. The Decembrist uprising of aristocracy in 1825 after centuries of supporting Tsarist Absolutism, showed that the nobility wanted political and social changes, specifically a constitutional monarchy and the abolishment of serfdom. The liberal nobility split from the monarchy; their liberalism reflected more of the Russian National Idea now. In general, Russian society was striving back toward its *pochva* (roots) and becoming disillusioned with the practice of Western Europe. Literature and theaters created comedies about some half-educated landlords striving to imitate European customs, or being against education. The most popular of these was Fonvisin *Row Youth*, a mother doesn't see the need for her son to study geography. "Our *Van'ka* (coachman) knows all the roads around."

The reforms of Alexander II in 1861 were of the greatest importance. The abolishment of serfdom and other reforms set free a tremendous energy on all levels of society. It brought a significant advance of economic, social, and intellectual life. The capitalist forms of Western economy were developing in Russia and the new class of the industrial workers from the peasantry was growing.

A new kind of intelligentsia was born in the 1830s, formed not only by educated nobility but by other classes, too, like the clergy and the state *chinovnics,* bureaucrats. Their political outlook was of Russian nationalism and their philosophy was secular humanism and idealism. One of the most widely debated topics of this period was the "meaning of history." Pushkin's *Boris Godunov* (1825), Glinka's *A Life for the Tsar* (1836), and many other historical plays, operas, paintings, and literary works dominated the cultural scene.

Peter Chaadaev's *Philosophical Letters* about Russian historical development served as the last impetus for a famous debate about Russia's past and the ways of the future. This movement split the intelligentsia into Westernizers and Slavophiles. Chaadaev expressed an entirely pessimistic view of Russian history. Tsar Nicholas I said Chaadaev belonged in a psychiatric hospital because of his unpatriotic ideas and he was the first thinker in Russian history who was treated for psychosis on the Tsar's orders. Each camp, the Westernizers and the Slavophiles, was opposed to both Nicholas I's regime and the Western bourgeoisie; each sought to borrow Western ideas and culture but without Western practices that were unfair to people. The attainment of social justice was the aim of Russian political struggle.

The intelligentsia had a mystical faith in the simple Russian people; this attitude formed the basis of Russian nationalism, messianism and the populist movements. The belief in the Russian peasantry was tied to the hopes placed in the peasants' communal life, which was now called *mir* or *obshchina*. Alexander Herzen was an outstanding personality, a leader of the Westernizers, and the son of a count, who had to live abroad and was greatly disillusioned with the Western bourgeoisie. He concluded that Russia would not need a capitalist phase in economic development, but it could go through a socialist revolution and have a communal form of social organization.

Herzen's protest against Western society was based on the reasoning that the contemporary generation had only one God and his name was "Capital" (Money), which corrupted the body of Europe, it is painful to see that this was a Europe in which they had believed. Christianity, revolution, everything had grown shallow. Herzen agreed with the Slavophiles about the peasant *obshchina*, but for the Slavophiles *obshchina* was an expression of Christian brotherhood, for Herzen this conveyed the socialistic instinct of the Russian people and a form of social organization. The aim of Herzen's struggle was social justice and freedom.

Changes in our Class

Our class content was changing; a number of pairs who were dating did get married, some to the other faculty students. They hurried to marry to be sure to receive jobs in the same region. The wedding parties in the dorms, as well as congratulations in our faculty's newsletter became usual *scenas*.

For several days, Lena didn't come to the Library. We wondered what happened and decided that I should go to find out. Her family lived in the workers' region in their own small house which her grandfather had built.

Lena's mother met me and fell on my chest, crying bitterly. "Lena's boyfriend of over two years broke up with her. They were planning to marry. He said he doesn't love her and doesn't want her. Lena had tried to commit suicide and I'm watching her day and night."

Lena was in her room. She looked at me with cold eyes I never saw before. She didn't want to talk to me. Finally she said that she was not going to continue her studies. The experience with her boyfriend made her understand people, how they are deceitful, dishonest liars and egoists. She didn't want to live in this world.

I persuaded her to go with me to stay with us. The next day, I left Lena with my mama, who talked to her not about her boyfriend, but about Lena, her character and life. She opened up the truth of our decision and consequent behavior after the tragedy. In the evening, all of our group came and we told her we loved her and needed her to be with us. The next day, Lena was in the Library. For Mama and me our shut-off past because of our trauma was again open.

One of our classmates, a very nice fellow, was in love with Lena, but she brushed him off. When I saw him in the Library, I told him Lena was free. In the spring they were married, and both were very happy.

The Radicals

For the pupils of Herzen, the radicals Nikolai Chernyshevsky, Nikolai Pisarev, Vissarion Belinsky, and many others, the political struggle became their revolutionary aim—the creation of a new Democratic Russia. The Westernizers' movement split. Belinsky, a literary critic, was not only a supreme authority of literary criticism but he expressed the ideals of Russian progressive society; he was the "conscience of Russia." His departure from the camp of the idealistic philosophy of Hegel to the camp of atheistic socialism had tremendous influence on the evolution of the view of all Russian intelligentsia. In his letter to Prince Botkin, a fellow revolutionary, Belinsky stated his revolt against God by saying that he wanted from Him an account of all the victims in human history; he didn't want happiness for himself if his human brothers were not taken care of. Dostoyevsky repeated this idea in Ivan Karamasov's rebellion against God in his novel *The Brothers Karamasov.*

In the '60s and '70s, Chernishevsky became the supreme leader of the radical intelligentsia, which was now in opposition not only to the Tsarist's regime, but to the liberal "fathers," the previous generation. Ivan Turgenev in the novels *Fathers and Sons* and *Rudin*, Fedor Dostoyevsky in *The Possessed*, Chernishevsky in *What Has to Be Done* and other authors depicted this time as a political split among generations. Chernishevsky called for class struggle against Tsarism and capitalism. He professed the materialist philosophy but personally was an ascete of high morals, an idealist. He was a precursor of Lenin and Bolshevism. Chernishevsky's fate was the same as that of the many thousands of Populists who followed his ideals, mainly young, idealistic students who went to the villages to educate and organize the peasants. After spending years in the Peter and Paul's Fortress, he was sent to Siberia for eighteen years and came back physically, but not psychologically or morally, broken.

The Populists of the '70s were zealots of a new belief—the emancipation of the Russian people. For this idea they went to their deaths, just as two hundred years before the "old believers" had burned themselves in the churches for, as they thought, their pure and uncorrupted Christianity. After the Populists, the new revolutionary Bolsheviks followed them on the way to Siberia for the same ideals. Reading the lives of those revolutionaries and their passion for truth, we worshipped them and felt our insufficiency, our acceptance of injustice. They were real human beings.

The distraction of the Populist movement by the government changed the essence and trend of the intelligentsia. They divided into groups and factions. Some joined a terrorist organization which carried out a number of terrorist acts, including the assassination of Tsar Alexander II. Lenin's older brother Alexander took part in the aborted assassination of Tsar Alexander III and was executed for it. This had a profound influence on Lenin's life.

Sophiya Perovskaia had led the victorious bomb squad into action against Alexander II on March 1, 1881. She was a former school mistress and a Province Governor's daughter. Lamentable inefficiency of her public execution together with her four accomplices broke into scandal. Similar to this happened during the execution of the Decembrists in 1826. A famous comment of one of the victims was: "My God, they can't even hang a man decently in Russia."

Still others found a new class, the proletariat, and started organizing a real, not utopian, class struggle. Russia was changing: the workers' class and the capitalist-industrialist system were growing and the nobility's estates were disappearing. Anton Chekhov in his play *The Cherry Orchard* depicted this period excellently.

In the '90s, Marxism came to Russia to stay, in contrast to Europe, where it did not find a warm nest. Georgy Plekhanov, a Marxist educated in Europe, introduced it and the Russian Social-Democratic Party was born, which consisted now of the intelligentsia and self-educated workers. Lenin made an iron troop of the professional revolutionaries, the Bolsheviks, aiming to take the power of the State and abolish Tsarism.

Russian intelligentsia was the only formation like this in the world, made up of idealistic, fanatic, selfless, educated people, organized as would be an Order of the Moral Knights. As we know, the intelligentsia prepared the Revolution which annihilated the Russian autocracy and communism conquered and annihilated the majority of these intelligentsia. In the end, we had a clear picture of the development of the ideas and forces which planned and accomplished the October Revolution.

The October Revolution 1917

We were contemporary with many of these developments. The October Revolution had triumphed. It was an absolute change, an interruption of the whole previous period of history. Power was taken by a new class of people who immediately fulfilled their main promises: land was given to the peasants; peace had been achieved; factories were given to the workers; freedom. These smart decrees established trust and belief in the new government in a great part of the population. Almost all of these new managers of the country were professional revolutionaries. They were selfless fanatics, serving an idea—the improvement of the people's lives. They spent the larger part of their lives in jails and in exile. It's natural that their style of behaving remained with them from their days in jail: a suspiciousness, secretiveness, and intolerance. It's possible that some of these characteristics were brought to the new system of government.

246

Only the Proletariat victory had value. The Bolsheviks promised to abolish all privileges and Lenin did it. But soon the picture started to change. After an attempt on Lenin's life in 1918, a bodyguard was assigned to him. But why not for all the leaders? they asked. Soon all of them, down to the provincials, had bodyguards.

Later, Stalin's policy of bribing, and at the same time terrorizing the Party functionaries, usually the Old Bolsheviks and those in higher echelons, included initiating special lists—a nomenclatura for additional material "goodies." The lists grew longer both with names of people and the substances they were to receive. Even now, it's hard for me to understand and explain the shameful behavior of the higher echelons of the Party, the "Old Bolsheviks" who silently accepted these anticommunist conditions. They had not been afraid in the past to face death, jails, and exile for the sake of their ideals.

The "Kremlin's wives," who shared with their husbands life in jails and exile, were organizing children's orphanages, kindergartens, schools for the illiterate adults, and many other social institutions. They didn't have time for the kitchen, so domestics became a necessity. With time, the new view superseded the old; *nam polozheno*, we deserved it. The abyss between the Party functionaries and the people grew deeper, and a new privileged class was born. The Tsars and the nobility had privileges as a norm. It was inhuman, but there was no deceit.

Stalin and the Party deceived the people. There occurred a split between the promises of the Party and the reality. The Revolution had promised to abolish the cruel world of autocracy but instead, Stalin created an unheard of world of terror and cruelty in which the human being became a "zero," not even worthwhile of notice. The enthusiasm of the masses and the great success in building socialism on the one side and the senseless terror and rejection of human rights on the other brought about the most decisive split in the minds of the people.

We believed in the Marxist concept, that not our consciousness determines our being-existence, on the contrary, it's our existence that determines our consciousness. Its logical conclusion was that the future socialist society of equal people would have humane values. But our contemporary society is not humane, it practices the "class struggle," hence it's not socialistic.

We were rejecting a creed of the violent class struggle and the violent Revolution as the only way to change for the better people's existence. Violence didn't bring tolerance and peace. We thought the Russian people's belief in truth, specifically that of Tolstoy and Dostoevsky whose basic values coincided with the truth of socialism, had to win in time. The truth as understood by Dostoevsky: "...as an expression of the fight of good versus evil on the battlefield of men's hearts."

Were we naive? No, we comprehended reality. In our small group of five, we trusted each other and were not afraid to express our secret thoughts. The most painful question we discussed was: Is the Revolution dead?

Lena, a daughter of an Old Bolshevik, became very angry at this question. "How dare you even ask such a question! Our Revolution is ill. It would be unnatural, abnormal if such a gigantic world upheaval as our Revolution didn't have from time to time a high fever."

Yes, we were in doubt about our Revolution's direction. We believed it would be corrected after Stalin's death. But we stoically believed in socialism as the future economic and social formation of the human race.

8

Final Thoughts

My interest is concentrated, specifically on the problem of what kind of society was created in the Soviet Union during a period of over seventy years; what progress was made in achieving a society of social equality, economic satisfaction, freedom, and human fulfillment. For me, it is not simply an intellectual question. In my childhood, youth, and adulthood, I happily served those lofty ideals of building a socialist society. The entire population was harnessed and pulling the country forward, and many were serving the country with great enthusiasm. I left the Soviet Union during WWII, but since 1961, I have watched closely the life and development of the country as part of my job teaching Russian culture and language at the State University of New York at Buffalo. This enabled me to visit the Soviet Union, and a few times for prolonged periods of cultural exchange.

Let us briefly summarize the balance sheet of positive and negative outcomes of building socialism or false socialism in the Soviet Union.

In the very beginning of the Revolution, land was given to the peasants and factories became the property of the State with the workers taking part in their management. At this stage of development, economic equality was not expected. The principle was payment according to work performed. Workers enjoyed the security of their jobs, month-long paid vacations, often in rest homes for free. Pensions were at age 55 for women, age 60 for men. The government or industrial plants built housing for their workers who paid a meager rent. There were children's nurseries and kindergartens at the plants or at the government institutions. The clubs, libraries, and sports facilities often were the responsibility of the plants or the state institutions and free for the workers. There were clubs for school children where they had various activities after school.

In spite of the permanent shortages in personal commodities, and the low standard of living for the majority of the general population, there was no real poverty and no homeless or hungry people, excluding the abnormal period of collectivization. There was free medical care and the larger plants had their own polyclinics. Education was free, from kindergarten through doctorate degrees. Higher Education students even received a good stipend every month. New colleges were opening up everywhere. For instance, in the early 1970s, the Soviet Union possessed more than 800 higher educational institutions with 4.5 million students, as compared to 105 in pre-Revolution Russia with 127,000 students. Also, take into account the damage inflicted by the Nazis during WWII on Russia's cultural wealth. Over 80,000 schools, higher educational and research institutes were destroyed. Even estate museums, like Leo Tolstoy's Yasnaya Poliana, Pushkin's Mikhailovskoe, Tchaikovsky's Klin, Chekhov's Yalta House, and others were ravaged. Now all are rehabilitated and rebuilt.

The achievements in literature, music, theater, cinema, and art were hard to overstate. Although the entire culture was forced to express the idea of the greatness of building socialism, the interests of a person had to be directed to the fulfillment of that great idea. There was no shortage of examples of extraordinary human deeds that provided all the arts with an abundance of great dramatic facts, even though strict censorship was never asleep, which limited free creativity.

Notwithstanding inadequacy, shortages, and unfairness, the economic, social, and cultural achievements were outstanding. Not diminishing the government's role, these were the people's achievements, created by their enthusiasm, heroism, and intelligence. The means used to achieve these aims had been created by Stalin and were coercive in contradiction with the political aims. The principle of social equality and belief in its attainment which inspired the Revolution was changing and not in favor of the workers and peasants, although the idea of an egalitarian society was publicly intensified. Even Stalin presented the country with his "God-like" revelation that a socialist society in the Soviet Union had already been built and that they were living in that society.

Actually, the society of inequality and oppression abolished by the Revolution had again gained strong ground in Stalin's socialist country. The "new class," consisting of the Party and the Political Security (NKVD) bureaucracy and the intellectuals who were Party members was in place and had power and big privileges. Stalin's rule abandoned the main principles of socialism: democracy and freedom. The entire population, as well as the individual human being, in actuality had no rights and the masses' belief that they were the masters of their country was losing ground. Stalin had an unjustified mistrust toward the population and he divided all citizens into two categories: the "reliable" and the "unreliable." The most dangerous feature of this system was the profound split it created between word and deed. The canonization of hypocrisy, lying, and double talk made wide roads from Stalin down into the lower bureaucracy and society as a whole. Uncontrolled violence and terror against the Party members and the general population became the norm.

It's impossible to comprehend those ten years of high terror, from 1929 to 1939. It was a state of mass hypnosis or psychosis. Imagine the millions of *Zeki, Gulags* prisoners, who knew well their own innocence but accepted the notion that "it is needed for the Party, hence the Motherland," because our country is encircled by enemies who are trying to involve people in counter-revolutionary activities against the Soviet State to destroy us. They had to pretend that they were in the service of those counter-revolutionary forces, to make people vigilant. If it was needed for the Party, they were ready for anything: to pledge themselves, even their families and friends as spies, breakers, provocateurs, and wreckers, and not consider it an act of villainy. The author Lev Kopelev, who knew several different forms of GULAGS from his own experience, gave clear pictures of these kinds of psychoses in his reminiscences (Lev Kopelev, *Utoli moya pechali*, Ardis, 1981, in Russian).

We knew a tragic sarcastic joke: *When an arrested person insisted on his innocence, he was told, "Of course you are innocent. We know that. That's why you have gotten only ten years instead of the execution squad."*

What kind of economic, social, and political formation was that? The scholars provided a number of answers, mainly that this formation was socialism. Understandably, it was the most acceptable political answer which satisfied both existing capitalism and socialism systems. The greatest tragedy for the socialist movement in the world was Stalin's discrediting of the idea of socialism in the name of

251

building socialism under the banner of Lenin. This happened in the country that was the first in world history to start a new social-political-economic formation and to provide an example for other countries. As a result, a viable idea was killed.

To qualify the Soviet Union as socialist meant doing a serious disservice to the idea of socialism, although its great economic and social achievements, including cultural ones, can be qualified as a kind of socialist system. But the absence of democracy and freedom, and instead during Stalin's rule, an all-embracing terror and oppression of the entire population, made it impossible to qualify the system as socialism. All wonderful ideals of the Revolution were washed in blood. Voltaire, the French philosopher of Enlightenment, once said that tolerance has never brought Civil War; intolerance has covered the earth with carnage.

Why did it happen? According to my understanding, the horrors of high Stalinism were neither the by-product of the Russian political heritage nor the natural development of a socialist system. Even though the Russian heritage is a tradition of absolutism with restricted freedom, the mass political terror against the population was not practiced. It would be unjust to explain it as systemic, that the nature of the system of socialism is not workable. It's true in practice the system didn't produce conclusive results. For an impartial judgment, it's important to recognize the singularity of subjective cause, "Stalin's inhuman rule," which determined the development of the Soviet system.

At the end of 1988, the extraordinary political novel *Children of the Arbat* by Anatoly Ribakov was published in Moscow. A broad discussion developed immediately which was centered on Stalin's image. Two renowned publicists, V. Chubinsky and V. Kavtorin, reflected the opinions of the country.

Ribakov undertook the very brave task of creating the truthful character of Stalin, his inner psychological world, the motives for his behavior and decisions. Stalin was undersized, with narrow shoulders, low-brows, a pock-marked face, and a traumatized right hand. He had a poor and humiliating childhood, was expelled from the religious Seminary, and later felt inferior to his highly-educated fellow revolutionaries. All of these may have created wounded ambitions and a craving for self-assumed power which was transformed into pathological cruelty and revenge.

Ribakov, through devising Stalin's inner monologues, tried to find the logic and conformity in his views and deeds characteristic of his whole life. In one of these, Stalin, after seeing his friend the Old Bolshevik, who was now a diplomat and with whom he had been in Siberian exile, expressed his inner thoughts about "them"—the top leaders, his friends.

"*They* were convinced that *he* was fully indebted to *them*. *They* were wrong. The true leader took power by *himself* and was indebted for this only to *himself*. Otherwise, he was not a leader, but *their* creature. *They* did not select *him*. *They* had not helped *him*, but *he* had raised *them* up to the top of state power. In order to be a leader, even a monarch had to destroy his close surroundings, which used to see in him their marionette. So did Peter and Ivan the Terrible (Stalin exaggerated it, specifically about Peter). *He* would not be the exception. That which Lenin called bureaucratic corruption was the only realistic form of governing. *His* bureaucracy, apparat, had to carry out without any denial, *his* orders. Did *he* have such an apparat? No, not yet. The apparat, which was created during the struggle for power considered itself as the associate in the victory of the Revolution, but not the instrument of the leader. *He* had to get rid of this old apparat. Certainly *they* would become *his* enemy, so *they* must be destroyed. *He* must create a new apparat and keep it in fear. This fear would be transferred down to the people."

Are these masterful monologues simply the author's inventions? The general opinion was in agreement with the author. In one interview, Ribakov explained his method. It proceeded from Stalin's real actions, his deeds, which certainly reflected his thoughts. He acted exactly in this way. He strengthened his role by creating an atmosphere of general fear in the country and hypocritically covering this antihuman policy with accusations that the enemies supported by capitalistic countries were spying on and wrecking the Socialist State.

At the XVIIIth Congress of the Communist Party in 1934, some delegates wanted to unseat Stalin as the General Secretary of the Party. After the Congress, 1,108 out of 1,966 delegates were arrested and executed or sent to the GULAG on Stalin's orders; out of 139 members and candidates of the Party's Central Committee, 98 were destroyed. They were accused as enemies of the Soviet people. Stalin established himself as the only true disciple of Marxism and of Lenin, which meant that to be against him was to be against Marxism and the Socialist State. Some people still believed him because we knew very little about what was going on at the top, and in the whole country.

Stalin knew that many top Party bureaucrats wanted Sergey Kirov, the popular more liberal Party Secretary of the Leningrad organization instead of him, so on December 1, 1934, Kirov was assassinated. Stalin accused the Soviet folks' enemies, but it was his work, organized by Yogoda, the Minister of Internal Affairs, on his orders. Later, Yogoda himself was executed on Stalin's orders as an enemy. He knew too much.

According to Ribakov, Stalin's thoughts were: "History had selected *him* as a leader because only *he* was in possession of the secret of supreme power in the country, only *he* knew how to rule that people, *he* knew their character. Lenin proposed first to develop private farmers and slowly, maybe in a whole generation, to organize the peasants into collectives. *He* did it in a few years. The psychology of the private owner had to be suffocated in the Russian *muzhik*. *Muzhiks* had to be simply workers in the collective farms. The peasants wanted a strong hand, a 'Father.' Only *he* could provide that."

Ribakov reconstructed the inner logic of Stalin's feelings and deeds, trying to find the basic regularity in his actions. The most constant characteristic was his treason against people and ideas depending on the conjuncture:

- At the beginning of his revolutionary activities he was also an informer for the secret Tsarist police.
- Treason against his friends and fellow revolutionaries who put him on the top. He destroyed them using perfidious ways of deceit.
- Treason against Lenin's policy which he promised to uphold in a solemn, dramatic, public oath during Lenin's funeral.
- And finally, treason against the idea of socialism and the Soviet people.

Scholars gave a number of answers as to why. Probably the closest to the truth was Stalin's pathological craving to hold his absolute personal power at any price and to be a member of the club of history's great personalities.

A certain system was needed for that kind of governing. The

Party, with almost 20 million members, was tightly centralized and a highly disciplined institution which was the intermediary between the government and the people. The *Nemenclatura*—the few million priviledged elite—was the policy enforcer and the source of Stalin's unprecedented power. Although this political base of the social structure was never admitted. "Dictatorship of Proletariat," that deceitful dogma, was proclaimed as the political structure of the state.

Why did people remain silent? They were confused, not knowing who the enemy was. Many still held the belief that Stalin was the righteous and strong leader for this historical period who fought the "real" enemies of the Soviet people. We did not know the truth; there was no freedom of the press and expression; ideas did not develop, those of socialism obdurated became dogmas which people repeated after Stalin-like religious rituals or as a demogogic shaman chorus. Probably the main cause of this behavior was many people still believed in socialism in spite of many mistakes and injustices. This belief was still strong in the '30s, although after 1937–38, a peak of Stalin's bloodbath, the political sobering down was secretly widespread and indifference to Socialist ideas started to expand. All these reasons: contentment, fear, and the inability to publish or to speak- were valid, but there was yet a deeper cause for the silence. Our intellectuals and writers, who expressed themselves even mildly in the Western or domestic press or literature told some of the truth about what was going on, but they had the feeling that they were traitors. They realized that they were strengthening the reactionary forces against the Soviet Union abroad and at home. We students supported these views.

Another point is that Stalin's crimes were so monsterous that normal human logic was not able to comprehend them, much less believe that such a thing could happen. It's still very painful for me, as well as for millions of former Soviet people, to accept the tragic fact that the honest passion and heroic feats of millions was ruthlessly trampled under the soft boots of the Oriental Despot from the small mountain village of Gori in Georgia Joseph Dzhugashvily (Stalin). The silent agreement of his frightened Politburo showed that they were not worthy of being leaders. On the other hand they realized that their secret, swift execution would not change anything. They would be known as the secret enemies of the socialist state.

Some historians have advanced the idea that Stalin was a "historical necessity" for the backward Russia surrounded by a hostile capitalist environment. Using violence, Stalin collectivized the private peasants and made them work to provide the means for industrialization. Although there were other ways to develop. Lenin, Bukharin, and others proposed slower, more economically practical and humane ways of transformation. As an excuse for the excesses and crimes, a Russian proverb was used: "When you chop trees, chips fly."

In 1922, after a number of strokes a sick Lenin wrote his famous letter to the Party Congress: "Stalin is excessively rude, and this defect cannot be tolerated in one holding the position of the Secretary General. Because of this, I propose that . . . Stalin should be removed from this position . . ." (From Khrushchev's 1956 address to the Twentieth Party Congress of the Communist Party of the Soviet Union). Trotsky, Zinoviev, Kamenev, and others from the left Party wing worked hard to save Stalin and did. But later they were executed on Stalin's orders. No doubt Stalin was a very strong and prominent figure, a skilled master of charming people. There is a long list of the victims of his charm including Andrew Barbus, Thomas Mann, Leon Foitvanger, and Bernard Shaw. As a rule of life, lies have nothing to cover themselves, except for violence.

In his exceptional book *Let History Judge*, Roy Medvedev wrote that the evaluation of Stalin's heritage by many historians, including one of Stalin's best biographers, Isaak Deutscher, leads to different views. While condemning Stalin's crimes, some made the simply unbelievable case that the building of socialism in a backward country like Russia could not have been accomplished without cruelty and the creation of a despotic totalitarian state. But Stalin transformed the backward peasant country into a mighty industrial power. He put the ideas of the October Revolution and Lenin into effect. They agreed that the price was very high because the task was very difficult.

Medvedev disagreed with such reasoning. I certainly support his views. It was not Stalin but the October Revolution that opened the road to education and culture for the Soviet people, to the nationalization of all the country's wealth, which made possible rapid expansion of the economy. The destruction of the intelligentsia actually slowed down this process. The prisoners of the concentration camps built thousands of industrial objects, canals, railways and roads, and pipelines. But industry would have developed faster and better if free workers had been employed. Victories gained by the Soviet people were accomplished not by Stalin, as was often said, but by the Soviet people in spite of Stalin's crimes and mistakes.

"The price our people paid, its sacrifices, underline not the difficulty of the task but Stalin's cruel recklessness" (R. Medvedev, *Let History Judge*, p. 869).

He maimed the psychology of the Soviet people—his most hideous crime. "Evil rulers," says the Oriental proverb, "find no refuge even in the grave." In spite of all logic and explanation, as a Russian I felt profound shame in the face of the world community that we were so foolish as to worship such a shrewd villain, brutal dictator, and a simple charlatan. He was as the dwarf Zekhas from the Hoffman fairy tale who had the magical power of ascribing to himself other people's achievements, and of shifting off onto his close comrades his own crimes and mistakes. In Stalin's case, he accused them of those crimes and demanded their execution.

In the 1970s in Moscow, I heard many jokes. Here is one of them:

Lenin is resurrected. After several days of walking and talking with people, he goes to the railroad station. The guard asks him: "Vladimir Ilich, where are you going?"

"Back to Switzerland to start over again."

It won't be just to characterize the Soviet Union after Stalin as dreadful, although democracy still was an anguish wish. Changes started with Khrushchev's antistalinist political reforms. At the Communist Party Congress in 1956 Khrushchev in his four-hour dramatic speech denounced Stalin's crime against the Party and the people. The process of destalinization culminated in 1956 in liberation over seven million political prisoners from GULAGs. They were the "lucky" survivors, the other, at least twelve million prisoners, died in GULAGs, not counting millions of those who were executed by their local NKVDs.

The skeleton-like figures wearing prisoner's rags had "decorated" every living place across the huge country. They returned to their own societies and dramatic confrontations between them and their torturers and falsed informers often happened. As the poet Anna Akhmatova wrote: "The Russians are eyeball to eyeball—those who were imprisoned and those who put them there."

The same moral and political question the Jews' Holocaust survivors asked: Who had been responsible for their suffering? Why are those victimizers not yet punished? The "memory" of what happened was a duty to those who survived, that it won't happen again. I don't forget my father and husband, and I don't forgive those who sent them to their deaths. Although as a Christian I have to forgive.

After Stalin the struggle between Soviet conservatives and reformers was played all the time, even during the conservative Brehznev's rule.

Continuity of the Khrushchev reforms was the dissident movement in the 1970s, which evolved into Gorbachev radical changes. American and Western information services had misinterpreted this dissident movement. They mistake the liberal or human rights movement for all Soviet dissent. In reality, it was the least popular because they had no viable program for changing the Soviet system. Soviet, as well as now, political dissent had always consisted of many conflicting outlooks and movements, ranging from the far left to the far right. Most popular were, and even more so now, Nationalist ideas, also of different range. Another was social equality demands. The Russian Nationalism, in its main form is understood as love to the own country, but not excel it above all others, which is chauvinism. The Nationalism or Patriotism of Russians is justified in full. From the incipience of the Russian state it had been invaded constantly by different powers and countries from the East, West, South, and North to mention just a few invasions in modern history. Russia destroyed on her territory the mighty Swedish Army in 1709; mighty Napoleon in 1812; coalition of the 14 states in 1918–22; and finally Hitler's Army in 1945. Russia's geography and geology—endless wide plains and immeasurable natural resources was always a strong invitation for invasion.

The nationalist position of the Russian people and the majority of the political bureaucracy did not support some of Gorbachev's reforms, especially his foreign policy of one-sided concessions, specifically after he gave up to the West strong military position in Central Europe which Russia had after WWII as a result of destroying Hitler's war machine. For most Soviet citizens that final glory in victory gave sacred meaning to their personal tragic losses. Especially veterans felt injured and cheated. Certainly America and Europe did not support Gorbachev's reforms; they did not have need in the strong reformed Soviet state.

In the 70s when I was in the Soviet Union a few times, I faced a whole range of different opinions and feelings. At the faculty cafeteria at MGU (Moscow State University) normally I joined the various groups of the faculty members and they knew who I was. Most often, there developed a normal discussion about the educational system, politics and life in the USA. The other groups who present intolerable socialist ideology bitterly attacked me, as they said, for my treason in leaving the Motherland during the War when the country was bleeding almost to death. They said, I had the impudence to come see their life now and cast dirt on them. I was surprised at myself; I was not afraid anymore like I was seven years before when I came back for the first time. Then they considered me officially still a Soviet citizen. Now I defended my case. But what entirely saddened me, even put me at a loss, was that the others were strongly critical of everything at "home" and highly praising of everything "abroad." In spite of my strong pain in the past, I also had a feeling of gratitude for my education and the development of my humane character. For them to have gratitude to the State was not modern, not popular anymore. I told them about my attitude and feelings and they practically laughed at me, saying that I was still using old-fashioned "double thinking." It became clear to me that the Soviet Union was in a period of skepticism, criticism, and political disunity. What would follow? Certainly not sacrifice for the sake of working people and enthusiasm for building a new just society. Nevertheless, the economic condition of the population was considerably improved.

At the end of the 19th century, the idea of communism was brought to Russia from Europe. At the end of the 20th century, the new ideas about market economy, "getting rich," is again the product of the West's ingenuity. In both cases, they were not well fitted on Russian soil. Although communal life mentality was normal state of mind historically. It would be decidedly better for Russia, with her heritage from both the West and the East and her deep indigenous ideas and customs and the communist ideology over 70 years, to develop her own unifying ideas and ways of accomplishing them and become an integral part of the world economy and society.

In the past, I sincerely believed in a wonderful, bright future for humanity. Christianity and other world religions gave people faith, which is based on love, tolerance, and compassion. The diffusion of these beliefs in saving the world was often accomplished by brutality, such as the Crusaders, the Inquisition, the religious wars, schisms, and more which still exist in various forms. Is this the fault of Christian and other religious teachings, of the guidance they give to the people? Basically, the answer is "No." I am drawing a parallel with socialism. Was the basic teaching of socialism faulty or unworkable? No definite answer. Although I believe in possible positive socialist formation, not of the Stalin vintage. But a violent revolution was and is not a practical necessity. As a consequence, the established system created power in the hands of a single political party and that party's total economic, social, and political control. The last brought an oppressive regime and finally an omnipotent psychotic dictator who was never elected by the people and answered to no one. The time of Stalin and afterwards, taught an important lesson: "If socialism is not combined with democracy it can become a breeding ground for new crimes" (Roy Medvedev, *Let History Judge*, p. 873).

Modern time Russian history is the history of the mass sacrificed on the altar of the social justice.

What is the state of Russia presently?

I have some first hand information, but mainly my previous knowledge and belief in Russia and her suffering and ever optimistic people help me understand the situation now.

Russia stands on the crossroads: the old road of totalitarianism ended, the new road is still in the process of defining and making it work.

Disintegration of the Soviet Union happened unexpectedly, quickly and chaotically, with the result that many industrial plants, commercial and other institutions were taken by the Party and "professional" mafia without any compensation. The secure legal foundations still are not established everywhere. In 1917 and in 1991—in 74 years, which is just a short moment in history—a country was utterly destroyed twice. The old systems, beliefs, and values were declared antihuman and obsolete. A full crisis of ideas and values is taking place again. The created emptiness was filled up fast with everything from former centuries, like magicians and charlatans; religious sects of questionable teaching and morals; paranormal beliefs down to shamans; prejudice; superstitions; fortune telling and many others. The Russians are emotional people and have sunk themselves in vodka much more than ever. They don't see much good in their new future. Some are corrupted and have lost their aim in life and their

260

identity as trustworthy human beings. Yevgeny Yevtushenko said that culturally Russia was always a great nation, except in its political life and its intolerance. Once we had forced collectivization, now we are forcing capitalism. The first we have to erect a statue of responsibility and then a statue of liberty. Tolerance and responsibility, not polarization, is becoming more and more the hope and struggle of many Russians. A process of improvement, a search for new values has started.

Some people found it in Russian Orthodox Christianity. Others, primarily the youth have noticeable interest and attraction to humanism, the center of which is at the Moscow University. The "Russian Humanist Society" is expanding over the country. It publishes the popular magazine "Common Sense." Many scholars are active organizers and teachers. Valeriy Kuvakin, Professor of Philosophy at M.G.U. is Chairman of the "Russian Humanist Society."

The basic tenets of the Russian humanist movement was freedom of beliefs and thoughts; critical thinking and value of human reason; humanist moral and ethics, high level of self-discipline and civil responsibility. The most important for change is reliance in oneself, not in government, and creation of a humane society based on law.

The pervasive disease of our times is a loss of the unity between the practical life of a human and his spirituality, the going process of dissociation from moral values and traditions. Human beings are losing their ideals, which is a search and struggle for a better and more just way of life for the whole human race, not just stronger, chosen societies. Continued division among the human societies would breed revolutions and distractions. Adherence to basic values, social justice, peace and agreements among nations according to law and the people's will has to become the aim for humanity.

9

World War II

Graduation from University. Life in the City.

It was Sunday, June 22, 1941. A few days previously, I passed my last State exam, the History of Philosophy, and was now relaxing. Suddenly, I heard a loud radio from our neighbor's apartment, a voice I recognized at once as Molotov's. He was saying that our cities, and he named them, were bombed by the German military air force. I put away all my books and realized that life was going to make another sharp zig-zag. Woman gathered in our building's huge pleasant backyard, full of trees, bushes and flowers. Mama was there, too. There was no panic, but the news crushed all of us.

I went to the Faculty and Mama went to Grandpa's apartment. The family had left a few days before for Alma-Ata, Kazakhstan, where Nina's theater was performing for a whole year, and my cousin Boris was staying there with his family.

The wide hallways of the Faculty were filled with students and faculty members. There were no noisy speeches; the mood was subdued. Boys brought a standing cathedra from a classroom and short Kassiy Markovich was now over our heads. He delivered a short prophetic speech.

"We are at the beginning of a crucial time in the life of the country and in our own lives. It will be much more devastating than the Civil War. You will dream about our present time as if it were a living fairytale. In a few days, you are going to answer your country's call, and instead of books, you'll carry rifles and machine guns, or guide planes or tanks, but remember: you are the leaders in this never before seen bloody war. I can now tell you the outcome. The pillars of the Revolution will be moved to the west. I am going to telegraph a request to be assigned to active duty in the Army."

A few days later, we gathered at the Faculty. K. M. gave us instructions as to when and where to receive our diplomas; the formal graduation had been canceled. At the end of his speech, K. M. became extremely emotional, praising us, and giving us advice for this new period of our lives. He congratulated several couples among our students who had just married. Then simultaneously we started singing as one, and it was not "International," but a very popular song that expressed our feelings and our minds at that moment:

As the light blue fog
Our youth passed by
And with its deceitful eyes
It enchanted us.
Only for you, my beloved
This song of a swan
Only for you, my beloved
This song of love.

As the folk story tells it, the swan sings only once in a lifetime, just before dying. Incredible emotions engulfed us as we said good-bye to each other, embracing, kissing, and crying. We felt that it was good-bye forever, and it was.

Every day life changed. Before, it was like the skin of a zebra—black stripes alternating with white. Now, our zebra-life lost all her white stripes. In the programs of the schools of higher education were military training classes, more or less like the ROTC in the United States. Each graduate had to have a military specialty; I was a nurse and a sharpshooter. Soon after the beginning of the war almost all our boys were taken to military schools to be lieutenants. And after a few or several weeks of training, they were sent to the front. In a few days, the majority of them were killed or taken prisoner. This tragic news was brought by one of them, "our" boy Zalman, who was very strong and able to run out of the Germans' encirclement and come home before joining another regiment. We received a blood-curdling first-hand picture of the frightful destruction and chaos going on at the front.

I received my diploma with honors in the Rector's office. Mama congratulated me and we cried. Imagine what a happy celebration it would have been if Papa and Misha were here! But Misha would already be in an officer's uniform, probably on the front line. No, as a scholar working for the important field of defense, he would be excused from active duty. I became so happy because Misha would not be killed. Isn't this peculiar, the rationally inexplicable human psyche? Perhaps deep down I still did not accept that Misha was dead.

Kharkov did not escape the lot of the other cities. On the contrary, it was bombed throughout the war, either by the Germans or by the Soviets, because the city changed hands a few times. The bombings were not heavy, however there was much destruction. The christening of the bombing was memorable to me, starting two or three weeks after the war began. I was in the city park about four blocks from home. It was like a news club. According to war regulations, people had to be inside before dark. I was rushing home when the air-alarm sounded and in a few minutes, just a block in front of me, the first bomb landed. Along with the others, I fell on the pavement. With time, we became used to this constant small bombing and didn't pay much attention to it.

But once I had an experience of life. In the daylight, I was walking home when the alarm sounded and the bombing started. I ran to the closest shelter, a small one where there were a few women. On the floor with makeshift bedding, a woman was in labor and it was a hard one, a premature, unexpected birth. The women were helping her and asked me to bring water. The crazy bombing didn't stop. Then suddenly a newborn human cried. And a woman commented, "He is saying, 'Stop this bloody game; I came to this world to search for happiness.'"

Kharkov was changing fast. The governmental and scholarly institutions were packing and leaving to go behind the Volga River or the Ural Mountains. Smoke and the smell of burning paper hung over the city, the archives were set on fire. The lines of freight trains were endless, carrying from the west to the east on open platforms the machinery of the plants and factories that had been taken apart to be hastily assembled in the new places behind the Volga River or Ural mountains. There were times when even military trains to the west were second priority on this Kiev-Kharkov line. Regular civil transportation ceased to exist. The Germans were fast approaching. Kiev fell. Poltava fell. We knew Kharkov would be next in a few weeks. It was an important strategic position: a railway hub leading to the

Northern Caucasian oil regions (and farther to Iran and Iraq), to the Caspian sea basin and lower Volga, the Crimea, and to the north the Moscow region.

The stores were selling all their goods. The lines of people, which included my Mama (although she was not well), were endless. The other people were leaving. Some lucky ones left with their institutions or factories which received one or a few railroad freight cars or open platform cars, but many were going on foot with bags on their backs, just walking in the eastern direction from village to village.

Sofa Rosenfeld's father was the director of a scientific institute and he received one freight car for certain important equipment. His family and a few others, mainly Jews, had preferential treatment because it was already known that they were an endangered species. Hitler killed them all. Sofa told me that her father would try to take me with a small suitcase as a member of the family. But I could not leave my mother. Her health was failing. At the same time I had to leave, having received a martial law order from the Ukrainian Ministry of Education to take a position as Director of a seven-year school in the city of Tomsk in Siberia.

Mama asked me to leave but I decided to stay. I thought that maybe she would get better after a rest. Besides, we gathered quite a bit of food. Then slowly we would walk from village to village to the east and in the Volga region we would be able to take a train. I received this advice and some important papers of support from the Oblast Department of Education. Mama's health became worse.

Authorities left the city. People opened all the stores and warehouses. Of course, it was disorder, but people themselves tried to keep the best possible order. Some who were grabbing everything, however, were saying in a week or two they would have enough food and other necessities. The Germans were not stupid; they would help people of a strategically important city like Kharkov.

For several days, we heard cannonades to the west and south of the city, which were getting closer. Then, it all stopped and the air bombing started, which was much worse than usual. Silence fell and it was a strange feeling, but we understood that there was no hope anymore. The battle for Kharkov was over. Our house residents were outside in front of our building. We saw a company of our soldiers moving fast between the houses down to the river. Women called to them. They came and asked for water. In a minute, the women brought them water and food, kissed and blessed them, crying and wishing for their survival.

A lieutenant, a handsome Georgian, stepped up to me and said, "*Krasavitsa* (a beauty; it's customary in Georgia to call young girls *krasavitsa*), give me a good kiss." I embraced him and we kissed like lovers.

"Your kiss is a talisman for me. It will save me. Look, if they tell me to fight for you, I will. They are telling me to fight for the Motherland, I do it. But I don't want to fight for Stalin."

He was saying this loudly and was not afraid. We did not know how to react. Some soldiers said, "It's okay. We agree with his words."

It was clear that the Army was in a deep political and moral crisis and this crushed us. There was no other force in the country which could fight the enemy.

Germans in Kharkov

About thirty minutes later, we heard the noise of motorcycles and several Germans rode on our street close to us. There was no exchange of smiling or handwaving. It was unbelievable to imagine Germans in Kharkov. It was October 21, and I didn't expect anything good in my life.

The city's power station was bombed: no lights; no transportation (trolley buses and tramway); no water; no sanitary canalization; no food; and soon starvation began. The first need for survival was water. We were lucky, living close to a river, about a half hour walk, and people opened up a couple of old water wells. Twice a day, I brought water, once from the river and the second time good water from the well, each time taking two buckets. Mama and our *dwornic* built a small brick stove in our kitchen. Bricks were left all over from the bombed buildings. Then he brought quite a bit of coal that was now no longer being used to heat the building. Each family, each human was fighting the critical battle for mere physical survival.

It was close to two weeks since the city was occupied and suddenly the loudspeakers on the trucks around the city were thunderously playing the Germans' military marches and asking people to come to the Dzerhzinsky Square at noon on Sunday for German

**Kharkov 1941. At entrance to the Oblast Communist Party Building.
Germans hung the partisans.**

military command instructions. Ina came and we went over there. Hundreds of thousands filled the square, mainly women and older men. On the balcony of the former building of the Oblast Communist Party Committee were thundering loudspeakers and the Nazis' flag hoisted high in the air. Then a group of German officers appeared with a young, strong man in just a light shirt, his hands tied, and a big placard on his chest with the words, "I am a partisan." They put a rope around his neck and hanged him from the balcony over the main entrance. Then they left.

Not one word was spoken; only the loudspeaker continued playing the victory marches. The crowd got quiet and in a few minutes, people ran away in horror. After a while, Ina and I came closer to look at that unfortunate man. We could do it; we were already hardened by life. But we were wrong. Emotionally we were not in the state to look at that poor young man. The Germans were leaving the building, passing by us. Not one glance was given; they just assumed airs. We slowly walked down Sumskaia Street and in the opposite direction the officers were strutting, usually in pairs. Not one gave us even a little way. We had no choice but to step off the street; the cleared pass in the snow was very narrow. No one said, "*Danke.*"

"Let's pretend that we're immersed in conversation and don't notice them."

So we ran into them, nose to nose, stopped and looked straight into their eyes. No smile. The haughty Germans gave us way. We politely said "*danke.*" They understood our message.

At home, Ina was very nervous and told me she planned to go into the partisan movement. Mama said that if she did, then her mother could stay with us. I felt calm in my mind.

We saw now how they treated the intelligent majority of people in a big city—as if we were not people at all. Imagine what they were doing to our peasants! I think they had already lost this war, in spite of the fact that their military conquest would continue. In the past, the Germans won a lot of battles, but always lost the war with Russia. Because it's not enough to be just smart—they have to be wise.

Events were happening fast; on two big connected squares of the city center, the Germans "ornamented" each electric pole with a hanging body. Each had an introduction card on its back: "I am a partisan" or "I am a Jew." I didn't want to see it, but my neighbor Ira told me, "You are a historian. You have to see it."

Although I and millions like me heard and knew about Stalin's NKVD expertness in torturing and killing our own citizens, we didn't actually see or read about it. But the Germans openly demonstrated their savagery. It was simply impossible to reconcile the Germans' Hegel, Kant, Schelling, Goethe, Schiller, Beethoven, Wagner, and many others, in general their great culture, with what we saw, heard and read now of the Germans' actions. It was clear to us we were lacking some sort of crucial knowledge about the past or contemporary Germans, or both.

A burgomeister (not a "head" or "chairman") appointed by the Germans and his government made some improvements—electricity and water started to run, although with limitations. Early in the morning, thousands of women pulling sleds were going in all directions to the villages to barter their things, like shoes, clothes, the most needed items such as soap, nails, utensils, and thread for basic food. But every day those unfortunate women had to go farther to reach new villages that still had some food left. I went several times, walking hundreds of kilometers. The winter of 1941–42 was very severe, usually 20–30 Celsius below zero.

Recalling that time, I am very proud about our people's high moral qualities. We never heard about women being robbed or attacked in a time when all around were hungry people. Often, I was walking alone because I couldn't walk as fast as the others. Night would fall when I was still on the road, not able to get to the village during daylight. I'd knock at the door of the first *izba* where there was a light. Usually he or she would open the door and say "come in" with no questions asked. They would help remove the heavy clothing and then ask my name. In ten to fifteen minutes, they would give me some good thick *borshch* (vegetable-cabbage soup) and a lot of black bread. Later, I'd be on a straw bed on the floor with some kind of pillow and a blanket. And I always felt happy to realize that there were still a lot of good people in the world.

In the morning they gave me a simple breakfast and a big piece of bread with something for lunch. They never asked for pay. But people, myself included, always prepared some items or gave them some money.

Peasants complained bitterly about the Germans. "They come into your house screaming like crazy. You don't understand what they want, but they hit you anyway and take what they want and leave, still screaming. Our young boys and some girls, really children, left for the forest to join the partisans. The Germans will not be here for long; we will take care of them."

Here is a shortened version of my article that was published in the Buffalo University newspaper in the 1970s:

Three Pietas

Michaelangelo's *Pieta* stands before me in St. Peter's Cathedral in Rome. This ageless masterpiece excites admiration for the magnificence of artistic achievement and wonder for the human spirit exposed by man's boundless creative ability.

The sculpture evokes a mood of solemnity, not sentimentality, and there is strength in this grief. My own mood reflects this: I have a smile instead of tears, a result of an adoration for perfection.

Then other thoughts and images start to invade my mind. I think of how this eternalized moment, the moment of Christ's death, affected the human race, how it shaped our civilization, because the idea of this moment is Selfless Love when innocent life sacrifices itself for the sake of all mankind.

Yet how could it happen that our whole planet is covered by people killed in violent acts of humans against humans? How can we save ourselves? This age-old question bothers me no less than it did millions of people before me.

Pain engulfs me when the images of two other *Pietas* emerge. They do not raise admiration—they create deep despair.

I see the *Pieta* on the Mamaev Hill at Stalingrad's (Volgograd) National Memorial to the fallen in the Stalingrad battle of 1942-43. Extremely impressive, this memorial complex, with its artistic and psychological qualities, belongs to the most memorable and powerful. High in the middle of the hill I saw a huge bulk of marble: an eternal mother holding on her knees the dead body of a soldier. She bends over him, covering his face with a light scarf. Standing there I wept bitterly because my grief and frustration were so strong that I was not able to hold back my emotions. For what purpose were about half a million lives destroyed here? Those who died were the finest young people of two nations. Our soldiers had to defend their land from the attack ordered by evil men.

In my mind the landscape changes again. Now I see endless land and plains without a horizon. Everything—the sky, the land—is all white. Sometimes it is clear, other times there is just light, the clouds are transparent. I am walking in this amorphous, sea-like environment. I am walking slowly, dressed heavily in a long sheepskin coat and felt boots, with scarves over my head. The temperature is reaching 40 Celsius below zero. The time is February 1942.

The Germans occupy the Ukraine and my city, Kharkov. If you can imagine a city of nearly one million people before the war left without electricity, without water and a sewage system, without heat, and of course, without food. The weakest have died from cold and hunger; they had been waiting for help from a non-existent source. Among them are two of my university professors. One of them is a professor of Classics, Ippolit Nikolaevich. I had come to help him, bringing him a loaf of bread, but I am too late. I find his childlike body in a small coffin, made of half burnt boards, put together by neighbors and standing in his empty bedroom. The body is frozen like the ground which is hard as rock because the temperature is 40 Celsius below zero. For my professor, as for many hundreds of dead, there will be no funeral.

The strongest, the survivors—and I am one of them—go to villages and exchange necessity items for basic foods like grain, flour, oil, and any other food. Once I told this story to my students and asked them what, in their opinion, was the most necessary item I exchanged with the peasants; their answer: toilet paper! I was shocked into realizing again that Americans, a nation which power is decisive for the present and future of the world, are the least realistically informed people. We exchange for food anything we have, but mainly we barter with items like soap, salt, nails, thread, and all kinds of clothing, especially shoes, socks, and heavy stockings.

I walk alone through the snow because I am too tired to keep up with the others. It is the sixth day of my journey. I have walked over 200 kilometers carrying pounds of food on my sled. In front of me I see Kharkov. I notice that a group of three women who had passed me have stopped for a short moment over some dark object.

Suddenly I realize that I am standing in front of an unforgettable *Pieta*! A girl, probably about ten-years-old or so, and lightly dressed, sits in the snow, holding in her lap her little brother who cannot be more than five or six years old. They are a perfect frozen statue. And who sculpted it? Hitler and his countrymen—or perhaps all of us, members of the human race, who have lost our ability to identify with what is human and what our purpose should be here on earth. We have supported, and still support as our powerful leaders, evil men, dangerous fanatics, who, instead of resolving peacefully human conflicts, use violent means.

I walk faster, looking straight ahead. My heart is cold, and the frozen statue is erased from my mind. Not until much later does this memory return to me to stay forever with my other painful impressions of war.

Life in the Occupied City

In the city, the Jews were ordered to the camp at the Kh.T.Z. (Kharkov's Tractor Plant) about fifteen kilometers from the city center. It was a heartbreaking picture; almost all of them were older people, sick and undernourished, barely able to walk, pulling a sleigh, sometimes with one who couldn't walk at all. People saw young girls

271

among them, too. During those days of the Jewish eviction from the city, people tried to stay inside, knowing that no one could help them, or otherwise would face their own arrest and be sent to Germany or even be killed on the spot.

The Germans once more demonstrated their anti-human, misanthropic dispositions. Hunting on the streets for younger people increased considerably. The Germans grabbed people and sent them straight to Germany as *Ostarbeiters* (Eastworkers), but in fact, slaves. Families didn't know where their family member was until they received a letter from Germany. My mama begged me not to go outside but it was impossible. I had to get a job which at least sounded important in the City Government or its institutions. I found it as an Inspector in the Personnel Department of the City's Markets Administration, now free and flourishing, are trying to make some rules and order.

Now that I could walk the streets safely, I wanted to check on some of my friends, Riva and Clara among them, both Jews. But other people were living in their apartments now and said they didn't know anything about them. Ina's mother was so happy to see me. She hadn't heard from Ina in about a month. Psychologically, she was very strong, but now all her body was shaken and her self-control had noticeably forsaken her. Ina's friend since high school days was left behind by the Komsomol for underground resistance work. He took Ina and others to the partisan underground groups. As I learned later, the plan was to place Ina as an interpreter in the higher or middle echelons of the Germans' commanding officers.

Then I visited another University friend, Nadia. I couldn't believe my eyes. She radiated happiness all around, looking like a Venus with her beautifully developed figure. On the couch, sitting comfortably, was a German major. Her father was a known communist in the second largest plant in the city (Ch.T.G.Z.). He left when the plant was evacuated, leaving Nadia and her mother behind. Nadia's sister and her husband were also evacuated with their plant, leaving their two small children with Nadia and her mother. Nadia had to take care of four people. She found a way by taking German officers as lovers for the time their company was staying there, a week or a few months. Nadia said they were nice gentlemen, taking care of her family, and good lovers. An irony of life or of fate—a daughter of an executed "enemy of the Soviet folk" became a partisan, while the daughter of a known communist became a German prostitute. In the end, both were killed.

I liked my job. Really, it was a "nothing to do job": giving out licenses, watching for proper sanitation. But as I found out much later, the job in the Markets Administration was quite lucrative. The administration (just a couple of bosses) opened a big buffet food place. Mama wanted to get a job there; she was resting a lot and felt much better. I obtained that job for her. She prepared different kinds of salads and sometimes helped at the counter.

In the city's condition of hunger and lack of basic sanitation, it was not unusual for infectious disease to easily spread. An epidemic of typhus hit the city. In the middle of December, Mama felt sick; a doctor came, diagnosed her with typhus, and a few days later an ambulance came and took her to a hospital. I don't think the word "hospital" could really apply—there was practically no medication, very little food, and it was only a little warmer than the outside. I wanted to take my mother back home, but it was absolutely out of the question, especially to a region like ours where the Germans were heavily concentrated. Even relatives were not allowed inside the hospital.

I saw my mother through a window. Every second day I brought good soup for her, but I was doubtful that the nurses gave it to her. On December 27, I noticed that my mother was lying uncovered. I insisted on seeing her. The doctor came, let me in, and told me that death would come in a few hours. I was with my mother, but she was unconscious. In the early hours of December 28, 1942, she departed. The doctor told me that her whole body was very weak, especially her heart and lungs. With such health conditions she would not survive even with good care. The years of terror had destroyed her. On December 31, I buried my mother. Only Ina was with me. Now I was entirely alone and I felt free to do with myself what I wished; to live or to die. No barriers left!

At this time, good news came from the front and boosted people's mood: the Stalingrad battle was developing successfully for our side. Tragi-comical live "entertainment" for the people of our city was being performed by the groups of Italian and Rumanian soldiers. The Germans encircled Stalingrad and in November started the famous battle. The Russians directed their initial attack against the Italian and Rumanian position in the north link of the encirclement and it was smashed. In December, the remnants of these armies were trudging through Kharkov. It was like a masquerade, a carnival. The poor soldiers were not dressed for a Russian winter, wearing light overcoats, small hats, and no gloves. They took what they found from the peasants, like sheepskin coats, felt boots, different kinds of blankets, mainly crude quilts, and shawls. The funniest looking thing was that many soldiers were wearing women's kerchiefs on their heads and *lapti* on their feet. *Lapti* were old-fashioned peasant footwear woven from birch bark, though they were no longer worn. Instead of rifles, some soldiers had guitars and other musical instruments on their backs. Our people lined the streets and greeted them with fun, and pity. Many of them showed evidence of frostbite on their faces, hands, and feet.

The German 6th Army was distracted and on February 2, 1943, Field Marshall Paulus and twenty-three generals were taken prisoner with over one hundred thousand officers and soldiers. It was the second defeat for the Germans. The first happened in December 1941 at the battle of Moscow, when their myth of invincibility received a big blow.

The psychological effects of the battle of Stalingrad were immense on both sides. Morale was bolstered tremendously in the country; the military initiative had passed to Russian hands. The Russian thrust continued with the Germans in retreat, and on about March 12, the battle for Kharkov began.

Fire, Our House Destroyed

The German Panzer troops were stationed in our backyard. On the night of March 15, I was exhausted, fell asleep and dreamed that our building was on fire. But it was not a dream. Ira was at my door, screaming, "Fire!"

We ran downstairs and saw people packing, making bundles, but some were standing inside an entrance. The fire started in the middle of the building. Tenants of the apartments close to the fire, some with their children, ran outside on the street and the German soldiers shot them. A few bodies were lying over there. All the people were staying inside. Probably our building was well-structured, each entrance separated from the other, so the fire was localized and developing slowly. We heard shots from the backyard and saw two women with white flags who wanted to speak to the commanding officer. He didn't listen, just screamed at them, "In this building you hide partisans. From that window, a partisan shot at us and wounded a soldier. You know that you will pay with your lives, burning inside or being killed by us outside. We will save our bullets if you stay inside."

Now we knew our fate. In our entrance, all of us, probably about twenty people from eight apartments, were sitting on the stairs. There was silence, except for a woman caressing her child, a boy of about seven years of age who was crying.

A man broke the silence. "It looks like we have a choice. To suffocate here where we are sitting now or try to run along the street closer to the buildings, all of us at once."

We were discussing which way would be better to die. We thought running would give some of us a chance for survival.

Later, I thought many times of this tragic event. Why were we so calm, accepting our fate? We knew there was no other practical way out. And psychologically, maybe even unconsciously, once more we succumbed to this condition, hoping for the better. In my mind, the pictures of the past: Misha, Papa, Mama; were developing like a movie. And I thought about the persistent lines of Nadson's poetry:

> It was a short-lived life
> It was a lot of grief.

But there were no regrets, no self-pity in my heart. Life had become more of a burden to me. We figured out that the fighting was going on along the river, a twenty-five to thirty minute walk from us. Smoke started to fill up the entrance and we moved closer to the basement. Suddenly, we heard the Germans starting the tanks and in about ten to fifteen minutes, they were gone. We had cheated death again.

Now people were trying quickly to save some of their belongings, running up and down stairs or throwing things through the windows. I stood in the middle of my room and didn't want to save anything, because I would be shot as a daughter and wife of the "enemies of the Soviet people," having stayed with the occupants, and mainly because I had disregarded a martial-time order. Ira called out, "Start moving!" I bundled my clothes, bedding, and some other things, including my personal documents, and threw them out the window. The hardest was parting with the letters, family photographs, some papers, and pictures of weapons as chronology of the family history.

"My beloved Grandpa, forgive me for I am not able to fulfill your wish," I said.

These pictures were on cardboard and were bulky and heavy. But the real reason for the decision not to take any family pictures and papers was that I did not believe in my own survival. For these last few days of my life, I wanted to have peace in my heart and clarity of mind. I am past; I am doomed.

Ira told me to gather her and my things together. In a half hour she appeared with the key for our new apartment on the other side of the street in the former NKVD workers' building empty now after the German officers had left it. We moved in. Ina found several bottles of wine; the Germans had left in a hurry. She opened a bottle, put some food on the table and said joyfully, "Happy Birthday!" Now I realized it was March 15, my birthday. I was twenty-nine. All the terrible deeds of the past night became immaterial; we realized that we were alive and drinking good wine. We fell asleep on our bundled bedding on the floor.

Soviets Are Back

Banging at the door awoke us. A Russian officer stepped in and we were sincerely happy to see him. We kissed and hugged him, asked him to sit down, poured him a glass of wine and gave him some food. He was an intendant officer.

"What am I going to do with you folks from that burned building? You've occupied all the apartments in this building which belongs to us, the military."

He informed us about the situation on the front and in the country. "We've started to chase the Germans out of our land." He promised not to throw us out of the apartment, but if he had to do it he would find another apartment for us. He left and we were so happy to have seen again a good human in military uniform.

Groups of Russian soldiers displayed funny, pitiful pictures, wearing *valenki*, felt boots without galoshes over them. The snow was melting and their *valenki*, as well as their feet, were wet and cold.

276

We noticed a number of the soldiers were blind. It was sun-blindness, the result of walking or riding for hundreds of miles over snow-covered, white sunny fields. In spite of their shabby appearance, they were a noticeably different army than what we saw in October 1941 when they were leaving Kharkov. Now they knew the Germans would be defeated. That had tremendously boosted their fighting mood.

Once I was walking along the main street, Sumskaia, when I saw a group of officers walking toward me and suddenly one of them called to me, "Nina, what a surprise!" They stepped up around me; all of them were SMERSH officers. The man who called me was a general, my old friend from the Oblast Department of Education, Vasia X. SMERSH was the special NKVD political unit in the military which watched over the entire military apparatus. They were ruthless and brutal. But the demoralization of the fighting forces in the first two years of defeat was stopped and discipline restored at a high level.

Vasia was a second, after Novak, in our Department of Education. He was a new type of Soviet bureaucrat—not noisy, not a chatterbox, but well-educated, with a good knowledge of history, literature, and philosophy. Vasia was soft-spoken, ready to help anyone in the department. Everybody liked him. He was a tall handsome man, sweet and engaging in his relations with people, but crafty and artful, a real devoted soldier of Stalin.

Once, he was arrested and Novak told me that he would be back in a few months. Saying this, Novak looked straight into my eyes with a strange smile on his lips. Then he added, "Be careful in your talk with Vasia. You understand that my remark is just between us." In other words, Vasia was an informer for the higher-ups in the NKVD. After being released from jail, he told people that we could trust the NKVD which did not punish innocent people like himself.

Vasia sent his "boys" away and looked for a place for us to sit and talk. We found it in a back room of a store.

"I can't believe you are so stupid as to stay in occupied territory," he said. "You know nobody can save you. You are doomed. Maybe our misfortune would help you. Probably in a week, we will leave Kharkov again, but in a couple of months we will be back to stay. If you don't want to be shot, then put a bag on your back and walk east. About sixty kilometers from Kharkov in Kupiansk you will take a train and travel to Ufa (the Capitol of the Bashkir Autonomous Republic on the main line to Siberia, just before the Ural Mountains). In Kupiansk, you will see my friend, a military 'boss,' and he will help you. In Ufa as well, you will meet my friend and he will take care of you. I am giving you all the official papers and papers for my military friends that you will need.

"Do you remember you called me a 'bad boy' because I was unfaithful to my wife and liked romances? Now, she has paid me back many times over. I am going to divorce her. But to be truthful, it is my fault. You know that you fascinated me. Your openness and sincerity somehow helped me to think and to try to be a little better human. I am depressed in spite of my high position and the fact that the war has started to unfold successfully for us. The path I am traveling throughout my life is a version of mutilation of the human soul: in my personal life, I had too many liaisons with women, these have not left any warmth in my heart, only feelings of loneliness and guilt. In my line of work, I have many times abandoned the moral criteria of a human being. I thought I had clarity of purpose, but it was wrong. In reality, we accepted Dostoyevsky's Smerdiakov principle, 'everything is permitted.' In our case, we did it for the sake of the Revolution, causing boundless suffering for our people. Now I have a tormenting duality in my mind, the result of my awakened conscience. I believe my confession will be between us. If I outlive this war, then I will go to Ufa where I have a number of good friends. Some are from Kharkov. I'll become a director of a school and if I succeed in bringing up some young students to be better humans than I am, I'll consider my life to have been worth living. I will find you and ask you to marry me."

Vasia gave me all the necessary papers. He kissed me and looked into my eyes with pain in his, and left. I knew he was sincere and in deep moral pain. Maybe seeing death all around made him feel his immoral past and approaching end.

Ira decided not to go with me. I packed my bag and went to the cemetery to say good-bye to Mama and Grandpa. Then I asked some soldiers how best to get to Kupiansk. They said it was impossible. There were no roads; thousands of tanks and cars were going through the roads and making deep, black slush lakes in many places. The thawed fields were not much better. I went to the railroad station, but no luck.

A few days passed by and in the morning we saw German soldiers on the streets. Momentarily, I realized I was left with only two choices: to stay in the country and eventually be shot to death or to leave Kharkov and for sure the country, because there was no way that Germany would win the war. I was thinking that to leave my people and my country forever was the same to me as being dead. I tried to chase away thoughts of this decision from my mind. I still had a few months to think. I continued my work, but the question of what to do was on the minds of many of us who were not able to leave the city. We stayed with the enemy in occupied territory, this put us in the category of the suspicious element, collaborators with the enemy.

Stalin's Flexibility

Stalin displayed great flexibility when mortal danger threatened the Soviet state during the first two years of the Germans' victorious advance. He used every means to strengthen Soviet patriotism. On November 7, 1941, Stalin stood on top of Lenin's mausoleum and said to the country and the armed forces, "Let the manly images of our great ancestors—Alexander Nevsky; Dmitry Donskoy; Kuzma Minin; Dimitry Pozharsky; Alexander Suvorov; and Mikhail Kutuzov—inspire you in this war.

It was practically an end to specific Soviet patriotism. Particularly in the Red Army, Tsarist-time Nationalist slogans and measures were introduced as well as military awards and orders in the name of famous field marshals like Kutuzov, who defeated Napoleon, and Suvorov. Slogans to fight for "Mother Russia," replaced ones like "Proletarians of all countries unite," and "Fight for a 'Socialist State.'" The new National Anthem now stressed the Russian people's role: "Unbreakable union of free-born republics, Great Russia has welded forever to stand," instead of "International." Peace between the Soviet government and the Orthodox Church was initiated. The Patriarkhat was reestablished. Stalin's reconciliation with the Church was important not only inside Russia but equally for the Balkan countries specially of Christian-Orthodox in constructing a political bridge for the revival of Panslavism. Finally, the Comintern was dissolved. This measure made a strong impression abroad. There were more reforms.

Hitler's Ignorance

In contrast to Stalin, Hitler and his government were not only lacking a flexible policy toward the people of the Soviet Union, but their unbelievable ignorance about life, the psychology of the people, and the culture was exposed. Hitler clung stubbornly to the illusion that all problems would be solved by purely military means, by force. He and the others did not believe that "inferior" Slavs could defeat the "superior" Germans. Did they know their own history? Or had they doctored it according to their philosophy? Stalin and Hitler were the indivisible pair in this respect. For Hitler, the Eastern Slavs were simply "swamp-dwellers," subhumans whose sole reason for existing was to serve the Germans in the attainment of their goal of Lordship over the world. We witnessed the Germans' cruel treatment of the population.

The result of the slave labor operation was soon noticeable in the occupied territories. The population, especially the young villagers, fled to the woods. The partisan groups increased to millions and paralyzed the Germans' delivery and communication systems, attacked reserve units, dynamited roads, bridges and munitions depots. The rural population expected that the collective farms would be dissolved. It did not happen. This was one more reason why the entire peasant population became absolute enemies of the Germans.

From among the millions of prisoners of war, the Germans recruited thousands for auxiliary units in the German army. Partly, it was for the prisoners' self-preservation to escape the camps, the "death camps" as they called them, and partly to free Russia from Stalinism. This found its fullest expression in the Vlasov movement: Andrey A. Vlasov, a general, was taken prisoner with his regiment. It was in the prisoners of war newspaper, *Dobrovolets* (The Volunteer), that we saw in the spring of 1943, Vlasov's "Open Letter," in which he declared the program of his movement. It consisted of two major points: a) Fight for the abolishment of Stalin's Bolshevism, and b) Preservation of the "single and indivisible Russia." He was a Russian patriot. This point was against Hitler's program for the division of Russia. Vlasov's plan was suspended and he was sent to the mass prisoners' camp.

At the end of 1944, when Russian Armies fought on German territory they remembered the "Red General" and recalled Vlasov. Certainly they didn't accept his theory that Russia could only be conquered by Russians. Anyway, it was too late. In the end, Vlasov's troops (R.O.A.) were interned by Americans and handed over to the Soviets. Vlasov was executed in Moscow, as well as all his officers, and the soldiers were sent to Siberia.

In the 1970s, when I was on the cultural exchange at Moscow State University, I liked to talk and argue with students. Once they attacked me for, as they insisted, the dishonorable and politically blind behavior of America in handing over Vlasov and thousands of his soldiers to the Russians. My explanation that the USA acted according to the agreement between the Allies did not convince them. "People don't believe the USA anymore."

After the battle of Stalingrad, the Germans resumed in a front line west of Kursk (southwest of Moscow) flanked by the cities Orel in the north and Belgorod in the south. There were concentrated the largest forces of panzer-tanks formations on both sides in the entire Russian campaign, close to eight thousand. The battle was going on for over a month along a line of several hundred kilometers, making it impossible to take care of the thousands of bodies on the fields and in the disabled tanks. The stench around the region was so strong that it made many people sick. Even in Kharkov we could smell it.

Leaving Kharkov

At the beginning of August we saw disorganized German soldiers from defeated troops coming from Belgorad Shosse (thruway) into Kharkov. We understood that it was the end and we had to leave. On August 8, trucks from the Markets Administration brought those who had to leave to the railroad station. I had no thoughts, no feelings. I just wanted to leave, realizing that I was a small leaf on the waves of the world's ocean. Who cares? The future didn't look better than the past.

The long wait at the station was nerve-wracking. The air was dominated by Soviet Air Force planes, which flew over us, but did not bomb. The German *Luftwaffe* was almost extinct. A train with many open platforms took us; it was an organized evacuation. The mayor of Kharkov, a lawyer named Semonenko with a strong personality, had good relations with the German Command and was able to do a lot for the city. Semonenko with his important people and the German Commandant of Kharkov were in only one passenger car. Where were we going? He promised, "Not to Germany." Our plan was to cross the Dnieper to the right bank and stay in Vinnitsa. Many times, we had to wait on the side tracks, letting military trains go by. Once, a Soviet bomber escorted us for about fifteen minutes, flying very low. We were again ready for death, but it was just a psychological attack, a really terrible one. Our defense was to have the children and women stand up on the platforms and wave white or red kerchiefs or any piece of clothing. The aviators saw it and finally put out a white flag and left.

Life of a Refugee: Vinnitsa. My Second Marriage.

In Vinnitsa, we stayed as the "Kharkov group," quartered in the townfolks' homes. I was sent to live in the home of a widowed wife of a colonel and her younger sister. They were very much Polish, old-fashioned ladies. For instance, the younger sister normally addressed the older one as *Polkovnikova*. Colonel in Polish is *polkovnic*, his wife was *Polkovnikova*. They were nice, but quite formal ladies.

Our group had a kitchen/dining room in the school building where three times a day meals were served, paid for by our mayor's office. Each of us had to work in the kitchen. In Vinnitsa I learned that the city had acquired horrible fame, like many other places. There was a killing ground on the outskirts of the city, encircled by a tall wooden fence and barbed wire. There the NKVD at night killed thousands of people brought by trucks. These killings continued for several years and the numbers and names of the victims were not known and certainly never would be. People lived on one side of this ground and they heard shooting when the executioners didn't run loud tractors or trucks to cover the sound. Sometimes they heard screams and even the words, "Oh, God, why? We are innocent."

Now those huge graves holding probably up to one hundred corpses each were opened and corpses dug out and arranged in long rows. Every day hundreds of people were looking for their loved ones. I was there, too. More than once, I was thinking, "Papa, maybe I will find you." I knew what clothes he wore. That was the way people tried to recognize their loved ones—by pieces of clothing that they had worn at the time of their arrest. The stench was bearable, or I just didn't notice it. There was a mass Christian funeral for those bodies a few weeks later. They were buried in new mass graves in a very emotional Christian ceremony. Here was revealed the entire inhuman Stalinist system.

The front was moving closer to us and the Germans were retreating. What to do? This question didn't leave our minds. Nobody wanted to go to Germany, understanding what was waiting for that country in the near future. The fate of single people like myself was particularly disturbing. As I said: "If I were to be killed, that would be good. But if I were to be wounded, who would help me, take care of me?"

A single man, 39-year-old Andrei Tretiak, started to pay attention to me. He was a good-looking, robust man, a pleasant, really "merry chap." He liked to sing and had a good voice. It was easy to be with him; we told each other our life's stories. They were similar in the sense that we each had had happy and successful, but different, lives until 1938.

In that year, he was arrested as a member of a counter-revolutionary organization of wreckers in the commerce system of the city. He was a director of the biggest grocery store, the only one in the city, where a large assortment of merchandise not found in other stores—including some from foreign countries—was available, but the prices were high. It was located on Sumskaia Street just opposite the wide and splendid entrance to the City Park with the famous and excellent monument to Taras Shevchenko. All the members of this organization were sentenced to death which was usually carried out right away. But not in this case. Almost a year passed by and every night he was waiting to be taken out and shot to death. He lost his mind. Finally, after a whole night of formalities, they threw him out of jail. He did not comprehend what had happened to him or what he had to do now. For a whole day, he sat at the jail wall. In the evening, two men who had noticed him sitting there in the morning came and took him home. What happened in his case was unusual. The main figure, the organizer, was somehow cleared of all accusation and the case fell apart. His lawyer was Semonenko, our city mayor. After about a year of psychiatric treatment he was back to his work as Director of the Food Market.

In a few weeks, we were married by Semonenko, a mayor of our city in exile. In spite of the growing tension around us, we were happy. A pleasant surprise—Andrei showed me a good-size tobacco pouch full of gold coin rubles in five and ten denominations. He had an exceptional talent for commerce and organization. The city mill, which the collective farms around were using, was bombed just before the German occupation. Andrei hired workers and found the necessary parts and machinery in the wrecked factories and built a new small mill. From early morning until late at night a line of people and the horse carts from *kolkhozes* with grain to mill were standing there. They paid by a certain percent of flour. So Andrei opened a bakery. He could make a lot of money, but he didn't care, understanding the shaky situation of the war. He hired many people and helped them well. But those gold coins, which he bought, saved our lives more than once.

The Soviet Army crossed the Dnieper River to the right bank. Semonenko announced that we had to move to Germany and in a day we were on our way traveling in passenger cars. Andrei became very restless, running many times to Semonenko's car. Then he told me secretly, "We are going to get off the train in Lvov (Lviv in Ukrainian), but we had to get permission from the German Commandant. I've already told Semonenko you are pregnant and have developed pain and even started bleeding. A doctor said that you can't travel in such a condition."

It was, as we say, *tufta*, Andrei's invention. The doctor came and gave us a paper saying I could not travel and we got off the train in Lvov. The Commandant allowed only two other families to get out.

Lvov

In two hours or so, Andrei found a rental and we settled in the Ukrainian environment, the hot place of Ukrainian politics. Two political factions, the leaders of which were Bandera and Melnyk, were struggling among themselves. As we understood, the difference between the factions' outlooks was not so intolerable as to justify a great bitterness, even killing between members.

Lvov is an ancient, interesting and fine city. Walking through it, one can recognize different cultural influences. First among these was Kieven Rus, then Polish which was prevalent, and then Austrian. The influence was noticeable in the language, architecture, and customs. Lvov was the Capitol of Galicia, part of the Ukraine. For centuries, Galicia was under Polish rule, then Austrian. In 1793, at the second partitioning of Poland, the Ukraine was again united but as part of Russia. At the end of the nineteenth century, Lvov became and continued to be the center of Ukrainian nationalism.

The Red Army again was closing in on us. We had to leave and Andrei found out that several other families like us were prepared to go and each bought a horse with a covered wagon (like Americans going west). So, in a few days Andrei bought a good horse and wagon. We started our journey from Lvov, Ukraine, to Augsburg, Germany which lasted from March 1944 to May 7, 1945 when we crossed the German border.

Not far from Lvov in Sambor we were taken for the first time by the German patrol and brought to a Commandant. He told us in categorical, high tones that we were able bodies and had to work in Germany. Andrei knew how to take care of such a situation: the *Herr Commandant* got a five ruble gold coin and we had all the necessary papers. A similar instance happened many times and the coin performed the magic. In the time of war when paper money had no value, gold was "The Majesty."

We and a few other families went across the green border to Slovakia, traveling over the serpentine roads of the Carpatians. It happened that the German horse carts transport was going and we followed them. They were expecting the partisans to raid them, so they were walking and advised us to do the same. In a small village near the border, we parted from the other families. They went on and were killed by partisans. We stayed behind. Over fifty years have passed since then and I still wonder what really happened. Did I truly see the image of that big man who blessed me, or was it a mirage created by my excited mind? I don't know but it saved our lives.

Life in Slovakia: Work in Hospital

Traveling through Slovakia left a bright, pleasant spot in my memory. Geographically, it is a beautiful country; valleys along quite high mountains and low hills, clean and neat villages. But what simply hit me were the stores full of everything in a time when Russia was hungry and all of Europe was half starving. I was in doubt that I ever saw such an abundance of food, clothes, and other necessities. But the people were real jewels: understanding, kind and natural. Always, where we stayed overnight, they invited us for supper and breakfast and very rarely took any money. The answer was: "We are Christians. You are in need of help. We help you."

The Slovak language is much closer to Russian than Polish or Czech, so in a short time I was able to read, write, and speak Slovak, and Andrei talked, as he said, almost like a native.

Our longer stay was in Preshov. From there we traveled to Ruhzemberk. On the way, people stopped us, invited us to their homes and asked us the same question. "Why did you leave your country?" The anxiety of the people was high; they didn't know what to expect from the approaching Red Army.

At Ruhzemberk, we rented a small, two room house standing in the backyard of the owner's home. No one had lived in it for some time. The owner cleaned and repaired the outside and we cleaned and whitewashed the inside. The houselady hung clean curtains, gave us sheets, blankets, towels and other necessities. There was enough furniture. After two days of work, we got a nice, clean little house and felt comfortable and happy. Soon Andrei took a job, using our transport to deliver sacks of flour to Ruhzemberk bakery from the mill about ten or fifteen miles away. The city, the second largest after Bratislava, the Capitol, was beautifully organized—a pleasant city on the hills of the Carpatian and Tatra mountains.

Here I learned that I was pregnant. I wanted to have an abortion. Andrei was against it at first, but then he agreed. I had not been afraid to face anything in life, but this time I was in terror. It was irresponsible for us to have a child when we were stateless, homeless, and didn't know what could happen to us tomorrow. I saw several doctors in the city. Each of them told me that abortion was against the law and no doctor in the country would do it. "Have the baby. Believe in God and in people. They will help you." Now I thank God that I didn't do anything in the line of "women's help." And I have a wonderful daughter, Lucy.

A few days later, a German soldier came and gave me an order to appear immediately in a German Military Hospital (at school) and he guided me there. The officer-administrator told me that they had received wounded Russian soldiers and the Slovak nurses didn't understand them. They found my name in the city's registrar of refugees and that I was a nurse. He gave me a nurse's head dress and took me straight to the room. It was a big former classroom and looked like anything but a hospital. On the floor, lying on straw mattresses, were the wounded. Several beds were occupied by officers.

I said aloud, "*Zdravstvuyte*, Good day. I am going to be your nurse and I will try to explain the condition of each of you to the doctors."

At once, this suffering mass became loud. "*Sistrichka* (diminutive of sister-nurse), *Sistrichka,* give us water, help me lift my hand, my foot, etc."

So I started working. What I first saw made me sick and I ran into the lavatory and vomited. But I realized that it was my task to fight a war against lice. They covered all the boys and were all over them. I saw that their faces, hands, and bodies all were bloody and scratched. They were in their dirty, torn uniform clothes. Only the officers had hospital gowns. I ran to the head nurse, a Slovak woman.

"I know the condition and what should be done, but . . . there is only one thing left for us to do: take off their clothes, take them outside, and spray them thoroughly with lice lotion (which I obtained with much difficulty). And then wash them, though we don't have warm water. I'll give you two or three women to help."

Andrei was very upset and told me that the next day he would obtain a release for me from the German Commandant of the city. He knew how to do it. I said, "No. I want to help our boys."

Early the next morning when I entered the room, I heard nice words. "Our angel has come. She is here." And I felt dejected happiness to be with them. After breakfast, I explained what we were going to do in the war on lice. They were as happy as small kids. "Lice is the number one enemy, worse than the Germans."

It was not an easy operation to take off their clothes because almost each of them had hand or leg wounds. As I found out, the heavily wounded were shot to death.

I asked the head nurse to give us some sheets, so the blankets could be taken for disinfection and then their mattresses also were sprayed. Finally, the room was cleaned and the soldiers and their clothes washed. At the end of the day, the four of us celebrated victory: each soldier was clean and lying on a fresh white sheet, covered with another sheet. Now it looked like a makeshift hospital.

Each day I faced some kind of crisis: the patients who developed gangrene were taken out. Nobody knew where. Very limited medication was given to my soldiers; practically nothing was given for pain, and some were in agony. The head nurse told me that the doctors didn't like my interference and to stop asking them for help. So I bought some medication for pain in the drugstore and gave it to the soldiers who needed it.

Once, in the morning, I had just entered and greeted them, when a captain said to me loudly: "I am telling you officially, and you have to report it to higher-ups, that that soldier (and he pointed to him) is a liar. He is a Jew, not a Tadjic, as he says he is."

All the patients became infuriated. Another officer told him, "You are a *zhlob* (villain). Why do you want the life of that child? He is 17 years old. Have you still not had enough blood?"

I realized that I was in a precarious situation, so I ran to the head nurse and told her.

"It would be better if we did not know about it. I have to report it, and you should think of how to save that child's life."

I talked to Khadek from Dushanbe, the Capitol of the Tadjic Republic. The soldier was circumcised. That's why the captain decided he was a Jew. Khadek told me that all males in his tribe were circumcised. He was extremely frightened. The German officer came.

"Ask him if he is a Jew."

"No. I am a Tadjic." He was trembling and crying.

"Why is he circumcised?"

"All our men are always circumcised."

Then the officer asked me, "Can you tell by his language who he is?"

"His accent in Russian is clearly from Central Asia and is closest to Tadjic," I said. "Some Central Asian tribes still have this ancient ritual of circumcising. I am a historian. I've studied these customs."

The officer turned around and left. That was all over.

The majority of the boys were from the Ukraine. When I spoke Ukrainian to them, they were excited. We talked about war and politics; I told them different stories. They especially liked to listen to stories about the famous battles like Borodino, the battle between Napoleon and Kutuzov near Moscow. I recited poetry to them. Then we started singing Russian and Ukrainian songs. The boys forgot their pain and their young voices sounded strong. The head nurse and the officers ran in and watched us in amusement. From then on, every day, we enthusiastically gave a "concert." The mood in the room changed; there was laughing and joking. They called their room "the home of rest and entertainment."

A German doctor came more than once and watched us. Then he made some remarks to me to the effect that those who tried to conquer the Russians are fools because people with such soul are not conquerable. In about a month and a half, they were transferred. The parting was very emotional for them and for me.

The city's burgomeister called a meeting of all residents to discuss what to do in the situation. He asked us to tell them about life in the Soviet Union. We thought about what we should talk about. We knew that the Slovaks were quite conservative, especially politically, much more than the Czechs. At the meeting, we both talked, trying to be balanced, saying what was good, what was bad, and why we left.

The next day, late in the evening, the partisans came, asking us to let them in, promising they would not harm us. We knew that if they wanted to kill us they would do it anytime, anyplace. Two of them entered and the others were left outside. They gave us their orders in very strict words:

"Give the Slovaks a more truthful and better picture of life in the Soviet Union. Don't exaggerate Stalin's terror. Your family was executed because they were secret enemies. Think carefully about what you are going to tell people. Otherwise, we'll take you as our enemy. We won't harm you, Nina, because you are with child. We don't kill even a pregnant mother-wolf. But later we will find you. Now we can sit down and talk like compatriots of different political camps."

Andrei put vodka on the table right away and I served something to eat. We asked them to call their comrades inside. Two came in and then they rotated.

Now the talk was of a different kind. I started a discussion about Stalin's terror and the fact that my family were honest Soviet patriots and so on, and a heated disagreement followed. I made the statement: "I was, and probably always will be, for the Socialist form of organizing human society, but for real democratic socialism, not Stalin's type of oppression and terror."

Then they told me that there were a couple of comrades from Kharkov at their partisan base. They remembered my name was in the newspapers. "We knew you did nice things for children, especially orphans."

I asked them if they had heard the names of Ina Khristenko and Dmitry Vasiliev. They were somewhat surprised. "Yes. Those names are known to us. How do you know them?"

I told them that Ina was my closest friend at the University and I knew Dmitry through the Obcom of the Komsomol and he was my good friend.

"Ina is dead. She did a lot for our country. She was an interpreter for a German general and our agent. On August 8, 1943, when the Germans were leaving Kharkov, our Air Force bombed the retreating army and she was killed with the general."

I was thinking what a coincidence it was that on August 8, I left my city, thinking that it was the end of my life.

"And Dmitry is a very important organizer in the partisan forces. His name is different now."

We talked a lot and they left late in the night. We parted as friends—enemies. Shaking hands, they thanked me for taking care of our boys in the hospital. It looked like they had penetrated everywhere. They advised us to leave in a few days and told us what roads to take.

Andrei became seriously sick. He hurt his back carrying heavy sacks of flour. The doctor put him in bed and I nursed him and took care of our Vaska, a beautiful horse. Finally, we were able to leave, but after a few days on the road we stopped in Illava, a nice town on the western border with Czekhia in the foothills of Bije Karpaty. Andrei had to be in bed. We stayed there for several weeks until the middle of April 1945.

Once, when I was in the market, a young man stepped up close to me and said, "Privet. Greetings from Kharkov." He smiled and disappeared.

I understood his message. It meant, "We are watching you. Don't talk against us."

We faced another problem: we had run out of money. It was particularly important for Vaska to have food, mainly oats. The gold coins weren't too popular yet over here. I decided to go to Ruhzemberk, which was like a home for us, and sell a couple of coins there. Andrei agreed, so I took a train and it was less than a couple hours' ride. I made a successful business transaction and after supper was counting my money together with my former houselady where I was staying. Suddenly, we heard a massive air raid and bombs started landing all around. It continued, wave after wave. My hosts were frightened to death. It was a baptizing for them. The retreating Germans were concentrated downtown which was smashed almost completely. It was an American or English raid. Even for me, it was the worst bombing ever.

The bombing stopped and we went out. It was a dreadful picture—smoke and flames all around but our home had not one scratch. My hostess ran to help people. Soon she brought back a group of frightened children and made them comfortable in our former small house. A man with a horse and carriage was collecting wounded people to take them to the hospital. It was like a bad nightmare.

Then my hostess came in, excited. "Did you see that just behind our house a bomb landed but did not explode? St. Mary wouldn't allow your innocent unborn baby to be killed. Your baby saved us and our neighbor." And she and her neighbor kissed and blessed me.

The owner came and told me the same thing. "All the people are saying that it is God's will that only one house, ours, is saved without a scratch. St. Mary saved a child and we are all lucky." He said that the railroad station had been bombed and that the Germans were leaving the city and going west."

"I have to go. My husband will lose his mind."

"There is only one way. We will have to go to the main road and try, maybe a German will take you, just to the next railroad station. It's on their way."

We tried and a German soldier from a subsidiary regiment took me into a cabin. He was worn out, all dirty with soot. He looked at me with pity. "Baby in this inhuman time? Scary. Last night I lost all my friends." Tears were flowing down his dirty face.

The trains were being taken by Germans. Finally, one train was given to us.

It was late evening when I arrived home. Excited people gathered around and asked what was left of Ruhzemberk. Walking on the road, I recognized Andrei's figure in front of me. He was walking slowly, crying aloud and gesticulating wildly. I could see he was in bad shape. Coming from behind, I embraced him. His reaction was most unusual. He looked at me, embraced me, stopped crying, and sat down softly in the dirty snow-slush of the road. He calmly started talking with God as he would have done with a human sitting next to him, saying how many times God had helped him, saved his life. Andrei asked God what He assigned him to do. I sat down next to him.

A horse carriage with people in it approached us and they helped us get up. Now we were walking home and Andrei was completely quiet, happy, helping me to walk because I was utterly out of strength after twenty-four hours of going without sleep, rest, or food. He told me of the plans he had made while sitting in the railway station. He would go to Ruhzemberk, find our bodies, bury them, and then he would live over there with us, who were the most dear people in his life. Since that time, Andrei felt a closeness to God, often talked to Him, and got a wonderful inner tranquility.

From Ilava we went over Karpaty to Czekhia. We felt a change in the political climate. "We are waiting for our brother-Russians. Why are you running to our enemy, the Germans?" And many were not friendly to us.

We were going through the city Brno and as we were leaving it, heavy bombardment started. We ran to a safer place, but Vaska was so frightened he tore the reins and ran away. Andrei ran after him, actually under the bombs.

There was much devastation and destruction left after the bombing. An ambulance was picking up killed and wounded people. After a considerable amount of time a policeman finally listened to me, but couldn't help. He advised me to sit and wait. A few hours passed and an unbelievable thing happened. Vaska came back alone and greeted me in his way. With difficulties, I obtained a bucket of water for him and gave him his dinner of oats. It sounds funny, but it was one of the happiest moments of my life. I kissed and caressed Vaska and he understood it in his animal way and was laughing. He was an exceptionally smart horse.

Andrei finally came back, almost half-dead. I was truly happy to see him. This bombing was one of the scariest moments in my traveling. I was alone in the street with no identification, nothing on me or with me.

Crossing the German Border, May 6, 1945

We tried to cross Czekhia as fast as possible. Some Red Army tanks caught up with us when we were approaching the German border in Bavaria. The road was packed with refugees, both foreign and German, who stayed in Czekhia because of the bombing. Many of the Germans' children stayed over there for safety purposes. Now the small children were being carried by some sort of transport and the older ones were marching along the road, usually in uniform. They were really beautiful, healthy children.

We got to Eisenstein in Bavaria, Germany, a border town, on May 6, 1945. We watched how the invincible German army was disintegrating: small platoons crossed the border, entered residents' homes, and came out in civilian clothes and then each went his own way.

The Soviet Army was a few miles away. Night was very troublesome. In the morning on May 7, I fell asleep and dreamed clearly that Vaska got on his hind legs, roared, and slowly disappeared. Andrei woke me. All the people were ready to move through the front line which was about two or three kilometers away. At the front of our transport was a long line of children on wagons or walking. All the wagons and we, as well, had white flags. It was raining lightly and the children were wearing military raincoats.

We were moving through the forest on a narrow road. Suddenly machine guns began shooting and I heard the noise of bullets all around me. Andrei screamed, "Get out and fall on the road!" I was trying to do it when I saw Vaska get on his hind legs, roar, and fall down dead. Exactly what I dreamed.

The shooting stopped. There were some wounded, some killed, two kids among them. People were asking each other who did it. Andrei ran to the front and then came back. Tanks were moving toward us; the wagons were moved out of the road and into the forest. But here was ours, a horse laying across the road and a heavy wagon standing on the road. A tank stopped and we talked to them in German. They didn't understand and then I saw a white star. Andrei and I were speaking in Ukrainian between ourselves and one soldier in the tank asked in Ukrainian, "Who are you?"

Happiness—we understood each other. They were Canadian troops on American tanks. Andrei was crying. What was he going to do? he asked, pointing to me as I was already very pregnant. The commander of the tank took Andrei and they went back. I talked with the soldiers, and meanwhile they removed our smart, beautiful

Vaska. The ambulances continued taking the wounded people. Later, I saw my husband coming, smiling happily and leading a new horse. The major of the troop gave it to us with its document to replace the one that was killed.

Refugee Life in Germany and the Birth of My Daughter

Our perennial question—"Where to go?"—was back. Some people had heard about the Kharkov group because it was really unusual, the only organized group among the émigrés, concentrating around Augsburg. It was not far and in probably three or four days we were in Haunstatten on the outskirts of Augsburg. The rumors were right. Semonenko was there with some of our people. Basically it was a DP (Displaced Persons) Camp for people of the Baltic states, and some Ukrainians and Russians.

Semonenko settled us into an apartment with two rooms, a big kitchen, bathroom, and a big entrance hall to be shared with another family, a lady with a small child and pregnant with another. Her husband, Dr. Saykevich, was with the Ukrainian Army. Nina Saykevich did not know where he was until one day he knocked at the door.

We were in the American zone and pretty soon the UNRA took good care of us. We were provided with food, and with different living quarters. In the past, it was military cavalry camps. Now, all the houses and stables were empty. Some of our people lived in the houses, and some in the stables, which were cleaned and partitioned with hanging blankets.

On July 14, I gave birth to a healthy, beautiful girl, ten-and-one-half-pounds, Ludmila-Lucia. Andrei decided to exchange the horse for a cow so that Lucia could have fresh milk from a healthy cow. In addition, he received money, chickens, and rabbits. A peasant was taking care of all our animals.

Several months later, a new terror started, the screening and forced repatriation of former Soviet citizens. That's what Stalin wanted according to an agreement between Allies. We were friends with an Estonian family, so they gave us a paper saying that they knew us from their city where both of us had lived. In our official papers, we wrote that we were Estonian citizens. During the first screening, an American CIS officer called an Estonian lady over and

**My husband Andrei Tretiak and Lucy at about
ten months old in 1946.
DP Camp, Augsburg, Germany.**

told her to talk to me in her language. She did, mixing Estonian and Russian, and I answered her in Russian (practically all Estonians spoke Russian) and we conversed with smiles. She told the officer that I spoke Estonian with a strong Russian accent. At the second screening, the officer knew quite a bit of Russian and he caught me. The truth came out that we were Soviet citizens and would be repatriated.

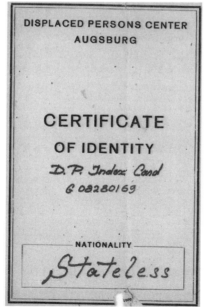

DISPLACED PERSONS CENTER
AUGSBURG

CERTIFICATE

OF IDENTITY

D. P. Index Card

G 02280169

NATIONALITY

Stateless

My certificate of identity, Germany, 1947.

Now, Semonenko was saying to all of us each time when the military police was to come to catch us like dogs, he knew a few hours ahead of time and told us to run into the fields or hide. I threw some diapers and food for Lucy and food for us into her carriage and we ran far into the fields, sometimes staying there for hours. People's nerves got short. Were we criminals? Or did we have the right to political asylum according to the Charter of the United Nations? Who was going to be the first who had some papers to prove it? Semonenko was gone and there was no help anymore.

I decided to take a risk. We knew that the screening officer was unpleasant and looked like he was against us. We had no choice.

We were called for screening. I went into the officer's office. "Sit down," he said.

But I stood. I was really mad. "Here is my Soviet Union passport." And with force I banged it on his table. "Here is my Kharkov University diploma." And I banged that on the table. "Here is an original paper about our apartment search during my father's arrest by the NKVD." Banged that on the table. "Here is my mother's and my petition asking about the revision of my father's case with all the explanations. And here are the two official answers to our petition."

I told him about my first husband's case. Then I asked him to let my husband in to explain his own case. After Andrei's presentation, the officer asked us many questions. In the end, he said it looked like we had the right to political asylum. He gave us a temporary paper so that the military police wouldn't bother us. After us, our people started to speak more straightforwardly. All of us wrote letters to First Lady Eleanor Roosevelt, who, as U.S. Ambassador to the U.N. took right care of us. For that, we gave sincere thanks. The "dogs catching" stopped.

The Ukrainian-Russian group from the Haunstatten camp was transferred to the Ukrainian DP camp in Dillingen, also not far from Augsburg. The old questions were again on the top of our life agenda: What to do next? Where to go? Which country would accept us?

Lucy had two Godfathers. One emigrated to Australia, the other, Kravchenko, to Argentina. He had a brother over there who owned thousands of acres of land in the prairie. He didn't have children and he gave half his land to his brother, also childless. And he, Lucy's

Godfather, gave half of his land to her. We were friends. Andrei had known them for many years. There was a very sparse population there and it meant that we would have to live with our cattle and animals. What would happen to Lucy? She was a very smart, intelligent, and beautiful child. We decided to wait and see, but we were taking Spanish lessons.

I realized that my education in history and philosophy had no practical use. I enrolled at the two-year nursing school; a year of theory and a year of working practice. After graduation at the end of 1948, I got a job in the camp's small ambulance hospital. Later, in 1949, we found out that the American Doctors and Nurses Association wanted nurses to work in the USA in the retarded children homes, or the tuberculosis hospitals. I submitted all the necessary papers. It was not the first time we had submitted papers. A number of people with relatives in the USA did it and were waiting for the initial permission for years. But we were called for a screening in a short time. Okay, we thought, this was not a big deal. Many had gone through several screenings and were still in the camp.

Several weeks later, we were called for a second screening and shortly after that to one more. Then nothing happened for several months. The majority of people's cases ended in that way and we were no exception. At the beginning of 1950, we were called by the American Embassy representative, had a long talk, and then he gave us an initial entry permit to America and some papers to fill out. "Start preparing. You will be called to Hamburg Haffen."

Andrei sold the cow, a funny moment. Lucy was very proud of my "*kuyovka*" (korova) cow. Someone told her that her father sold her "*kuyovka*" and they were taking her out. Lucy ran through the camp to the stalls, the cow already on the truck. She screamed, "I don't allow you to sell my '*kuyovka*.' Bring it back to the stalls." There was a lot of crying until her father put her on his shoulders, went to town and bought what Lucy wanted: two big dolls. The next day she brought them to the kindergarten.

"I sold my '*kuyovka*' and bought these dolls. We don't need '*kuyovka*' in America. But I don't know what I'm going to do in America without my seamstress." This got a good laugh in the camp.

Lucy's birthday party, July 14, 1950, Dillingen Displaced Persons Camp. A week before our departure on our way to the USA. Lucy is second from the right. Next to me is Yelena Shishatskaia and her son Alex, now a Professor of Architecture at West Virginia University. Yelena's story: an opera diva in the Kharkov Opera, a lyric coloratura soprano, called a "voice of the century." She had guest appearances in all leading operas starting with Bolshoi and Kirov. By Stalin's personal permission, she had guest appearances in Berlin, Vienna and other European operas. Her husband, a modernist architect, was arrested and executed. Her career was finished. During World War II, the Germans took her to Germany for her to perform. She came to the USA in the 1950s and died in the 1980s. (Alex Karter, W.V. University)

Coming to the United States

In Hamburg, we embarked on the *General Holbrook*, a military ship hastily adapted for civil passenger use. The crossing from Europe to America was long and very inconvenient. We were with at least fifteen to twenty people in a huge room at the lowest level, with a cement floor, previously used for ammunition storage. In addition, the turbulent ocean made us very sick. But Lucy was running and I was very much afraid about her.

Once, a ship's officer came with her along with an interpreter. He told us a lot about himself and his family. We listened and wondered until he said he wanted to adopt Lucy. At first we did not take it seriously, but he was persistent. We told him Lucy was not for adoption. The next day he came again and gave us a good hint that we also would be helped. People around us advised us to see the Captain of the ship immediately. The three of us did, and in addition to that, we gave him a written statement. The Captain took it very seriously. He called a female employee and told her to look after Lucy and to be sure that she got off the ship with her parents in Boston. The officer did not bother us anymore and stayed away from Lucy.

It was August 31, 1950, the last screening at the ship, and we were free. The American Ukrainian Committee was our sponsor on the grounds that the American Nursing Association was providing a job for me.

Now we could go to see the city of Boston. That first impression is still with me: the young men and boys looked the same as ours. They walked, behaved, gesticulated, looked, and dressed like our boys did at home. We walked around very excited and noticed that all the people were very similar to us. It made us feel that way because the Germans had behaved differently from us. We felt finally we were at home, a wonderful, unforgettable feeling.

We were sitting on a bench not far from the harbor, watching people. Then I noticed that on the ground around the bench were pieces of white bread. It surprised me. In my childhood I was taught, as were all of us, that to throw bread away was a sin. Later, in the pioneer organization, we learned that throwing bread away was antisocial behavior.

Andrei laughed at me. "You are in rich America. It's time to change your outlook and behavior."

America is a different world and experience, one where a human being has a free hand to build his or her life according to their own intelligence, will, and energy.

A Few Thoughts About WWII

The Great Patriotic War, a war of "grandeur and grief," was not forgotten by the Soviet people and never will be. Just to touch on tragedy expressed in the simple statistic—every family in the country lost one member or more; only three percent of men between the ages of 17 and 20 survived. Many young women were not married. State and society's need for children became a problem.

This National war "for the Motherland" had started changing the relationship between the Communist state and society. Specifically, the traditional Russian values received importance not less than official revolutionary ideology. Glory of victory gave to the Nation moral and practical satisfaction and pride: the destruction of Germany's war machine resulted in Europe's freedom; creation of the Eastern European communist states became not only the buffer zone against another invasion, but above all was spreading the communist ideology. The Soviet state became the great world power.

P.S.: Since my student years, the ideas of the philosopher Nikolai Berdiaye have never left my mind.

Why does a human who is by nature a free and creative creature use these gifts so often unsuccessfully? Why are his knowledge and skills he so often turned against himself, in oppression and distraction of his own race? Why when he so self-confidently presents himself as a master of the world, but then becomes a slave of those forces, which he created—technology and social order?

Our world is the object of our soul.

Family Pictures and Documents

Step-daughter Kathleen, her husband, John McNeish,
and their daughters, Abbie and Jennifer, 1988.
(Photo © Duval)

Lucy and Ronald's wedding, in their home, 1981.

August 6 was an extremely significant and happy day for Nina Tretiak, Accounting, Cleveland, because she achieved a goal she's been striving for ever since her arrival in this country late in 1950. She became a citizen of the United States.

Among her prize possessions commemorating that day are an American flag, and a personal letter from the Honorable Michael A. Feighan, Cuyahoga County Representative in Congress.

To Nina, who was born in the Ukraine, the most valuable thing she has acquired in her adopted country is LIBERTY. Having lived in two distinctly different countries, she is enthusiastic in her praise of the way of life she now enjoys.

Pride also shows in her face as she talks about her 14-year old daughter, who is an honor student at Lincoln High School.

An article about me becoming a citizen of the United States of America, 1958.

Charlotte Lösel, sister-in-law, and myself. Germany, 1973.

303

**Konrad (Bill) Shields, step-son, and
Kathleen McNeish, step-daughter.**